PRACTICAL
HOME OFFICE
SOLUTIONS

"The good life means
living in the place where you belong,
being with the people you love,
doing the right work—
on purpose."

Richard Leider,
founding partner of
The Inventure Group, Minneapolis, MN
as quoted in *Fast Company*,
February/March 1998 issue.

PRACTICAL HOME OFFICE SOLUTIONS

Marilyn Zelinsky

McGraw-Hill
New York   San Francisco   Washington, D.C.   Auckland   Bogotá
Caracas   Lisbon   London   Madrid   Mexico City   Milan   Montreal
New Delhi   San Juan   Singapore   Sydney   Tokyo   Toronto

Library of Congress Cataloging-in-Publication Data

Zelinsky, Marilyn.
    Practical home office solutions / Marilyn Zelinsky.
        p.   cm.
    Includes bibliographical references and index.
    ISBN 0-07-063365-7 (alk. paper)
    1. Home offices—United States—Design.   2. Interior decoration—
United States.   I. Title
NK2195.04Z47   1998
643' .58—dc21   98-24786
                                                            CIP

McGraw-Hill

*A Division of The **McGraw·Hill** Companies*

1 2 3 4 5 6 7 8 9 0   FGR/FGR   9 0 3 2 1 0 9 8

ISBN 0-07-063365-7

The sponsoring editor for this book was Wendy Lochner, the editing supervisor was Penny Linskey, and the production supervisor was Clare B. Stanley. Interior design and composition: Ron Lane, Vincent Piazza.

Printed and bound by Quebecor/Fairfield.

McGraw-Hill books are available at special quantity discounts to use as premiums and sales promotions, or for use in corporate training programs. For more information, please write to the Director of Special Sales, McGraw-Hill, 11 West 19th Street, New York, NY 10011. Or contact your local bookstore.

 This book is printed on recycled, acid-free paper containing a minimum of 50% recycled, de-inked fiber.

To Steve, for helping me
to explore my heart's desire

Contents

Chapter 2.
Dilemmas of Planning Your Home Office: Hire a Professional or Do It Yourself?   51

Chapter 3.
Avoiding Home Office Hazards That Lead to Physical Pain   96

Chapter 4.
Why the Ancient Art of Placement Is Important for Your Home Office   131

Chapter 5.
A Bargain Hunter's Guide to Buying Home Office Furnishings   155

Chapter 6.
Real-Life Home Office Technology Needs   201

Chapter 7.
How to Kid-, Spouse-, and Pet-Proof Your Home Office   223

Chapter 8.
More Real-Life Home Office Dilemmas:—How Others Cope   243

Chapter 9.
Understanding the Telecommuter's World   287

Chapter 10.
Back at the Corporate Office: Could You Work There Again?   305

Resources   317

Index   325

About the Author   331

Introduction

I'll warn you now that this is not a book about pretty pictures. It's a book depicting the real world of what it's like to work in a home office. You'll find a handful of good-looking photos in this book—the rest are characteristic of how you and I really work at home. At least you'll know that you aren't alone. But maybe we can all learn a thing or two from one another on how to cope in the home office.

After reading one too many magazine articles about the home office, I became as dismayed as many of you are out there. The articles depicted one of three categories of home offices:

- Fantasy, upscale home offices of wealthy people designed by interior designers
- Fantasy, upscale home offices of interior designers
- Pretty, but unrealistic, home offices that all but ignore every aspect of ergonomics and comfort

Most articles fall into the first two categories and simply forget the needs of the average home office worker. Virtually all articles (with few exceptions) fail to address the everyday annoying problems, situations, questions, and dilemmas at-home workers face. Most of these articles trivialize the home office, making it look as though it's just a luxury to have the space in your home in which to put a desk and some pretty pillows and chalk it up to the magazine's version of a home office in order to satisfy the need for a trend story.

This kind of irresponsible attitude makes the home office look far from the serious place of business many at-home workers tend to live in 12 hours a day, six to seven days a week. I simply don't believe that design and lifestyle are exclusive from one another. How you plan and design your office is usually affected by your lifestyle.

For example, one couple, the Tureks, who are interviewed in this book, work in a basement home office. They have two children and live in a three-bedroom house. Their home office used to be in one of the bedrooms because the room has a separate entrance and a spectacular view from the sliding glass doors. Their two kids shared another bedroom. Because the kids were growing older and wanted their own bedrooms, the Tureks realized they had to move, and the only place to move was into the basement. They never thought about working in the basement, but lifestyle issues forced them to renovate the space. The result—a good-looking basement home office.

One expert on the home office says it best when it comes to reading articles on the home office that fall into the last category of pretty, but unrealistic, home offices:

"Even the home offices you see today in award-winning magazines are unergonomically correct and unsound. There are keyboards on work surfaces instead of on articulating keyboard trays, and monitors sit on the desk at an angle from where the person needs to sit because it photographs better that way. People take their cues from these photographs and then wonder why their necks, arms, backs, and shoulders are hurting," says Mark Dutka, owner of InHouse, a thriving furniture store in San Francisco that specializes in the home office.

Time and time again did I hear such remarks about articles (and books) about the home office.

In fact, articles about the home office never seem to take into consideration that most people who work at home—like me—don't have time or budget to fix up a picture-perfect home office, yet at the same time, need to find attractive—and attainable—architectural and interior solutions to their planning and design problems to acccommodate business and lifestyle needs.

Most articles don't take into consideration many of the lifestyle issues at-home workers face: family, isolation, barrier-free needs, lack of space, to name a few:

> **The question most people that pull together articles on the home office often don't ask is this: To what extent can redesigning your physical home office foster in you a greater sense of importance and self-worth that ultimately flows out into your work, to your clients, to your family, to your friends and neighbors, and to your community? If we don't take care of ourselves and our physical work space at home, then we are giving out the message to the world that home office workers are not to be taken seriously.**

This is quite a serious question we should all be asking ourselves for when most of us begin a home business, rarely do we invest in any time, or any money, to create a worthy space in which we can launch our fortunes.

A Real View of the Physical Home Office

I could never relate to any so-called solutions that these articles about beautiful home offices espoused. Don't get me wrong—I don't dismiss the beauty of a well-appointed, well-designed home office. I love looking at wonderful shelter magazines, but they don't speak to me. I'm not in the position to knock down walls, install a wall of windows, put in skylights, rewire the house, buy expensive furniture and filing systems nor do any of the other costly architectural detailing that make these home offices such appetizing places in which to work.

At the same time, I always wanted the office I had dreamed about having but never acquired in the corporate world. I wanted to work in a great home office. But it was up to me to define what I viewed as a "great" office and not fall into the trap of letting the press define for me what a "great" home office should be.

I wanted—no, needed—to read a book that spoke directly to me, filled with stories, experiences, ideas, and realistic—not idealistic—photos of home offices that I could indeed relate to, instead of looking at home offices that made me feel like the desk I was working on was one step above a bridge table.

At the same time, I became acutely aware that just about everyone has a home office of some sort, and most of them look as though they had been put together in an ad-hoc fashion. After nearly a decade of attending open houses while buying two houses and accompanying friends and family on house-hunting expeditions, I came to the startling conclusion that in most every home I trampled through, somewhere there was tucked away a home office.

I've seen simple home offices consisting of a luan door over two file cabinets, elaborate custom-built home offices, dusty home offices, paper-ridden home offices, and poorly lit home offices where one wouldn't believe the people working in them could actually be productive or happy.

There have been basement home offices, attic home offices, garage home offices, and spare-bedroom home offices. There were home offices that seem to spread out all over the house—if there wasn't enough storage in the dedicated home office, a spillover of papers and folders could be found in a corner of the bedroom, dining room, or kitchen.

If I had a dime for every home office I saw . . .

I paid little attention to the home offices I ran across in my early years of house hunting. I didn't understand back then exactly for what purpose a home office stood. Early home offices were simple: a desk with a typewriter or old computer. Piles of paper. Books everywhere. Today, I have a decidedly different view of the home office. Though builders haven't perfected what at-home workers require, nevertheless, whether I visit a condominium, a $200,000 house, a million-dollar house, or a builder's model home on the East or West coast (an addiction I cannot rid myself of)—inevitably, there is room for a home office (typically called a "bonus room" or "study") in the floor plan.

For instance, one model home I visisted in Connecticut had a floor plan in which a small bonus room was built off the master-bedroom suite marketed to potential buyers as either a "nursery" or a "home office."

No doubt the home office has become the room of the 1990s and beyond. Most of us have a hard time setting up and designing our main living space so we turn to shelter magazines and books to ease the way. But how can we be expected to turn a space into a professional, working environment when it's been done most of our lives for us in the corporate arena by professional office designers?

Who Should Read This Book?

After seeing dozens of home offices and talking with dozens of at-home workers, I realized I had to write the book I was initially looking for to help me out of my own dilemmas. So to help you—and me—out, I've written this book based on nine criteria, and I'm happy to say that I haven't caved in on any of the criteria:

◆ The book would not include photos from design firms that depicted perfect fantasy home offices designed for wealthy clients.

◆ The book would include photos of products and furniture from manufacturers if they were shown in a photo of someone's real-life home office. If a real-life home office photo was unavailable for this book, the furniture would have to be worthwhile enough so that the readers of this book would fully appreciate seeing the product.

◆ The book would include photos of real-life home offices whether or not they are well-designed or complete disasters (again, you aren't alone!).

◆ The book would include lots of shots of my home office so you can identify with me, knowing that just because my background is design doesn't mean I have a perfectly appointed home office and that I've made, and will continue to make, all the decisions you are now facing.

◆ The book would *not* include any highly styled fantasy home offices designed by an interior designer or architect unless the offices could illustrate something absolutely relevant to the reader or expand on an experience such as in Chapter 2.

◆ The book would discuss the advantages and disadvantages of all types of home office furniture from ready-to-assemble to commercial-grade furniture.

◆ The book would include firsthand experiences and accounts of people who *really* do work at home in order to give the book the vox humana—or human voice—a phrase for which I credit author Studs Terkel.

◆ This book is *not* intended to be a primer on technology (there are too many great magazines out there on the subject that you can easily refer to), and the technology chapter will discuss only how real-life, at-home workers have handled their own technology problems and issues.

◆ And lastly, this book would be *fun* to read.

Whether you are a corporate worker who brings work home once in a while or whether you consistently take work home on a daily basis, moonlight evenings or weekends, telecommute one to five days a week, or are thinking about or have embarked on a full-fledged business in your home, you're bombarded day after day with a mountain of informaiton about the home office that can be, quite frankly, over- or underwhelming. This is a book for everyone who has a keen interest in the home office—the workplace of today and tomorror—for the workplace is a central theme and concern in almost everyone's life.

Through the help of other at-home workers who have gone through the same experiences you are now facing, this book creates the framework to help you embrace and better understand the benefits and consequences of planning, designing, and actually working from a home office.

I've taken large portions of interviews from many at-home workers who express their innermost feelings about working from home in their work space. The many funny and heartwarming stories and insights of home-based professionals or infrequent home workers in this book will give you information and help in easing the transition to your home office.

In addition, the comprehensive index will make it easy and fast to find the information you are seeking, whether it be about finding a file cabinet for $20 or about keeping the cat from chewing your documents or about finding worthwhile Web sites to tap into for home office furniture and other products.

What This Book Will Do for You

In this book, you will see how real-life home-based workers have solved design dilemmas and problems. I promise you that this is the first book you will be able to relate to, feel comfortable with, and apply the solutions from in finding to your current home office problems.

This book is written to be that right reference tool for you. I've listened and learned the questions and concerns that you need answered because you couldn't find the solutions anywhere else. In this book, you'll discover answers to the following questions I've heard so many of you ask.

◆ How can I find home office furniture that is inexpensive but will last for more than a couple of years?

◆ Interior designers are expensive; why should I hire them for a home office project?

◆ Why should I care about ergonomics in my home office, and what does *ergonomics* mean, anyway?

◆ What are some of the best tried-and-true home office design and lifestyle tips from real people who work in real home offices around the country?

◆ How do I kid- and pet-proof my home office?

◆ How do I set up and design a home office so that my friends and family take my business seriously?

◆ What is *feng shui*? Is it just a hoax, or is it important to consider when planning the design of my home office?

And there are many more of your questions on home office planning and design that will no doubt be answered within these pages.

In each chapter, you will find questions in need of solutions from people just like you who are home-based workers to whom you will no doubt relate.

At the end of the book is a special section designed especially for you. It includes a few pages of graph paper and a few pages of scaled universal shapes of home office items—products, and furniture—that will help you to plan and design your own work environment.

I encourage you to use this section. Cut out the universal shapes, copy them, and figure them onto the graph paper! It's a creative, fun experience that will save you headaches in the long run when you realize that your antique rolltop desk won't fit in your 8- by 10-foot dedicated home office room along with the three lateral file cabinets and two task chairs you absolutely must have in the work space! Use the graph paper if you choose to become your own planner.

My Personal Home Office Design Dilemmas

In my first book, *New Workplaces for New Workstyles,* I immersed myself in the world of telecommuting. I interviewed scores of people who worked at home, manufacturers studying the phenomenons and companies offering their employees the chance to work at home one or more days a week.

What I saw intrigued me. People might consider their home office a recliner in the living room or a tray table piled with papers that they can take room to room with them. Others use the kitchen table or the baby's high-chair for piling papers and the coffee table in the living room to hold their work. Obviously, none of this is a very efficient use of space no matter how large or small your home. But where could these people turn to for help?

That was my dilemma, as well. Although I had a wonderful dedicated home office, I still had problems with storage, lighting, and privacy with nowhere to turn for affordable answers. The articles on home offices that shelter magazines featured were unrealistic and styled by a photographer usually in a studio, rarely in a real home. The home office books on the market though beautiful, were filled with unattainable customized millwork or expensive furniture, and I couldn't garner any solutions from those pages for my own home office.

At the same time, because of my interest in home offices, I would often receive questions from acquaintances, friends, and family about problems they have with their home offices for which they needed solutions. It came to my attention that there is a need for a book on the home office for those of us with home offices that need space planning and design help. Realistic help.

I discovered the problems of working from a home office as a writer and part-time crafter-painter in 1994 when I moved into my second house. As lucky as I was to have a dedicated 8- by 10-foot room for an office and beautiful furniture from Herman Miller for the Home (which has now been discontinued from production), I quickly ran out of storage space and began to store stuff in the other rooms.

So I began to solicit free advice from designers. During public speaking engagements on home office design, I'd show slides of my home office that often resulted in laughs in the audience for how could a design writer live in such an "ordinary" problematic home office? I've had interior designers offer to come into my home and redo my home office, a luxury I cannot afford.

I've documented for you my own office adventures. After a consultation with a feng shui expert, I moved my home office from an 8- by 10-foot room to a larger 10- by 13-foot room after I renovated the first smaller room. Why did I do that? You can read about it in Chapter 4, "Understanding Why Feng Shui Is Important."

Home offices sort of evolve day to day, and it's hard to really plan and contain a home office set-up. You never know how much stuff you will accumulate from project to project. So home office workers don't need to see another tidy, stylish home office straight from the pages of a magazine. (How many of us use milk crates for storage in the home office but want a more attractive, yet affordable solution, for heaven's sake!) What we need to see are real-life problems, real-life solutions.

Our home offices will no doubt mature over time as we learn about our own individual quirks and nuances in the process of living and working at home. I hope that this book will become a reference, an inspiration, and a tool for you to use toward your own discoveries in planning, designing, living, and working in your own special home office.

Marilyn Zelinsky Syarto   Fairfield, Connecticut   mzelinsky@aol.com

Acknowledgments

Working at home can be isolating, but writing a book like this meant I was able to get out and meet a variety of funloving, heartwarming home-based workers. Not only that, but once you begin to work at home, you start to see who your true friends are once you don't have a corporate title anymore.

I lovingly acknowledge the emotional support and dedication I received from my family, friends, and colleagues—both old and new—for helping me settle into a work-at-home lifestyle. All of you have been instrumental in a multitude of ways throughout the sometimes difficult transitions and challenges of becoming a free agent.

To my mom, Ida, for sending me a stream of research on the home office. Thank you for instilling in me at a young age the courage and drive to write books.

To my husband, Steve, for providing me with the nurturing, patience, and love I so sorely need on a daily basis. And thanks for the wonderful and creative photographs, too!

To Bella—I couldn't ask for a more beautiful, meaningful, and fulfilling friendship of the mind and soul. Thank you for your unending words of wisdom.

To my former cubicle mate and current dear friend, Kris, I thank you for egging me on to become a free agent—you are the only element I miss about working in a corporate office.

To every single person who participated in this book, I am eternally grateful to you for letting me into your hearts and home offices. I thank you for taking the time to give me an honest picture of how you live, how you work, and what you've learned and hope to learn from being a free agent. I'm especially grateful to those brave souls who took photos of their own home offices for publication: Leslie Goddin, Linda Shea, Julie Taylor, Brian McGuren, Steven DeMartino, Michael Laessle, Maurice Blanks, Manfred Petri, Peter Baylies, and Maxi Cohen.

To everyone who let me into their homes with my camera—a million heartfelt thanks to Cindy Froggatt, Shannon Wilkinson, Mimi Akins, The Gustufson Group, David Grant Grimshaw, Cathy Barto Meyer, Lisa Wendlinger, Holly Gruske, Mary Davis, Barbara Mayer, Elaine and Rick Turek, Michael Love, and last but definitely not least, Lisa Roberts.

To everyone who lent me their opinions, insights, expertise, and support: Nancy Glenn, Tom and Gayle Gentry, Alison DeMartino, Lara and Renay Nieto, Jessica Taper, Lynn Bygott-Leahy, Marita Thomas, Jerianne Fitgerald Thomas, Jennifer Busch, Mark Dutka, Ellen Kolber, Deborah Quilter, Deborah Meyer, Paul Berglund, Marlene Green, Peggy Doughty, Jill Nance, and Susan Aiello.

To Marci Nugent, who edited both of my books—thank you so much for your thoughtful and joyful comments about my books!

To Penny Linskey, thank you for making the editing process of this book pain-free!

To Wendy Lochner, senior editor at McGraw-Hill, I send my deepest gratitude for your support. I have a tremendous respect for your invaluable insight into the publishing world.

Last, but never least, I once again must thank the higher powers that saw me through this second book project to its completion.

PRACTICAL HOME OFFICE SOLUTIONS

Figure 1-1. Cathy gives us a reality check of what working in a home office is like. (CATHY © 1997 Cathy Guisewite. Reprinted with permission of *Universal Press Syndicate.* All rights reserved.)

Myth versus Reality: Can You Find Peace and Productivity in a Home Office?

After I started to work from home full-time, I began to notice the following behavior of many people who work in corporate offices:

◆ They let voice mail pick up virtually all of their calls.

◆ They return calls after two or three voice-mail messages.

◆ They always sound out of breath because they are running to and from meetings or trying to meet deadlines.

◆ They are grouchy.

And most of them are fantasizing about what it would be like to work at home:

> **I'm just sitting in my sad little cubicle envying you. In my mind, you have the perfect life sitting in your home office meditating on the gently falling autumn leaves while writing acts of courage.**

This is an excerpt of a letter I received from a colleague who works in a crowded cubicle at a rather large company in the Midwest. I'll admit the autumn leaves are beautiful from my window and writing is definitely an act of courage, but it's pushing it to say that I have the "perfect life" working from a home office.

I believe that shelter magazines, along with a few well-played commercials on television, have perpetuated this idyllic vision of working at home.

"Having run out of ways to make a bathroom upgrade a must-read, they have embraced the home office as the last great decorational frontier," says Karen Stabiner, a work-at-home writer. "They see it as an Eden of cyberspatial bliss—the sleek modern desk that looks half the length of a football field...an overstuffed chaise...a skylight...a private bath" (see Stabiner, 1997).

Here's another splash of cold water for the home office–struck: "Despite what TV and print ads show, not everyone who works at home has a beautiful wooded vista outside of the window…and the vast majority of us do not set up shop in offices that remotely resemble the offices that magazine spreads regularly feature," says Alice Bredin, author (see Bredin, 1997).

Your decision to work at home full-time should never, ever be taken lightly.

I mean it.

The fantasy to work at home starts when the grass starts to look greener from the other side of the corporate fence. You've read one too many shelter magazines, seen too many television commercials. You're slaving away (just wait till you work at home!) in a less-than-inspirational–looking corporate interior in a Band-Aid-beige cubicle or bland private office with no windows.

Then, one day you have the lucky chance to work at home because of bad weather or you're a little too sick to sit in your office. Wow. You get a lot done. Working at home is pretty neat. It's downright idyllic! Now *this* is the life! If only you could do it every single day of your working life…

But note this comment from Tamara Hardy, a former fast-tracker who quit her job as a regional director for Ross Perot's 1992 presidential campaign to raise her three kids: "I gained weight, and my self-esteem dropped. Since I was hardly ever home while I was working, I knew no one. And it was hard to find people I had anything in common with" (see Lawlor, 1997).

The same kind of shocking realism that Hardy discovered as a full-time mother happens all the time to those who quit their corporate jobs to work from a home office. It helps to know that there are pros and cons to working from home and from the corporate office.

"Some days I think: This is it—a seamless melding of work and home, a full day's work without a full regimen of suits and commutes. Other days I think receptionists and water coolers are very civilized. I think sane people construct firewalls between work and family," says Betsy Morris, a writer for *Fortune* magazine who works at home with her husband who's an author and writer for *The Wall Street Journal* (see Morris, 1997).

The Work-at-Home Craze Is Centuries Old

Does everyone *you* know say that everyone *they* know works from home? It could be the truth. Before we take a look at some hard numbers about the work-at-home phenomenon, let's talk a little about the history of working at home.

The home office is not a new concept. Most of us have always had a small work space dedicated to paying our household and medical bills. Furniture manufacturers have always designed desks for the home (see Figures 1-2 through 1-4). And scores of writers, sales professionals, crafters, and other professionals have always quietly worked at home.

But the more formal, more structured, more mainstream tradition of working at home goes back a few centuries when families farmed together and practiced a trade in a shop attached to the house. The formal concept of working at home became a lost and forgotten workstyle for most people when the family farm started to erode in the late 1800s as the scale of manufacturing grew fast in the cities. Decades later the den with a desk made a quick comeback until televisions took over that room in the 1950s. People shunned the work-at-home concept up through the status-conscious years of the 1980s when it was politically correct to tell people you took work home for evenings and weekends. And there was an unwritten rule that you never worked at home during a workday.

1909   1909

1936   1937

Figure 1-2, 1-3, and 1-4 The home office has changed over the past decades. It started out with a simple boudoir desk for the home in 1909. The right idea starts to emerge in 1956 with desk compartments and more space. The L-shaped home office mimics the L-shaped secretarial desk prevalent in corporations at the time. Today, furniture manufacturers, like Sligh, take the home office as a serious market to be catered to, and they have designed furniture with space, compartments, and work surface to address the serious, at-home worker of today (see 1-4). (*Sligh*)

1959

1956   1965

Figure 1-3

Figure 1-4

Numerous economic and social changes that began to take place in the early 1990s have given the home office a fierce resurgence in popularity. In fact, here are a couple of interesting work-at-home–related predictions for 1998 from the management consulting firm Watson Wyatt:

◆ In response to the huge number of corporate mergers in 1997, next year will see another significant wave of corporate downsizing.

◆ A major company, probably in the service business, will exit its New York headquarters and have all but a few employees working at home in virtual offices.

These general predictions—driven by corporate decision makers—could have been made, and might have come true, during any one of the years in this decade. Wanting to leave a company is quite another matter, and lots of us want to do just that.

Almost 40 percent—or three out of eight people—in a nationwide survey about employee turnover say that money is not a factor in their decision to leave one company for another. The survey, conducted by the professional services firm of Coopers & Lybrand L.L.P., was given to employees in exit interviews conducted by the companies they were leaving. It showed that while 63 percent of the employees surveyed give "obtaining a higher salary" as one of the reasons for resigning, relocating (47 percent) and lack of career advancement (39 percent) also rank high on the list. Other reasons, in descending order, are "offered better position" (37 percent), "dissatisfied with position" (28 percent), "career change" (27 percent), "stay home with family" (27 percent), "dissatisfied with organization" (20 percent), and "miscellaneous," such as going back to school (20 percent).

"Most people feel comfortable saying they are leaving for better pay, but in many cases, the real reason is more profound," said Carl Weinberg, a partner with Coopers & Lybrand L.L.P., who specializes in compensation consulting. "To improve employee retention and avoid the high costs associated with new hires and training, employers need to identify the root causes of turnover. In our experience, there is usually a significant gap between the expectations of the employment deal that the employer created and the reality of the job. This gap weakens commitment and pushes good people out the door."

Corporate America is slowly beginning to realize where they falter, but they aren't moving fast enough to retain every employee who wants to walk out the door. Other findings of the Coopers & Lybrand survey show that the number of companies with a formal telecommuting program has more than doubled, increasing from 7 percent in 1996 to 17 percent in 1997; 43 percent of the companies in the survey offer child-care services, an increase of 30 percent over 1996.

How Many People <u>Really</u> Work at Home?

Take surveys with a grain of salt for they inevitably vary from month to month. The bottom line is that the work-at-home contingency is growing at a healthy pace. Dramatic statistics from a variety of sources* testify to the exponential growth of the work-at-home phenomenon:

◆ An estimated 47 million people currently work at home, either full-time or part-time.

◆ 14.2 million of those are running their own companies.

◆ 8,000 new home offices are started each week.

◆ Experts predict that nearly 60 million Americans will be working at home by 1998, up from 43.2 million in 1994.

◆ 23.7 million (of the estimated 47 million) use their home to catch up on work from the corporate office.

◆ You can equip a home office for $3,000—a 40 percent *decrease* in price since 1990.

◆ The work-at-home market accounts for $200 million each week in home office equipment sales.

◆ Products and services being produced and sold to this marketplace currently represent a $79 billion market and are projected to reach $132 billion in the next five years.

◆ A 1997 survey reports that 9.1 million people work at home as telecommuters three days a month or more (the telecommuting population does not include home-based entrepreneurs).

◆ There are 47.4 million full-time, home-based professionals in the United States alone, and they earn an average of $58,000 annually, according to Lisa Roberts, author of *How to Raise a Family and a Career Under One Roof* (Bookhaven Press, 1997, Coraopolis, PA).

* Sources include Specialists in Business Information, Business Communications Company, FIND/SVP, and IDC/LINK, 1997.

◆ The number of telecommuters in the United States has risen by more than 30 percent since 1995 to 11.1 million in 1997, according to Telecommute America, a public-private effort launched in 1995 to promote telecommuting.

◆ Almost 33 percent of total U.S. households in 1995 had at least one person operating a home business, telecommuting, or working at home after hours for their employer.

◆ The IRS reports that it expects to mail out more than 74 million Form 1099-MISC for the 1997 tax year (these forms are used by independent contractors and freelancers), according to *Fast Company Magazine* (December/January 1998).

◆ Out of 1,600 large and mid-size companies surveyed by William H. Mercer Inc., nearly 30 percent offer telecommuting and 60 percent offer flex-time programs to keep employees happy according to *Business Week Upfront* (November 24, 1997).

Yet another independent study breaks the work-at-home contingency down further. According to a study by Dr. Charles Grantham, president of the Institute for the Study of Distributed Work in Walnut Creek, California, no one has done a study of a large enough scale of U.S. residences to really assess who works at home. Grantham's research is based on data from the Bureau of Labor Statistics. He assesses the following three categories of people that work at home:

◆ Between 9 and 14 million American workers telecommute at least two days a week.

◆ In addition, 10 to 12 million Americans are home-based workers, running businesses from their home.

◆ Finally, Grantham's last category is the 12 to 16 million Americans who are independent contractors who work on projects for multiple companies. It's the category of the independent contractor that Grantham predicts will explode by the turn of the century (see Wells, 1997).

A Twist in Number of Telecommuters versus Home-Based Entrepreneurs for 1997

There were some surprising statistics in *IDC/LINK's 1997 Home Office Overview Report*. The work-at-home market continues to grow, showing the number of home office households reaching 34.7 million in 1997, up 15.6 percent annually from 1995.

But unlike past years, when home-based businesses were critical in expanding the number of home workers, 1997 has been the year of the corporate home worker—the telecommuter. Telecommuters and after-hours workers grew in record numbers over the past 12 months, and for the first time now outnumber those running a business from home.

Growth of Home-Working Households (in Millions)

	1995	1997	1999
Home office households	27.3	34.7	40.2
Income-generating home offices	18.7	20.7	23.8
Primary self-employed	12.2	13.2	15.5
Part-time self-employed	10.8	9.4	10.7
Corporate home offices	13.6	26.4	28.9
After-hours home offices	10.2	24.3	26.1
Telecommuters	6.4	9.1	10.7

Note: Because some households have more than one home worker, households can belong in more than one category. As a result of these "two-home-office households," the total of subcategories is greater than the home office group they compose.

Source: IDC/LINK, 1997.

Who Works at Home?

In 1995, Ameritech commissioned The Gallup Organization to conduct a study of attitudes and behaviors of people who work at home, or more exactly, self-employed home-based entrepreneurs. Gallup contacted by telephone 1,544 people who work at home in the Midwest. Here's what they had to say.

The Average Work-at-Home Respondent Is:

- ◆ Male (65 percent)
- ◆ 45 years old
- ◆ Married (78 percent)
- ◆ Lives in a suburb of a large metropolitan area (40 percent)
- ◆ Has worked from home for more than a year and a half.

How They Rate Productivity Working at Home:

- ◆ 68 percent say they are more productive working from home than working from their former office.
- ◆ 79 percent say that since they began working at home, they have been happier.
- ◆ 7 percent say they have been less happy since they began working at home.
- ◆ 59 percent say their stress levels have decreased from when they were working in their former office.

◆ 47 percent report putting in fewer hours working at home than they did working in their former office setting.

◆ 38 percent feel they are more respected by their clients or customers because they work at home.

On the Upside, Respondents Said the Biggest Advantages to Working at Home Are:

◆ Getting more accomplished with less distraction (26 percent).

◆ Increased flexibility (26 percent).

◆ Not having to commute (17 percent).

◆ Staying at home with family (16 percent).

As for Work-at-Home Hassles, the Biggest Disadvantages Are:

◆ Interruptions and distractions (30 percent).

◆ Feelings of isolation (18 percent).

◆ Lack of access to proper equipment (17 percent).

Tools of the Trade that Respondents Use:

◆ *Telephone:* 98 percent of respondents have a telephone in their home office. 31 percent say the telephone is the most important piece of office equipment.

◆ *Computer:* 46 percent say the computer is the most important piece of office equipment.

◆ *Office:* 74 percent have a room in their home dedicated to work-at-home activities.

Respondents Said They Would Like to Improve Their Home Offices By:

◆ Adding or upgrading a fax machine (13 percent).

◆ Adding additional phone lines (9 percent).

◆ Buying a computer or a faster computer (7 percent).

◆ Buying a new or faster modem (6 percent).

Respondents Considered Their Biggest Challenges to Be:

◆ Attracting new clients (14 percent).

◆ Finding and managing time (10 percent).

◆ Expanding business (8 percent).

◆ Staying organized (7 percent).

◆ 95 percent of the self-employed say they would make the same decision to become self-employed again.

Source: Ameritech.

Social and Psychological Reasons That the Home Office Is Popular Today

Look in any newspaper or magazine over the past couple of years, and you'll find many articles on the subject of "working at home." Why has this age-old workstyle suddenly become more popular?

What's wrong with work processes as they've been set up all along, you ask. Once you look at the holistic picture of where our society came from and where it's going, it's clear that the traditional corporate office doesn't work for many of us anymore.

We were doing pretty well working in traditional offices for over 50 years. But things began to rev up in the 1980s when technologies started to take over most of our lives. Working at home hasn't exactly hit us like a tidal wave, but we do feel the way we work is somehow *different* today, more so than ever before.

There are three critical business and social developments from the late 1980s to the late 1990s that explains how and why the home office has evolved into its current popularity. What's happening around us causes us to shift gears to view our experiences in a different way. What's changing is this:

◆ Technology

◆ Job functions and work processes.

◆ Lifestyle

Each development is contingent upon each of the others, and there's an undeniable common thread of change that runs throughout each issue. These three areas of our lives are shifting, and in turn, directly affect how, when, and where we work.

Developing Technology Levels the Playing Field of Professionalism for the Home Office and Corporate Office

Information technology is the big umbrella under which all other shifting patterns fall to create this continuum of change. It's the catalyst that changes the way we socialize, live, and work.

Ever since the first fully electronic computer was built in 1945 (called the *Electronic Numerical Integrator and Calculator*, better known as *ENIAC*), our work life has not been the same. From there came the Burroughs E-101 in 1956, a desk-sized computer. The modem debuted in 1966, the Internet was created in 1969 by the Defense Department's Advanced Research Projects Agency, and then Intel introduced the world's first microprocessor in 1971, the fax found its way into our lives in 1980, and from then on, we've been hooked on technology.

Technology wasn't always so easy to buy, however. At first, it was expensive and reserved for only those computer programmers who knew how to use and apply the technology or for those corporate executives who could afford it and who were willing to learn how to tinker with it. But today, high-speed modems cost less than $100, online Internet services are quite affordable, and cellular phones seem to be a fixture on everyone's ear as they walk and drive down the street. Even the once-hallowed technology of videoconferencing—found only in a multi-million-dollar executive suite—is more mainstream as the venerable Kinko's offers it to consumers at about $2.50 a minute per site.

What does all this have to do with the working at home? Well, the way technology is priced and accessible today means that the corporate worker and the home-based worker operate from the same playing field. What *they* can afford, *you* can afford. And much of the time, your home office technology will be more advanced than the technology you had in the corporate office.

In fact, when I worked on the staff of a magazine, I had to share a tiny, old Macintosh with about three staff editors and a handful of freelancers. In 1994, I was tired of fighting for time on a slow and antiquated machine, so I bought my own Macintosh Quadra 660AV machine and printer for my home office. In late 1995, a computer was finally appropriated to each one of the staff members, yet my home office computer was *still* more powerful than the one I was given at the office.

You can read more about technology for the home office in Chapter 4, "Understanding Your Technology Needs."

Unfolding Work Patterns Unshackle Us from Corporate Offices

A new study by Steelcase shows that only a handful of American office workers would take the corner office if they had their choice. Whatever happened to aspirations for the corner office? Apparently corporate protocol is changing the status game in today's office. When 1,000 office workers (split between men and women) were asked where they would like to work, only 17 percent chose the corner office, according to the Steelcase Workplace Index, a semiannual survey that gauges workplace trends in the United States.

It appears that the nature of work is changing and so are the places that people prefer to work. The top choice of the majority of respondents (34 percent) was to work in a home office rather than anywhere else. Other top choices for a preferred work environment included shared team space (15 percent), a cubicle (7 percent), and a think tank where individuals can have privacy (5 percent).

People are realizing that there are alternatives to the traditional 9-to-5 office day because they see that work can get done in many places and at any time of the day or

Figure 1-5 Pedestrians probably give a double take to the emblem on this old stone facade of a New York City–based bank's headquarters. Today, companies rarely use the words *home office* to refer to what they now call "global headquarters." (*MZS*)

night. Workers are beginning to value the more unconventional, flexible options that technology and forward-thinking managers provide.

Comfort and control are important to corporate workers, but they usually don't have as much control over comfort as the home office worker. An overwhelming majority (46 percent) of those responding said they spend eight hours or more at their work space regardless of where it's located. In addition, the majority of respondents selected a number of items they would like to change about their work space, many of which relate to comfort and control over their space. This suggests that because Americans are spending the bulk of their day in their work space, they place higher value on being comfortable and having control over that space. Participants said the following were most valuable to them in a corporate work space (participants were encouraged to select all that applied):

◆ More storage (27 percent).

◆ Better technology support (18 percent).

◆ More privacy (18 percent).

◆ More comfortable chair (17 percent).

◆ Better lighting (14 percent).

◆ More tackable wall space (11 percent).

◆ More space for impromptu meetings (10 percent).

Those responding to the "other" category mentioned a window or better view would be most valuable. Fewer than one-fourth of respondents (21 percent) said they wouldn't change anything about their space. In the home office, you can choose to have more privacy than you've ever had in a corporate setting, a more comfortable chair, better lighting, more tackable wall space, and a whole living or dining room for impromptu meetings, not to mention the possibility of having a better view than you do from your cubicle.

As one home office worker, Cynthia Froggatt, Froggatt Consulting says, "When you think about your home or apartment as an office, how many people get to have a kitchen, a bath, a stereo, and even a terrace in their office like *we* do!"

Why don't people strive for the corner office anymore? Priorities of workers have shifted. People still get downsized, older women have children and make the conscious choice to slow down their career tracks, and a younger, technology-savvy population is entering the workforce seeking out more flexible employment hours and work processes with less hierarchy involved.

Much of this has created a growing breed of worker, the *contracted employee*. The use of independent contract workers is expected to have grown to 35 percent of the total workforce by the year 2000, according to a Conference Board poll conducted in 1996 surveying personnel managers. And that will require a major reevaluation and enhanced flexibility in future space usage plans with a focus on home-based and off-site workplaces.

Thanks in large part to downsizing and to bright, eager, smart people who refuse to work for corporations without vision or direction anymore, the temp industry is growing and changing. Temps aren't being sought for just administrative duties but for more and more technical and professional duties. According to a survey by the American Management Association, over 200 companies that have downsized employees have brought them back onboard as contract employees, the largest being Pacific Bell.

Outsourcing is yet another growing working pattern that gives way to off-site office space. The downsizing of the mid-1990s has left companies with bare-bones staffs who have had no choice but to begin focusing on core competencies. This opened up the demand for outsourcing services and projects, and downsized employees who went on to become entrepreneurs were right there to fill in Corporate America's need for small, specialty-driven outsourcing companies.

Despite the demand for outsourcing, companies are still trying to hire, even in tight labor markets like this. But tight labor markets mean that workplace flexibility is as good as money in the bank:

Century 21 Radnock is the first full-service real estate company to offer our agents telecommuting via the information superhighway!

That's how the Century 21 Web site heading read in 1995. "Some agents are great prospectors but just don't want to be in the office atmosphere. That's OK with us!" read the page. Telecommuting is clearly a recruiting tool, not unlike what other companies are using today to attract job applicants.

That's just one in dozens of stories about companies using workplace flexibility to attract the best talent in tight labor markets. In a city with only 3 percent unemployment, St. Paul, a big insurance company in Minneapolis finds it easy to locate new hires and retain employees. Its secret weapon: flexibility. Alternative work schedules, four-day weeks, and telecommuting are the norm for employees at St. Paul.

A third growth pattern, thanks to technology, is the virtual work process. What is a virtual corporation? One way to describe a *virtual company* is that it exists and communicates mostly through an electronic infrastructure. Virtual workers feel hindered by the constraints of traditional offices. "I'm a technology consultant, but I'm a virtual employee. Our company is a 13-year old virtual company that writes software for hospitals. We have over 750 people in five offices around the country, but only 120 people work in those offices while everyone else is virtual. What that means is that most work is conducted on client sites or at home," explains Holly Gruske, a virtual worker who has a full-scale home office in her den.

Modern Lifestyles Require More Freedom

How many of us struggle to find time? Time to do anything! Single, single with children, married, married with children. Then, there's the care of aging relatives. Nearly everyone has a lifestyle issue that can throw a wrench into the balance of work and home.

More couples in their thirties are having children into their careers. Though more women have entered the workforce, many women who don't find corporate support with which to balance work and family drop out of the workforce to care for children. Many open up businesses at home.

Suburban sprawl has forced couples living in suburbs to face longer commutes to work. Increasingly, natural disasters and weather-related problems leave us without a way to get to corporate headquarters. More families have technology in their homes to allow telecommuting to happen in bad weather.

New job outlooks and lifestyle changes go hand in hand, influencing each other, paving the way for home-based businesses and telecommuting strategies.

Women and Telecommuting

A Bellevue, Washington, staff accountant had arranged to work part-time while on maternity leave, but when her child was born with unforeseen disabilities, it looked as if she was going to have to quit her job. That was until her boss refused to let her leave and worked out a way for the woman to work most of the time at home.

In today's changing workplace, CPAs, like many other professionals, face the challenge of better managing the complex demands of balancing work and life issues. In 1995, 53 percent of the new graduates hired by CPA firms were female, according to the American Institute of Certified Public Accountants (AICPA). Flexibility is the key to managing the new workforce, and the workhorse approach to structuring accounting careers is no longer appropriate in today's marketplace—one major reason why women leave the accounting profession before they reach higher levels.

The accounting industry is not the only one facing this issue. Many have tried to dissect and progress the insularity of Corporate America. The late Felice N. Schwartz was president of a woman's organization, Catalyst, when she prompted a national debate in 1989 with an article in the *Harvard Business Review* in which she asserted that it cost companies more money to employ women than men. She noted that women's careers were often interrupted, or ended, when they had children. She suggested that employers create policies to help mothers balance career and family responsibilities by giving them more flexibility in work hours and providing high-quality day care.

An uproar began almost immediately. Schwartz's proposed alternative career track came to be known as the "mommy track." Detractors voiced the fear that by raising the higher-cost issue, women would not be hired and promoted and that all women would be left with the primary responsibility for child care. Although Schwartz said her views were widely misinterpreted to mean that women are less ambitious than men, the fact remains that women with families face many obstacles in the workplace that men simply don't face.

Schwartz felt instead of letting women's talents go to waste, that the group of male executives who run Corporate America to this day address those needs in a meaningful way. She believed, she said, that there should be a "parent track." Perhaps the notion of telecommuting has answered Schwartz's call for flexibility in the workplace. But not everyone opts to telecommute for fear that it will be held against them by their managers and coworkers.

Generation X'ers to Demand Extreme Flexibility in the Workplace

At Lucent Technologies, telecommuting and other alternative office strategies are now used as a recruiting and retention tool. College hires increasingly ask about what flexible work arrangements the technology company provides. They ask if Lucent has a four-day workweek, telecommuting, or flextime.

Karen Sansone, alternative workplace strategist, feels they are driven to request those types of work styles because they've seen their parents work themselves into the ground and they don't want to repeat the pattern, she concluded at a seminar for the Telecommuting Advisory Council in New York City.

Most post-baby-boomers don't like what they see in Corporate America:

> **"Veal-Fattening Pen: Small, cramped office workstation built of fabric-covered wall dissassembleable partitions and inhabited by junior staff members. Named after the small preslaughter cubicles used by the cattle industry." From the definition of a cubicle that is given in the book,** *Generation X,* **by Douglas Coupland.**

The values the much-maligned Generation X'ers bring to their jobs might just result in a makeover of the workplace. There's good reason for this. First of all, those under 30 were the first generation to be raised in the Information Age, and their high-tech orientation enables them to be more productive, doing more work in less time using technology. That will result in their ability to meet the requirements of their jobs in a shorter workweek so they can spend more time with families and friends.

Gen X'ers also witnessed their parents' loyalty to companies being returned by being downsized out of their jobs. They saw a time of failing family values and a drained educational system. They don't want to repeat the pattern in their own lives, and they don't trust paternal Corporate America to pat them on the head and give them a corner office if they play the game right.

As a result, Generation X'ers are entrepreneurial in spirit, yet practical, fungible workers who tend to play devil's advocate in the workplace by asking to try new work processes and strategies, such as working at home.

Reality Check: Myths about the Home Office

Myth: You get to know your neighbors better once you work at home.

Reality: Most of your neighbors commute to their jobs, are stay-at-home moms, or are retired.

Myth: You can sleep as late as you want and take daily naps when you work at home.

Reality: Sleeping late once in a while is a luxury, but you start to feel slovenly if you get up every day too late while the rest of the world is slaving away. Sleeping late all the time is one way people sabotage themselves into thinking they are failures because they work at home. Most people feel too guilty sleeping late all the time, and in any case, the phone or fax wakes us up anyhow! Naps are great—a true luxury—but impossible if you have an assistant working in your home office.

Myth: You get to see your kids more often when you work at home.

Reality: If you get to see your kids more often when you work at home, chances are you aren't working very much. Working at home does not replace child care. There are real issues about working at home with kids. You'll hear some problems and solutions from people who have managed to work at home with kids in Chapters 7 and 10.

Myth: People that work at home have a one-minute commute.

Reality: Usually the commute to a home office is only a few seconds unless you live in a mansion.

Myth: People that work at home watch soap operas, shop, and eat all day long.

Reality: Well, I admit to watching—sometimes—the Martha Stewart Living show at 9:00 a.m., I manage to grocery shop at 7:30 a.m. on occasion, and I'm thrilled to eat my own cooking at a fraction of the cost and fat of lunches and snacks I used to eat when I worked in New York City. Which brings me to the fact that many people that work at home eat lunch in a civilized manner in their dining room, in their garden, on their deck, at the local coffee house, or park. This is much different from the times I found myself scrambling for an inevitably dirty table at the corner pizza place during a rushed lunch hour.

Myth: People who work at home are workaholics who never know when to stop.

Reality: This is tricky. My home office is located right in the central path of my home near the kitchen, living room, and main bathroom. I admit I go in to it one too many times during the evening and on weekends, a phase I hope will end some day soon. If you place your home office off the beaten path in your home like an attic, basement, or a room way, way down the hall or make it not so easily accessible by putting a screen around it, locking the door, and taking the key into another room, putting your home office in a lockable closet, or putting it in a closable (but not very pragmatic) computer armoire, chances are you won't be making pit stops so often.

Myth: Many articles and books say that a home office should have the following items in place so you don't have to interrupt your pace of work to run to the kitchen: a microwave, coffee machine, exercise equipment, and refrigerator.

Reality: To have everything in your home office from the microwave to a minirefrigerator to exercise equipment is baloney. Are you really going to sit there on a bicycle talking business on the phone? No. What's in the office should not relate to any other part of your life except to beautify and bring comfort into the space.

Second, most of us have enough problems storing files, so who has an office big enough to fit in a kitchen and exercise room?

Another point, who has enough outlets and electricity for a microwave, coffee machine, and refrigerator plus all of the other equipment in the home office such as a computer, fax, printer, and lights to all run at the same time?

And the last point, it's healthy to leave your home office for a change of scenery. When you worked for a corporation, did you enjoy spending eight hours cooped up in your cubicle or office without taking time out to walk around? No, you did everything possible to get out for a change of pace. It's okay to go into the kitchen! Most people who work at home weren't born yesterday and have a solid enough work ethic to know that taking a walk into the kitchen or any other part of the house is only a pit stop and that work beckons in the home office.

Myth: People who work at home are lucky because they get to pick their own furniture.

Reality: True, you do get to pick your own furniture, but inevitably, it won't be exactly what you want or need due to limited funds. You also may not have the room in your home to work on the 8-foot long antique pine dining table you have your heart set on using as a desk, and you are left with a corner of your bedroom in which might just fit a small card table.

Myth: People who work in a house are lucky because they have unlimited storage space in their attics, basements, and garages.

Reality: I admit I'm lucky that I work in a house versus an apartment, but I'm too lazy to store my files anywhere else but in my office space. Not only that, any time I've ever stored stuff in the basement, it gets all moldy and sort of wet due to the dampness of the basement. I won't store files in my attic because I refuse to pull down the stairs to climb up into a searingly hot crawl space to retrieve a file. Forget the garage—my car is already stored there! And there are places like Texas where it's impossible to find a home with a basement.

Myth: People who work at home are lucky because they get to work with their pets in the office.

Reality: It's great when the pet is quiet. In my case, it's not so great when the cat regurgitates on the floor in my office while I'm in the middle of a business call, gets upset and bites me when my modem screeches, starts meowing loudly when I'm on the phone because she's hungry, or chews up paper and pictures I have laying around. Actually, I just live with it and have learned the hard way (destroyed papers and photos) to shut my door so she can't go snooping around when I'm not in the office. You'll hear about other pet foibles and the home office in Chapter 7.

Coming to the Decision to Work at Home

I failed every test I took to assess whether or not I have the right stuff to work at home. Evidently, according to these tests, I'm not the entrepreneurial type. My husband, on the other hand, does fairly well on these tests, but he has no intention of ever working from home or having his own business.

My low scores never seemed to be a deterrent to my working from home. So I went on my intuition, and my gut feeling told me to leave my job and start making a living from my home office. My advice: trust your instincts, not those tests.

The other belief I have about making the decision to work from home is that it is entirely possible that you will be home based for some time, a few years or so, then go back into the corporate fold, and that's perfectly okay. Accept that life is a series of cycles.

It took me about two years to leave my job. It took a lot of soul searching and test taking. It doesn't matter how high your scores are for tests that assess whether or not you are cut out to work at home; making the transition from corporate office to home office is still a tough path to travel. I know people who seemed to have the perfect personality and drive to make it on their own only to go back to a staff position that caught their interest. Others who are shy and reserved are able to make it for years in their own business.

Before leaving my job, people warned me that it would probably be difficult to be home day after day. I didn't listen to them because they had never worked at home before so how would they know. How hard could it be? I already knew I could work at home. I had a dedicated room with great home office furniture in which I had spent at least one day a week informally telecommuting for the preceding few years. I absolutely loved those days I spent telecommuting, often dreading the trip into New York City the next day to my tiny cubicle.

I gave my boss six weeks' notice, and after the shock of my resignation, the teary-eyed calorie-laden good-bye lunches, one too many cocktails, flowers and fruit baskets, I couldn't wait to get started in my new life working from home. I went out, bought a fax machine, called in the phone company to put in a dedicated line for the fax, and I was on my way.

My date book began to look strangely empty with way too much white space after the entry of my last day at the magazine. Hmmm. Okay, I can handle this. Well, farewell corporate life!

I must admit that I thought for sure I'd be sitting in my home office twiddling my thumbs with nothing to do but hope and wait for a call, any call, from anybody.

I kept pushing that fear from my mind by constantly thinking to myself, *just how hard could it be to work at home anyway?*

First Few Months of Working at Home: A Diary

Week 1

Thankfully, Week 1 is a breeze. My husband takes a week off from his job so we can have the vacation we haven't been able to have for three years. It's an easy transition, but out of excitement for me, curiosity, and enthusiasm, he keeps asking me, "So, what is the first thing you're going to do Monday when you wake up to your new life?" It's amazing how you can dream about something, but when you actually do it, it's another story. I panicked because I couldn't get clear in my mind what in the world I would do that first day—I couldn't see beyond my first cup of coffee. Uh-oh.

Week 2—The Official Start of Life in the Home Office

I look at my home office, realize it's pitiful, a disaster, and take some photos of it for this book. I figure I'll keep busy by remodeling the office over the next couple of weeks. That should take up some time!

I spend about an hour deciding what kind of message to put on our voice-mail system.

After I figure that out and finish my first cup of coffee, I get an avalanche of calls. I'm actually busy. I bite the bullet and go get new cards and stationery designed. But wait, things are getting too busy—uh, wait, I don't have time to get this office in shape. Uh-oh. And this is the dilemma most new home-based workers find themselves in—no time to plan and design an adequate home work space.

Week 3

This week, my cat finally realizes that I'm not going back to working in the city four to five days a week. She just doesn't know how to handle this attention from me, and she becomes oh, so clingy at all the inappropriate times.

Week 3 is a blur, and I thank my lucky stars that I'm so busy doing things I really want to wake up each day to do. I am on the phone at least 20 times a day for my various projects.

And, on Thursday, I pick out a $2 can of yellow paint for my office and then go to the beach.

On Friday, I move an enormous amount of junk out of the office so we can paint it.

My husband tells me I look relaxed and I don't have that "commuter growl" on my face anymore.

I'm having a blast and can't believe the fun I'm having in this new life.

Week 4

Is the honeymoon over so soon?

My office is a disaster so I'm working on the dining room table on my laptop. My office smells from paint. I don't know where anything is. I interview a difficult subject for an article. I'm upset after this call and realize when I hang up that I have no one to vent to except the cat. So I tell her what I think of this lady I just interviewed. Oh, well—not the same as venting to my former cubicle neighbor. I can't go to lunch with my cat and continue venting as I would at the magazine. And I hesitate to call anyone at work because I don't want to bother other people who are "at work." Hmmmm. It's getting lonely here. My husband suggests starting my own local free-lance writers' lunch group. It's an interesting idea, it piques my interest, but for now it's on the back burner.

After a few more calls like this, I realize I should not talk to anyone else today. I go to the beach. Relief.

Over the weekend, we rearrange my office, move stuff back in but leave most of the junk sitting in the two guest rooms because I just don't know what to do with any of it.

Month 2

I realize I work more now than I did as a staffer! I literally have to drag myself out of the home office and shut the door, only to go back in there every so often for something or other. My deadlines are looming. Uh-oh, I'm becoming a work-at-home-workaholic. Not good. Goes against what I want to transform my life into.

I do realize that the life of the self-employed means busy times and not-so-busy times. I wonder when the not-so-busy time comes. Because I've never been busier (or happier).

I put up shelves and begin to decorate the office the way I want my office to be decorated (thank goodness it's not up to some office manager with a penchant for spartan cubicles).

Life is going along swimmingly.

I don't know why, but I suddenly panic about working at home, feeling as though I am being irresponsible about the direction I'm taking my career.

My husband saves the day by telling me I do have a responsibility to get into the home office every day to run a business.

A year later, I'm used to working at home. I've gone through a year's worth of cycles where I've panicked from having too much business or no business. I went through the panic of thinking I needed to find a staff job for income until work came to me out of the blue just when I needed it the most. I realized I *can* make things happen; I *can* generate projects! I have more overwhelming feelings of joy than feelings of anxiety about my life change. But I believe it was talking to people for this book that helped me to make the transition quicker and more smoothly than it would have been had I stayed in a vacuum about the issues of the work-at-home lifestyle.

Real-Life Traumas of Working at Home

Planning a home office is the fun part of working at home (so is the part about receiving checks). But there are psychological, social, and emotional disadvantages and advantages to working from home that the shelter magazines and the rest of the media fail to recognize.

Any book about the home office is not complete unless the downside of working at home is explored, for it is a reality in every home-based worker's life. The next section focuses on the realities and the pitfalls of working at home. Don't be discouraged—the rest of the chapter will feature the benefits of working at home to lead you into the rest of the book.

I liken the experience of working at home to having a baby—experienced women don't tell first-time expecting mothers the stark and scary reality of what happens when you get the baby home: You never sleep, you work harder than you've ever worked in your life, you truly believe that no one understands how hard you work, the isolation can drive you nuts, you may end up staying in your robe all day, you crave adult conversation, and staring at the same walls day in and day out without a break can make you think you're going insane. Now men who work at home can more fully understand how a new mom must feel!

Though I certainly don't regret my decision to work at home, I do regret that I didn't talk to anyone about these issues before I made my choice. I wish someone had warned me that the psychological trauma and transition I'd go through before finding true joy in working at home five (sometimes seven) days a week would be so frightening and consuming! But eventually I realized I wasn't alone. It wasn't until I began interviewing people for this book that I realized we are all alike and we are all in the same boat when we set up our first—and our third—home office.

Perceptions about People Who Work at Home

Not only do we have to deal with our own internal struggles and thoughts about our status as a home-based worker but we also have to deal with other people's perceptions of home-based workers. Most people who work in the traditional workplace think at-home workers aren't productive, have lost all self-worth, are out of tune with the rest of the world, or are destitute.

"During my first month as a free agent, I described my switch to a friend, and he responded, 'I really admire you for doing that. Most people wouldn't be able to handle the change in status,'" says Daniel Pink, former chief speechwriter to Al Gore, and now a consultant, in an article he wrote for *Fast Company Magazine* (see Pink, 1998).

The concept of working from a home office just doesn't compute for some people. When Betsy Morris, a writer for *Fortune* magazine (who incidentally works at home with her husband, a writer for *The Wall Street Journal*) had a phone conference with her small son's teacher about some problems the boy was having in school, the teacher politely asked: "Well, what do you and your husband *do*, exactly?" When Morris explained, the teacher went on to say that the reason that the boy was having problems at school was because "he's the only one who has to get up every morning and go out into the world" (see Morris, 1997).

Friends' and Families' Perceptions

A friend of mine told me to tell the person I was meeting for lunch to pick up the tab. "Tell him he should pay for lunch since you're not working right now." I tell her that I *am* working. "Well, you know, I mean you aren't working at a *staff* job." Truth is, I'm doing well in the money department as a self-employed author and journalist. Not only that, I no longer spend money like water on overpriced city lunches, $3 cups of coffee from Starbucks, spur-of-the-moment shoe-buying sprees, high-priced commuter train tickets, new business outfits every week, weekly dry cleaning, reams of pantyhose, and an endless number of unreimbursable cab rides.

A dear friend of mine picked up the tab for dinner because I'm "freelancing." I remember I used to pick up the tab for her when *she* was freelancing.

Back in 1989, when Shannon Wilkinson launched her art marketing business, Cultural Communications, people were shocked when she announced she was going to work from home. "My friends flipped when I told them about my freelance plans. This is before home offices were as prevalent as they are today. They didn't see how anyone working at home could make money. Alot of my friends and colleagues were shocked and some of them were nervous because they didn't return my calls anymore. So I panicked a little bit. I had just put down a couple thousand dollars on a house share in the Hamptons for the summer, which left me $400 in the bank. So it wasn't the best time to go out on my own. But, by the time I left my job, I had over $20,000 in business that had been referred to me which was practically my whole salary anyway! I proved to them I could make money working at home," remembers Wilkinson.

Today, people still say unnecessary, ridiculous, and insensitive things to home-based workers. Most friends and family will say to a home-based worker, "Hey, how's retirement," or "When are you going to get a real job?" Here's one telecommuter's story: "Most folks in my area commute to work in Manhattan or they are retired. People at the health club I go to joke with me that I'm semiretired. Even my son thinks I have a really sweet deal and thinks that I'm not really working. I'm working more now than I ever did! I don't know if anyone really understands this—most of my contemporaries are long in the tooth, and with mindsets from the old school of work ethics, and telecommuting is something completely different to them—they can't believe how good I have it," says Brian McGuren, a five-day-a-week telecommuter at Lucent.

"I think our friends are still waiting for us to get *real* jobs. It took time, but now that we have recognizable clients like Black & Decker and others, it's sinking in that we are a *real* business. Sometimes you have to give them name recognition before they take you seriously," says Elaine Turek, coowner of Big Daddy Digital, a home-based imaging specialty company.

Corporate America's Perceptions

I know of one corporate executive who actually complained to her publicist that a freelance writer interviewed her for an article instead of a staff writer. There are people out there like that? Does working at a desk located in a home office make the freelance writer dumb or less legitimate than if she sat at a desk placed in a corporate setting as a staffer? This is the first bad reaction the freelancer got from someone about her status. She's starting to sense the prejudice that Corporate America has about freelancers.

Many times, people who still work in a corporate office needle those who work at home with subtle, and not-so-subtle, remarks that can irritate or rankle even the most confident home office worker.

"I get a lot of comments from people asking me what's happening on the Oprah show, or they say to me that it must be nice to be able to sleep in. I feel fortunate that I was able to choose this career and go down this path. But people say to me 'you're so lucky to be doing this—maybe I should get into public relations and do it from home.' And I think, wait a minute! This choice took a lot of thought-out planning! It didn't happen overnight by any means. My goal was always to be able to work from home when I had children, but I started planning this way back when," says Jennifer Taper, a home-based media consultant.

Telecommuters often feel prejudices from coworkers who don't work from home. Oftentimes this happens when the telecommuting program is informal. When I worked at home once a week while working at the magazine, coworkers would say things like, "Going shopping tomorrow, eh?" wink, wink. They didn't believe I was going to work hard the next day to meet a major deadline. The problem, I believe, was that I was an informal telecommuter because there wasn't a formal telecommuting program in the company for which I worked. Others have felt the same sting of resentment, or they sense that there is just plain confusion among coworkers.

"It's an interesting psychological dynamic with coworkers because I'm a manager, and I work at home. I can tell that at times people think I'm too far removed from a situation to know what's really going on, and sometimes I feel that way too since you lose that consistency of communication by working at home. Sometimes something happens on a day when you aren't in and no one bothers to tell you about it.

"A lot of these perceptions are a matter of education. For instance, people will call and say 'sorry to bother you at home,' and I find that strange because I am working. I'm trying to get people to understand that I'm just as accessible at home as I am in my office. Those kind of comments indicate to me that they don't think I'm really working when I'm at home," says Jennifer Busch, executive editor and part-time telecommuter at *Contract Design* magazine in New York City.

Another problem with Corporate America is that they dilly-dally when it comes to paying self-employed workers. "I've come to the conclusion that some publications believe that their contributors live in a magical world where telephone companies will wait four months for payment without turning off service, and where the electric company supplies free power for the greater good," says Elayne Robertson Demby, a freelance writer in an article she wrote complaining about the leisurely way companies pay their freelancers (see Demby, 1997).

Neighbors' Perceptions

Neighbors pose an interesting dilemma. Most of them don't really understand the choice to work at home unless they do so themselves.

My neighbor caught me gardening during the workday and said, "How's early retirement?" Furious, I give him the standard response, "I'm working harder now than ever!"

I hope my neighbors see all the Federal Express packages I receive every day which is visual proof signaling that I *am* working. On the other hand, I hope they don't start complaining about the onslaught of one to three trucks daily in the circle, and I hope the trucks don't run anyone over in their rush to finish their deliveries.

Some neighbors think you are available to see them at any time during the day. The *Fortune* magazine writer, Betsy Morris, says that one time a neighbor interrupted her when she peeked into her home office window to ask if she had any bay leaves for a recipe.

"One of the hardest things about working at home is letting the neighbors know that I'm working even though the car is in the driveway," says Nancy Glenn, a telecommuter for Lucent Technologies. "One of my neighbors would pop in all hours, even if I might be on a conference call. It was very difficult for me to hit my mute button and run to the door to tell her I was busy. If I had to do it over again, I'd let them know up front that from 8:00 a.m. to 5:00 p.m., I'm in office mode. It was hard to tell my neighbor all of this, but now she's trained. In fact, she tells other neighbors not to bug me because I am working."

Julie Taylor, a home-based author and publicist, has different reactions from neighbors: "I don't know what a lot of the people in my building do because they are always hanging around, but I think there are a lot of consultants. They generally know I'm around a lot. My window is in a good position where I can keep an eye on things. I'm like one of those little old ladies who are constantly looking out the window. There are some kids across the way who know I'm home, and they call up to my window to come out and play! So I'll go out and talk with them for a few minutes, then go back to work. It's human, it's really a nice way to live and to work."

Other neighbors are confounded by the self-employed who are home based.

"We live in a neighborhood that's very mixed—very young and very old. Since both my husband and I worked at home together for 14 months, it confused the neighbors. The older ones probably worried about us thinking we were at poverty's door; one in particular probably thought we weren't working and didn't have jobs. She thought we were either independently wealthy or at poverty's door," says Jerianne Fitzgerald Thomas, publicist.

Oftentimes neighbors get the wrong impression when they see a relaxed home-based worker taking a much-needed break: "One of my clients lives in the neighborhood, and he works for a big corporation. He'd come home from work, and sometimes we'd bump into each other on the street; I'd be wearing sweats because I was biking in the park. I used to be embarrassed because he'd say things like, 'Oh, I see you had an early day,' so I would consistently reply to him, 'No, I'm just taking a break, I'm going back to work now.' Now, he gets it, and when I see him in the neighborhood, he doesn't say that anymore," says Cynthia Froggatt, strategic facility planning consultant.

Other at-home workers don't want their neighbors to know they have a home office. There are issues of security, zoning, and landlords: "I used to be nervous that my doorman would find out I work at home. The doorman may or may not know I work from home because I do get most of my mail at a post office box. But they may know by now because I have assistants that come up here once in a while. I never really said anything specific to them. What I've learned is that most landlords don't care what you do as long as you are not a manufacturer working from home. I'm very low key about it, and because I don't have a lot of meetings here, it's not an issue. A lot of people in coop buildings have maids, cooks, and helpers, and I know there are other people in the building here with businesses. I don't know them for privacy reasons. Someone told me in my old building that there was a man who ran a business out of his apartment, and he had five lines there. I have three business lines. That's a sure sign that someone is running a business," says an anonymous home office worker in New York City.

In the suburbs, it's quite different when it comes to installing phone lines. The man that installed my second line told me that it's so common for families to put in three to four additional lines for faxes, computers, home offices, and one for each of their kids that no one thinks twice about it anymore.

"I go out of my way to *not* let anybody know that I work at home in this apartment building. Of course, the doormen must know because I get packages all day long, but I never write to the rental agent on my letterhead and I use plain envelopes. I can't imagine that they would not let me do this. I just don't know and don't want to test it. I never even see the Fedex people because they see only my doormen," says a second anonymous home-based publicist who lives in New York City.

Our Own Perceptions

We finally get to the most dangerous of perceptions: our own.

Some of us don't feel, well, *serious* about our business if we work in a home office, like celebrity gossip columnist Liz Smith who recently moved out of her home office. "In keeping with what she calls her 'adolescent outlook,' she used to live a bit as a recent college graduate would, working out of an office in her Manhattan apartment. She now rents a second apartment for herself and uses her old one solely for business," said *New York Times* reporter Geraldine Fabrikant in an article about Smith's financial status (see Fabrikant 1998).

For most of us, when we first begin to work at home, and even years after we have begun to work at home, our egos can be fragile, our self-worth doubtful, our confidence wobbly: "When you first go out on your own, your confidence takes a nose dive. I wish it weren't like that, but I think that's how it is for many people until you gain experience. I didn't want to be perceived as a struggling, but talented person. From the beginning, when people called to find out how I was doing, even if business was terrible and no one had called me for three weeks, I'd say 'Great!' People like upbeat people, it generates business," says Shannon Wilkinson, president of Cultural Communications.

When we first strike out on our own, we could even be soaring with confidence and self-worth, and our ego is grander than ever. Either way is dangerous if we are to remain healthy about working at home. But you should know you aren't alone if you feel remotely under- or overconfident.

To keep me on an even-keel on days when I need a boost of confidence and motivation, I taped positive quotes all around my computer monitor and pinned others onto my bulletin board:

◆ "Willingness to trust the unknown takes courage," from *A Guide to the I Ching.*

◆ "Disperse invading doubt," from *A Guide to the I Ching.*

◆ "The greatest discovery of my time is that human beings can alter their lives by altering their attitudes," William James.

◆ "There is a prospect of a thrilling time ahead for you," and "If your desires are not extravagant, they will be granted," both sayings from Chinese fortune cookies.

The most creative solution to this comes from a posting on an America Online home office–related bulletin board from a home-based worker named Ken: "I went to the bank to get a new $100 bill. Then I headed to Kinko's and made a huge copy of it. It now proudly sits over my desk, and when I feel uninspired, all I need to do is look at it!"

It's those first few days, weeks, and months of working at home that you feel the most vulnerable: "The transition of working for a corporation to working for myself at home was really strange. I was so uptight about going out on my own seven years ago that I was down in my studio at 8:30 every morning because that's when I would have been at my corporate office. I was very disciplined about it at first—I would still go down there diligently even though I was getting more and more stressed because the phones weren't ringing off the hook and there wasn't the hubbub of the office I was used to. Now, I'm at the point where I wouldn't trade it for the world," says Manfred Petri, furniture designer.

"When you are unsure of your future and you are literally wondering how and if you will pay the rent next month, it's all-consuming. When you are by yourself sitting in your home office and your roommates are at work, the phone never rings, you can feel pathetic. It's hard to feel confident when you go to meetings in beautiful offices or luxurious homes. That's what I so clearly remember feeling in the early days of my freelance career," says Shannon Wilkinson, publicist and marketing consultant, in business for herself since the early 1990s.

"The money was really traumatic for me," says Sandy Horowitz* (names with an asterisk have been changed at the request of the interviewee), a publicist in New York City. "I was always standing in the grocery store holding a piece of zucchini wondering if I could afford it. I wore my old clothes until they became tattered and started to become very self-conscious that my clothes were three years old. I then couldn't afford to go to professional events that would cost $30 at a time. I dropped my membership and told them I couldn't afford to go to the events. I realized how unprofessional and ridiculous that sounded to admit such a thing.

"Here's a technique I've learned for myself to help me feel confident and successful. At the end of the day, think about everything you've accomplished that day, and tell yourself how pleased you are about your list. Force yourself to think about what you did do rather than getting mad at yourself for what you think you didn't do," says Horowitz.

There are others who have never felt funny about working from home because it's what they've always done or always wanted to do: "For most of my life, I've worked out of my home. I never even thought of my life in terms of where I'm going to work. The thing most forefront in my mind is what the work is that I'm doing and what it's about. The very first project I did out of college was my own television show and I produced, directed, shot, and edited it in my house. My home number was also the number viewers could call to give commentary on the show," says Maxi Cohen, independent film producer.

"When I was a child, I used to think that the coolest thing to do was to be a freelancer. I pictured myself as a freelancer, even though I didn't know what it was going to be. There must have been something I liked about the word *freelancer*. I always wanted to do it, and now that I'm doing it, I feel as though I was born for it," says Lesley Goddin, owner of Lesley Goddin Writing, Editing and Publicity Services.

Dealing with Isolation in the Home Office

The issue of isolation in the home office is a major problem that is never quite fully addressed in articles about the home office, and I challenge a psychologist or the like to write an entire book on the subject to coach home-based workers on how to deal with its stress. It's an issue that I didn't anticipate would affect me so deeply because I couldn't wait to get some peace and quiet away from a corporate setting.

"We need other people because we are grouped in herds," says Ron Goodrich, a psychologist specializing in workplace stress. "We are social animals. Groups reduce stress and make work psychologically meaningful."

Goodrich has studied at-home workers and discovered there are a number of disturbing consequences of working alone. "I've seen a loss of interest in life, some at-home workers are emotionally depleted, they lack sexual vitality, they have a difficult time opening up to others about emotional stress," says Goodrich. "They are productive, but they have no feeling of accomplishment."

Goodrich says much of this applies to the virtual office worker, the employee of a company that doesn't have a dedicated office to go to anymore and who must work at home, on the road, or at clients' offices on a full-time basis. "Virtual office workers fear they are being left out of decision-making processes, and they begin to feel more loyal to their customers rather than to the employer, then they end up leaving the company because of that lack of connection and alienation," he says.

Figure 1-6 Isolation is the number 1 complaint of people who work from home. At-home workers tend to use the phone and Internet more often to connect with the outside world. (*Sligh*)

Figure 1-7 If you thrive on the constant social interaction you have working in a corporate environment like this MCI office in Boston and feel that you can't enjoy a coffee break by yourself, working at home is most likely not for you. (*Steve Syarto*)

Psychologist Jessica J. Schairer, Ph.D., is a clinical psychologist specializing in the psychology of self-employment. Schairer has worked extensively with work-at-home gurus Paul and Sarah Edwards to study the needs of the self-employed. What she found is that isolation is the number 1 concern of at-home workers. During an America Online roundtable she participated on in 1995, most of the questions were about solving the isolation problem. "We recommend starting your own personal 'board of directors.' This is one or more other self-employed people with whom you get together on a regular basis to discuss what's happening in each of your businesses," counseled Dr. Schairer.

That's exactly what publicist Jerianne Fitzgerald Thomas did. Fitzgerald Thomas and another woman started an informal group of about 10 women who all have public relations businesses of their own and who work at home with the exception of Fitzgerald Thomas. Their goal is to meet quarterly to brainstorm on business problems: "Our goal is to brainstorm; it's what we miss about working for an agency, the brainstorming sessions with groups of people," says Fitzgerald Thomas.

Writer Barbara Mayer joined a similar group, called the Cross Pond Writer's Group, about eight years ago. They meet about one time a month for lunch to discuss projects they are working on, and of course, to brainstorm on problems. "I also try to make a point of going out every day," adds Mayer. "I'm not good at doing this, but I try since I'm single and don't have a partner coming home every night to provide companionship. It's one of the reasons I don't have a copy machine. I take little 'trip treats' for myself, go to the library to copy things, or to the post office. The local post office is a lot of fun! One of the people that works there is part of my writer's group."

Isolation is a problem that continues to dog virtual worker Alex Walker.* Walker works for a large insurance company on the East Coast as a loss control representative. He sees clients to evaluate operations, then submits reports to the underwriter regarding safety. Walker is in the field three days a week and works at home the other two days writing reports.

"In the last year, my company started an informal hoteling program so when we do come into the office to drop off reports, we don't have our own desk anymore—we share it with three other people," says Walker. "Before we started to hotel, we were doing a significant amount of remote work, but we'd go into the office more frequently."

Although Walker likes the flexibility of working at home, the fact that his company has "forced them out of the office" has been a source of stress for him. "The office has always been my primary source of friends, but I rarely see them now that we are quite virtual." Walker knows he needs to find other sources of friendship during the weekdays, but he is too busy working to give it much time.

For New York City–based interior designer Michael Love, the isolation of working at home grew too much to bear any longer. "I was getting insular. I'd start to say 'I'm not going to this or that meeting tonight, I might as well just stay home, I'm too tired anyhow,'" she says. "You think it would be the opposite, that you would want to get out of the house if you were stuck in there the whole day. Now that I moved to an office out of the home, I go out more than I did when I worked from home."

Single people admit it can be more difficult to work at home because isolation is enhanced: "I love this work-at-home lifestyle except for the loneliness. If I had a boyfriend, I would have it all," said an anonymous single work-at-home marketing consultant in New York City.

"The one thing this neighborhood is missing is a real hang out place where I could take my work, like a café where I'd feel comfortable sitting and working alone, but also a place where I could walk into and there would be some sort of group of regulars I could bounce ideas off of. I do that now by phone or e-mail. You find something like that at the Harvard Club. A Barnes & Noble that caters to at-home workers would be good, and so many people go there to do research anyhow. I want a place where there are people who don't think like me or do the same work I do. I was reading a friend's grandfather's autobiography, and he talks about how there was one restaurant in Rockefeller Center where in the 1950s, everyone who was in some kind of creative field would go there for lunch to talk over an idea. They weren't afraid to share ideas," says Cynthia Froggatt, a New York City–based work-at-home consultant.

One work-at-home publicist and writer, Lesley Goddin, who used to work for a large corporation in the stressful New York metropolitan area, moved with her husband to New Mexico to find a slower, more meaningful pace of life. She decided to set up shop in her condo to run her own business, a lifestyle much different from what she was used to. But she's managed to beat home office isolation in a variety of ways.

"One thing I liked about the corporate office was the camaraderie and all the developed friendships over time. But here, I've learned to develop friendships from other sources. One of my clients is a really good friend of mine. But it's a different type of camaraderie because you don't get to hang out over someone's cubicle talk to them about philosophy for hours. That's the only part that's difficult about working at home," says Lesley Goddin, publicist and writer.

Productivity: Do You Really Have to Be Disciplined to Work at Home?

After isolation, discipline is the second-most stressful aspect of working at home. Entrepreneurs who have started their own business, however, have different discipline problems than telecommuters. Home-based entrepreneurs may find the discipline they need through knowing they need to buckle down to be able to pull in a salary. They know they need to finish a project in order to collect a fee.

Telecommuters, on the other had, may find the discipline they need through knowing that they need to sit down and finish a project if they want to keep their telecommuting privileges afloat. However, they also know they are going to pull in a paycheck regardless of whether or not they finish a project on time.

Some home-based workers feel that society is just now starting to understand that working at home means business: "Today, a lot of people are beginning to realize that we're not playing office just because we are working out of our homes. However, people still call me early in the morning and say, 'did I wake you?' and I tend to think—'do *they* nap at work?' I have enough discipline and training to know that this is my job! I'm not playing. People who work at home are not playing! We're working for real money, and you have to take it seriously and discipline yourself. One way to take myself seriously was to have my office properly outfitted," says Linda Shea, owner of Dallas-based Shea Co., Web site designer and consultant.

Telecommuters are a different breed because they have a boss, a team, an employer they still need to answer to on a daily or weekly basis. Their motivation comes from another source: When you first start working at home, you tend to procrastinate a little bit because you are suddenly free. Then, all of a sudden the work comes and bites you at your back, and you learn not to put anything off because you just don't know what's going to happen next during the course of a day or week.

"People think that if you are not in the office you aren't working. So, we telecommuters say we have to work twice as hard to prove that we are in fact working. After you've done it for a while, you get over that, however. You know what your objectives are, and it doesn't matter if someone thinks you're not working because you know how busy you *really* are," says Nancy Glenn, telecommuter at Lucent.

Once you are disciplined, your productivity gains can go through the roof: "I always worked remotely at a Lucent satellite office, but now that I'm telecommuting, quite frankly, I'm working more hours now than I did when I was at the branch office. I'd try to get to the branch office by 8:00 a.m. or earlier, and I was on my way home about 5:15 p.m. Now that I telecommute, I get another 45 minutes of sleep and I'm in my home office 7:30 a.m. I work until about 6:30 p.m. but I could work here all night! I do pop in during the weekends to do some work. I'm working so many more hours, I think the productivity gains to companies that have telecommuters are very, very real!" says Brian McGuren, also a telecommuter at Lucent.

Others just can't discipline themselves enough to make a success of working at home. They need the structure of a corporate office to signal to them it's work time.

Noise and Other Distractions in the Home Office

When reporter Lynn Ermann set up her home office in New York City, she didn't realize that her neighbor would blast Slim Whitman music all day and night or that her block was a popular route for noisy emergency vehicles (see Ermann, 1997). She offers a tip for easing distraction in the home office: "If you live across the street from a modeling agency or [adult] club, sit far away from the window."

New York City, and other large metropolitan areas, were never havens of peacefulness. In fact, New Yorkers who have complained about noisy neighbors, busy nightclubs, shrieking car alarms, garbage trucks, blaring car horns, incessant dog barking, and more don't have to rely on retaliation or earplugs anymore. As of late 1997, anyone violating the city's new noise law will have to pay a hefty fine. If a New Yorker complains of a car alarm, the owner of the car will have to pay from $100 up to $750 (based on the discretion of the investigator on the complaint). Anyone jackhammering will face fines from $440 up to $4,200 (see Toy, 1997).

One New York City–based work-at-home consultant, Bob Livingston,* conducts business in his living room with the windows open regardless of the noise outside. "But the noise outside can be absolutely beyond imagination," he says. Livingston lives near a cluster of hospitals so he has the privilege of hearing constant ambulance sirens, taxi horns, construction, and squealing garbage truck breaks. "I sound like I'm calling clients from a construction site," he says.

Livingston spent $1,000 on a professional radio station voice processor that includes a compression system to cut out background noise. It's the kind of headset-microphone that sportscasters use at noisy stadiums. A phone hybrid coupler connects the radio gear into the phone line. This has solved his problem.

Although New York City–based consultant Cynthia Froggatt lives on a quiet block off of docile Fifth Avenue and Central Park, she has another problem: airplanes. Froggatt has a 10- by 15-foot terrace that makes a great outdoor office during warm weather. However, she's right before the flight path to LaGuardia Airport. "I used to rush back inside my apartment when a plane flew overhead. Frankly, people are so used to New York City noises, that they don't care when we are talking on the phone. I joke about incoming wounded and low-flying planes, but most people aren't bothered by the noise," says Froggatt.

Yet another former telecommuter found that his dog barked too much and disrupted his concentration. Pets can be a noise problem because they think it's time to play just because you're home.

I have somewhat of a different noise problem. I like to sit out on my deck in the summer and write or make calls. When I make calls, especially in August, the sound of the birds and the cicadas are so loud, I oftentimes have to take my calls inside. I'll get comments like, "Where are you calling from, a zoo?"

I would rather be calling from my deck than from a dreary traditional office during any season of the year.

The Volatile Issue of Maintaining Decorum in the Home Office

In 1997, Levi Strauss conducted a survey of 900 workers from large corporations and found out that more than half of those polled are allowed to dress casually every day of the week. Now that casual day is the everyday norm in Corporate America, why is every corporate worker so interested in finding out what the home-based worker wears or when they take a shower?

"I love wearing slippers to work. I need to have a dress code because I don't have my own," says Elaine Turek of home-based Big Daddy Digital.

Most of us are familiar with the MCI television commercial that depicts a young woman, dressed in pajamas and bunny slippers, videoconferencing with a conference room full of men in suits. She also tells us she hasn't showered all day. That commercial, on its own, has elicited much response from the work-at-home community.

Telecommuters and home-based workers either bristle at those implications, or they admit that they indulge in lifestyle choices they couldn't express when they worked in a corporate office: "I cringe every time I see the MCI commercial. You're setting yourself up for failure if you take that commercial seriously. You have to get up every morning as if you are going into a corporate office.

"I have a routine. I watch Good Morning America, get my coffee, change my answering machine to reflect where I'll be, pull in my e-mail. But I get dressed! Don't do *anything* in your pajamas even if your conference call is an hour before your usual routine starts," says Nancy Glenn, a telecommuter at Lucent.

There seems to be two camps about this issue. One camp says you *must*, absolutely, get dressed in work gear every day. The other camp—the one I belong to—believes in comfort wear such as leggings, sweats, robes (when I'm very lazy), and when I feel like getting dressed up—jeans!

"When I first began working at home, I found that after a couple of weeks of working in jeans, I didn't really feel like I had a business. I felt like an impostor. After a few weeks of hanging around in blue jeans, I changed my habits. I curled my hair, put on stockings and skirts—never corporate suits, but miniskirts, black leather outfits—very hip clothing. Wearing high heels at my home office desk makes me feel like the professional I am. I always put on makeup and style my hair, and always wear great accessories because I never want to be on the streets of New York City and run into a client without looking absolutely polished. At the end of the day, then I throw on a pair of jeans, and I don't feel like I'm in my office anymore," says Shannon Wilkinson, publicist and marketing consultant.

The issue of clothing and working at home set off quite a controversy in *The Wall Street Journal*. Columnist Sue Shellenbarger wrote an article in the August 20, 1997, "Marketplace" section questioning whether the press is portraying telecommuters as slobs (see Shellenbarger, 1997). She conducted her own survey of a dozen telecommuters. The results? Most shower and get dressed—at the beginning of the day. One work-at-home stockbroker Shellenbarger interviewed admitted to being a "scum bucket" who doesn't have time to shower. Shellenbarger says, "Telecommuters are a casual but clean, organized, focused lot," and they don't wear bunny slippers but rather prefer bare feet.

Work-at-home consultant Cynthia Froggatt responded to Shellenbarger's article by faxing her a letter expressing her concerns that American society thinks that someone can be productive only if they wear all the appropriate business trappings and suitings: "As for my personal telecommuting style, I dispense with the pajamas and bunny slippers, opting instead to work naked for the first hour of phone calling and e-mailing, then shower," said Cynthia in her letter to Shellenbarger.

Yet another work-at-home consultant wrote Shellenbarger roughly the same thing. "I'm often in my birthday suit," wrote Phidias Cinaglia of Utah.

Deciding what to wear—or what not to wear—when you work at home is one issue. After getting dressed, however, many home-based workers and telecommuters need to give themselves an extra ritual that signals to them that the workday has begun: "There's a telecommuter at Lucent who actually gets into her car and drives around the block to simulate the drive to work. Whatever works for you, do it! Walk the dog around the block before you start your day," adds Glenn.

Before interior designer Michael Love moved out of her Manhattan home office and into an office building, she also had a ritual that she used to begin her day: "I wouldn't go into my kitchen in the morning to make my coffee because I wanted to keep my kitchen as 'home' space. So, I used to go outside, go across the street, buy my coffee and bagel, turn around and come back into my apartment with my breakfast and eat at my desk, just as I would do if I were going into a regular office," says Love.

My own ritual is quite simple. I get up as soon as my husband leaves for work, do a half hour of yoga, then get dressed in leggings and a sweater, eat breakfast, have coffee while pulling in my e-mail; then I start writing until lunchtime when I take a walk outside with friends. I do admit that on certain days, I've worked in my robe until at least 11:00 a.m.! But I don't do it often because it's too embarrassing to answer the door in your robe and accept a package from the Federal Express courier!

The issue of napping is another subject of working at home that is sure to elicit chuckles whenever it's brought up in a conversation: "I was at a party recently when the subject of napping came up. One of the people in the crowd said, 'Alice, you *must* nap; you work at home,'" says Alice Bredin, author of *The Virtual Office Survival Handbook* (John Wiley & Sons, 1996). Irritated by that remark, Bredin said, "Sure, and every so often I get up, call my clients, and tell them to send me more money!"

But napping can be a reality for many home-based workers, and no one should be ashamed to admit to it! Haven't we all at one time or another craved a few minutes alone to nap when we worked in corporate offices? I once tried to open the door to a conference room where I used to work only to find out it was locked because someone was napping. And because we couldn't freely nap in a corporate setting, we'd drown ourselves in one more cup of coffee to keep us awake until quitting time.

The World Nap Organization, a group that studies napping, has numerous reports and surveys on napping on its Web site (http://www.bluemarble.net/~amyloo/wno.html). It recently reported that *Neo Tokyo,* a Japanese cultural magazine, featured an article on the Napping Shop in Tokyo, a business that visits companies with tents, earplugs, and eye masks so workers can nap on breaks.

Napping is becoming more legitimized in the post-Industrial Age United States, too. The Trends Research Institute in Rhinebeck, New York, says that naps allow the body to cool down, recharge batteries, and harmonize the mind. "When companies start realizing that napping makes employees feel better, it will be recognized as a productivity booster," says Gerald Celente, director of the institute.

If doctors, movie projectionists, and cab and limousine drivers can nap on the job, why can't the home office worker nap without feeling remorse? Some home-based workers already recognize naps as a productivity booster and don't feel one pang of guilt: "Now that I have an assistant, I don't take naps anymore," says Julie Taylor, publicist, author, and marketing consultant. "I'm in the office at 6:00 a.m. to call New York. I start my work-day that early. So by the time 11:00 rolls around, I'm ready for a few minutes of napping. I work long days and long nights since I'm always at an event or a seminar. I work hard, so I never felt guilty about taking a short nap."

Dining à la Home Office

One downside of working at home is that you don't have an expense account. So one free-lance writer, Pamela Margoshes, decided to start a unique ritual to save her money while allowing her to entertain and bond with clients at the same time. She invites clients over to her one-bedroom apartment slash home office in Washington, D.C., for lunch.

Admitting it was a bit of an experiment to see how her clients, mostly male, would fare while eating in her apartment, she nevertheless felt it was advantageous to the alternative of overpriced, oversalted lunches in crowded, noisy restaurants.

"Of course, there were negatives. My apartment hasn't much of a kitchen and is furnished postgrad," says Margoshes in an article she wrote about her experiences. "It is more Marge Simpson than Martha Stewart." She even threw a white sheet over a less-than-desirable part of her living room, only to rouse the curiosity of her lunch guest who thought she was sitting shiva.

Margoshes still gives client lunches even though, with over two dozen house plants in the living room, "my apartment tends to look more like a southern outpost of the New York Botanical Garden than someplace where serious business is routinely conducted" (see Margoshes, 1997).

Other Issues That May Deter You from Being Lured into a Home Office

Besides having to struggle with issues of isolation and lack of discipline, here are some other tid-bits about working at home that may sound disappointing to you, but it's part of the reality:

◆ One-third of home-based workers say they have gained weight while working from home, according to *Income Opportunities Magazine.*

◆ Most home-based workers can't easily take a vacation, says Alice Bredin, author and work-at-home expert. "Film for the camera and suntan lotion are minor concerns compared with letting clients know you won't be available, arranging for your phone calls and e-mail messages to be handled, planning for bill payment and invoicing while you're away, and taking care of security of your home and office," she says in one of her syndicated "Working Smart" columns.

◆ Your house could become a drop-off point for UPS packages for your neighbors who aren't home. Delivery people don't care if you're working—they just need a signature for the package.

You'll no doubt hear other horror stories about working from home, but take it all with a grain of salt, and learn from them.

Why Do Americans Quit Their Jobs?

According to the American Association of Home-Based Businesses, 46 million Americans have at-home businesses. But why?

69 percent have their own businesses at home for independence.

38 percent saw an income opportunity to work at home.

33 percent don't like working for a large company.

30 percent needed a change.

25 percent had a great idea for a home-based business.

20 percent were downsized.

18 percent were plain tired of the long commute to and from work.

8 percent cited family reasons as the factor in starting a business from home.

Source: American Association of Home-Based Businesses and Canon Personal Copiers, 1997.

Why People <u>Love</u> Working at Home

Please don't get me wrong—in spite of isolation, distractions, family and friends who think you are lazy or destitute, the absence of expense accounts and perks, the possible lack of clients, checks lost in the mail, and the real presence of a less-than-desirable home work space, there can be indescribable, overwhelming feelings of joy, bliss, gratitude, and elation that overcome people who work at home, feelings that corporate-based employees will never experience unless they take the plunge.

Why does it seem like more and more of us are working at home? "Free agents," the term *Fast Company* magazine calls self-employed Americans, independent contractors, and temporary workers, are leaving Corporate America behind in droves because they were tired of working incredibly hard for companies that lack vision.

Many at-home workers left jobs while they were looking for new jobs, and they never had any intention of becoming freelancers until projects snowballed, and before they knew it, they were in business. It happens all the time: Job hunters who end up freelancers can't seem to find a company they really want to commit themselves and their lives to: "After my boss informed me that my staff position was cut, I worked for him on a consulting basis as I was job hunting. I had several job offers from high-profile companies, and I didn't want any of them because I knew there would be inherent political and personality problems. After four months of looking, nothing felt right. At the same time, more people heard I was on my own and started coming to me for consulting jobs. That's when I realized the joy of not having to answer to a boss. I've been in business since 1993," says Sandy Horowitz,* a public relations and marketing consultant.

Remembering what it was like to be embroiled in office politics can make a home-based worker grateful for the solitude of a home office. One home office worker posted this on an online bulletin board:

> *Dear Friends,*
>
> *I found it quite beneficial to try and work at a client site a few days per week. It's nice to put on a suit…commute…listen to the office gossip…go out to lunch…fight the traffic home…and reflect back about all the baloney and office politics that I don't miss working for someone else! Then, I type up an invoice and fax it in!*
>
> *Bob*

Isolation is one thing, but if media relations consultant Jessica Taper had the choice between solitude and office gossip, she'd choose the privacy of a home office: "When I visit the law firm I used to work for full-time, sometimes I feel like I'm out of the loop. Being out of the loop can have its plusses and its minuses. Something might be happening and I feel like I don't know about it, but on the other hand, maybe I don't want to know about it! Feeling as though I'm sometimes out of the loop isn't about to lure me back to the corporate office by any means," says Taper.

Oftentimes going back to the corporate office means facing a long commute. That's one of the perks of working from home. No commute. Nationwide, the average commuter travels about 45 minutes a day, but for others, the commute to a corporate office can often take a toll on peace and productivity. What can a 1-minute commute to your home office do for you? It gives you that extra time to be clearheaded enough to get work done when others are on the road or on the trains traveling to their offices.

There are times that working at home is a financial dream come true. Dr. Todd LePine, known in Stockbridge, Massachusetts, as an old-fashioned country doctor, hangs a wooden shingle outside of his eighteenth-century farmhouse on Route 102 in the Berkshires. Why is he practicing solo and out of his home, no less? One of the main reasons is that his overhead is at least 10 percent lower than that of other doctors who work in big groups in fancier medical offices. That makes a big difference when about 50 percent of a doctor's revenue typically goes toward overhead, which can cause a large ripple throughout patient care. "I don't have to work as hard to meet my expenses, and since I don't have to kill myself, I can spend more time with my patients," says Dr. LePine (see Lahr, 1998).

Others love the flexibility of the work-at-home lifestyle: "I can't fathom how people who work at a corporate office all day get anything done at home. Do people take off half a day to meet the home security system representative or a contractor? People actually take a day off from work to do something as silly as that? I value being able to run to the bank or post office during off-hours," says Alex Walker,* virtual worker, loss control representative for an insurance company.

Home office workers make no bones about it: They like the fact that they can take care of small household chores during the weekdays instead of the weekend: "My day is much more full because I can take care of some of the personal things I never could when I worked at the branch office or in New Jersey. I can pop out of the house for 10 minutes to get things done, and I make up that time later in the day. I'm much more efficient in getting home and work things done," says Brian McGuren, telecommuter at Lucent.

More and more men are working at home in order to accommodate their family's needs: "Working at home gives us flexibility to fit our lifestyle right now since we have kids. My wife has the corporate 9-to-5 job with business travel. One of the kids always has to go to the doctor or comes home from school sick. When they come home from school at 3 p.m., they need to know someone is always home for them. I've never liked the corporate structure, anyhow," says Steve DeMartino, at-home graphic designer.

Does the Home Office Really Solve Work-Family Balance Issues?

For Bonnie Fuller, working from home solves her work-life balance issues. Fuller's plate has been full since taking on Helen Gurley Brown's illustrious position as editor in chief of *Cosmopolitan Magazine* in early 1997. When she first took the helm from Brown, Fuller had a newborn, was in the process of restoring an 87-year-old house, and was learning to edit the infamous, yet top-selling, woman's magazine worldwide (see Scott, 1997).

How did she do it?

Fuller worked from home when she could and used a headset for talking on the phone while nursing, hired a home-care nurse for her newborn to stand by at all times, and requested that her assistant come to the house when she needed her. Although Fuller was able to juggle work and home by working from her house, obviously this arrangement had its privileges that many of us don't have access to. What about the rest of us? Is it possible to balance our lives without relying on a bevy of assistants?

Most women and men say they wish they could find a flexible work schedule so that they can balance work and family. Yet in 1995, 55 percent of women aged 15 to 44 went back to their jobs within a year after delivering children, according to a study by the Census Bureau, as reported in a 1997 report *Fertility of American Women*. In 1976, only 31 percent of women in the same age group returned to the workforce within a year of giving birth.

Although many men and women decide to work at home to better balance work and family demands, a home office is not a substitute for day care if your child is quite young.

Most of the women interviewed for this book take their child to an outside day-care facility, or they hire an in-house nanny to look after the child during working hours. Nonetheless, they consider working at home as an opportunity to "be there" for their children, regardless of their age.

"Now that I'm a mom with a four-year-old son, the other appealing thing about being in a home office is that when he's going to school in two years, the all-day kindergarten is only two blocks from here. My ultimate goal is to work from 8:00 in the morning to 3:00 in the afternoon. Maybe he'll play while I finish up things in the office, but at least I'll be here, not somewhere else," says Sara Marberry, a marketing and communications consultant who works out of her home office.

Another work-at-home graphic artist with a teenage daughter feels the same way: "My daughter, Rosie, sees how much I work, but she probably thinks that if I had an office somewhere else, I'd probably *never* be home. She can call during the day, and I'll be available to pick her up from school. When you are available for your children, it's always much better for them. I always try to include her in my work when I can by having her help me out labeling slides, for example," says Kathryn Kimball, owner of K2PR, a home-based graphic arts business.

One work-at-home architect and mom made the decision to start her own business based soley on her daughter's needs: "When I knew it was time to go back to work, I struggled with the thought of going back to a corporation. I talked to headhunters when Sally started school, but I really wanted a flexible schedule. Yet at the same time I knew that I wouldn't be given the responsibility and authority on projects I wanted because the most important thing to me was at home. No one in a corporation is going to understand it when a parent says, 'Listen, my daughter is in a play at 2:00, and I have to leave work to see it.' Forget it! They *say* you can, but it's lip service. If I did that, they wouldn't put me on another major project again," says Mary Davis, a home-based architect with her own practice.

Best Places to Work from Home

PC World Magazine and *Money* magazine teamed up in 1997 to rank the nation's largest 300 metropolitan areas for working from home. Since California is the national trendsetter for telecommuting, 6 out of 10 cities in the Top 10 list to live and work are in the Golden State.

San Francisco won the top spot because it has a vast network of Internet access numbers, fast ISDN phone line connections, a high concentration of computer supply stores, and more copy centers per capita than any other city in the country.

Editors from both magazines gathered information on 300 cities from government and private sources such as the FBI, real estate brokers, the Environmental Protection Agency, local phone companies, Internet service providers, and courier services, and all the cities were scored to assess the quality-of-life and quality-of-work conditions for home-based workers.

Figure 1-8 San Francisco won best city to support work-at-home businesses and telecommuters because it has more amenities per square mile to cater to at-home workers. (*MZS*)

Top 10 Best Large Cities to Telecommute From

1. San Francisco
2. San Jose
3. Los Angeles
4. San Diego
5. Seattle
6. Oakland
7. Tampa
8. Orange County
9. Boston
10. Atlanta

Bottom 10 Worst Large Cities to Telecommute From

291. Santa Fe, New Mexico
292. Rockford, Illinois
293. Atlantic-Cape May counties, New Jersey
294. Glens Falls, New York

295. Benton Harbor, Michigan
296. Sumter, South Carolina
297. Wausau, Wisconsin
298. Sioux City, Iowa
299. Mansfield, Ohio
300. Lima, Ohio

Top 10 Midsize Cities to Telecommute From (Population 250,000 to 999,999)

1. Raleigh-Durham-Chapel Hill, North Carolina
2. Sarasota-Bradenton, Florida
3. West Palm Beach-Boca Raton, Florida
4. Santa Barbara, California
5. Jacksonville, Florida
6. Austin, Texas
7. Brevard County, Florida
8. Ventura, California
9. Fort Myers-Cape Coral, Florida
10. Madison, Wisconsin

Top 10 Small Cities to Telecommute From (Population Less Than 250,000)

1. Manchester, New Hampshire
2. Gainesville, Florida
3. Nashua, New Hampshire
4. Bryan-College Station, Texas
5. Naples, Florida
6. Boulder, Colorado
7. San Luis Opispo, California
8. Portsmouth, New Hampshire
9. Santa Cruz, California
10. Olympia, Washington

Source: PC World Communications, 1997. This survey will appear in *PC World* and *Money* magazine's April issues on an annual basis.

The Ubiquitous Tax Issue: A Potential Perk for Home Office Workers

The self-employment tax is quite a startling revelation for new home-based entrepreneurs (something corporate-employed telecommuters don't have to worry about even though they work from home). Self-employment tax is the dark side of having a home-based business because it eats up such a large chunk of your billings. However, on the bright side, becoming self-employed means you can deduct all of your expenses at tax time. So for every sigh you utter when you buy an office chair, or even something as small as a pen for your full-time home office, you can rest assured it's deductible and that *every* penny counts.

Most notable are the home office deduction changes for the tax year 1999 and beyond. The IRS has frustrated and denied deductions to many self-employed people who have a home office but don't use it regularly and exclusively for administrative or management tasks for a business that has no fixed locations such as plumbers, electricians, or computer repair services that work on customer sites. But starting in the 1999 tax year, that group of self-employed people may qualify for the home office deduction.

You can deduct expenses that are directly related to the building and upkeep of your home office as long as the office is used on a full-time and exclusive basis for your work. For example, painting or repairs made to the specific area or room used for business can be deducted in full.

The IRS does give pretty clear guidelines for who can deduct home office expenses in its *Publication 587, Business Use of Your Home.* If you clear the guidelines, you can deduct a business percentage of the direct expenses you pay to keep up and run your entire home such as real estate taxes, deductible mortgage interest, casualty losses, rent, utilities and services, insurance, repairs, and security systems (note again that this may not apply to telecommuters who also have a corporate office to work in, which means that the home office is not that person's exclusive place of business).

To figure deductions for the business use of your home, find the business usage percentage. You can do this by dividing the area used for business by the total area of your home. You may measure the area in square feet. To figure the percentage of your home used for business, divide the number of square feet of space used for business by the total number of square feet of space in your home. If the rooms in your home are about the same size, you can also figure the business percentage by dividing the number of rooms used for business by the number of rooms in your home. You can also use any other reasonable method to determine the business percentage.

For example, your home measures 1,200 square feet, and you use one room that measures 240 square feet for business. Therefore, you would use one-fifth (240 ÷ 1,200), or 20 percent, of the total area for business. As another example, if all the rooms in your home are about the same size and one of the rooms is the home office, then you would use 20 percent of the total house for business deductions.

Also remember that the basic local telephone service charge, including taxes, for the first telephone line into your home is a nondeductible personal expense. However, charges for business long-distance phone calls on that line, as well as the cost of a second line into your home used exclusively for business, are deductible business expenses.

There are lots of twists and turns with home office deductions, but it's well worth it to get the correct IRS information. And whatever you do, don't forget to pay your estimated taxes if you are self-employed!

Do Home Buyers Want Houses with Home Offices?

According to a Coldwell Banker, a major real estate company, the most desired additional room at the turn of the century was a sewing room, and it was considered a luxury item at the time. Today, we will find bonus rooms and great rooms on new construction floor plans. And space for a home office is fast becoming a criterion of home buyers today: "We planned on buying a house into which I could move my office. We looked for a house with that in mind. We looked for a house to provide me with an adequate office space plus all the other things we needed. Was it hard to find? Yes and no. You can always find something that fits your needs if you have enough money. When we were looking, I did find myself walking into some of these houses thinking I could never work there, or that one has a space for a home office, but it was too small a room. It is hard to find something to balance all the criteria of living *and* home office space," says at-home Sara Marberry, in Chicago.

Plano, Texas, is filled with home-based businesses, and it wasn't too hard for media consultant Jessica Taper to find a house with a built-in home office: "The house already had space off the family room tucked into the back corner of the house that was set up as an office. Someone had this house built for them, but the deal fell through and we bought the house. We knew at the time we bought it that it would be the perfect home office for me. But if we ever decided to move to another house, we would definitely look for a space that would be a home office. It would be a criterion."

But in tight urban markets where space is at a premium, apartment dwellers may start out looking for an apartment with a perfect home office, but plans fall short: "When I first began working from home, I lived in a tiny little apartment and worked in a corner of my living room. I had to move because my entire apartment became overtaken with work. I looked specifically for a two-bedroom apartment so that I could have a dedicated office with a door to close. It's not what I have though. I looked at two-bedroom apartments so I could use a second bedroom as an office, but the rooms were so tiny. In New York City, lots of one-bedrooms are cut in half to create a two bedroom apartment. What I found is a walk-through apartment with two living room-type spaces connected by archways. In one of the spaces, off to the side nearest the window, I carved out a space for my home office," says Marita Thomas, home-based editor, of *Fine Furniture International*.

Home-based marketing director, Lisa Wendlinger, and her husband will soon be looking for a house outside of New York City where they currently live: "We will definitely look for a house with space for a home office. Sometimes there are houses with space above the garage, and it will have to be separate enough so that my little boy doesn't know I'm there. It's ideal to have a room in a house that has a couple of different doors from which you can exit. But a separate entrance to a home office is really the perfect situation," says Wendlinger.

More and more people are adding space for a home office as a criteria for house hunting. Trying to find a house with adequate room for a home office set-up is not just on the wish list of full-time home-based workers. Those who work from their homes a couple of days a week need a decent home office, too.

Take the case of Jennifer Thiele Busch, executive editor of *Contract Design* magazine. When she gave birth in 1995, she was lucky enough to forge an arrangement with her manager to work at home two days a week from her house in New Jersey instead of commuting to New York City. She'd like to increase her arrangement to three days a week at home if her job allows for it in the future. Though her present home office is less than desirable in relation to her needs, she is making plans for a future home office: "Right now, my home work space is the quintessential, horrible, home office. I work in a corner of my basement, and I have to walk through piles of junk to get to it. I'm next to this tiny basement window, and my washer and my dryer are behind me. Sometimes they are running, and I have to stop them to do an interview, and other people hear them humming in the background!

"When we move to a new house in a few years, I am definitely going to buy a home with a home office in mind. We'll look for a garage with a room over it or something of that nature. But working in these conditions is giving me insight into what I want in a future home office in order to be comfortable. If I can't find a house with another wing or area, I'll just use a fourth bedroom as a guest room and home office. My ideal home office will have huge windows that look out over the backyard," says Busch.

There could be hope for home-based workers who seek space in a house or apartment for a home office. Builders have slowly started to add a home office in the form of a guest room as the first space you see when you walk into a newly constructed house. The rooms are usually small, 8- by 10-feet and higher-end houses have a designated home office with built-in bookcases and rich woods.

Mark Tilley is trying to help builders identify what makes a more desirable home. Tilley is president of IBACOS, Inc., which stands for Innovative Business and Construction Solutions, a firm dedicated to research and development of better homes.

"Today, the average stay in a home is 12 to 17 years," Tilley says. "Because they are living in their homes longer, homeowners want lasting performance and product integrity."

Tilley identifies a list of features that home buyers are most anxious to find when looking for a house, two of which are related to the home office. He tells builders that they should locate a home office adjacent to the main living space, not isolated from family members, and to insulate walls to minimize noise and other distractions. In addition, he tells builders to construct a well-wired house to allow connections for television, computer, security system, video, telephone, and Internet access. Another interesting point that Tilley makes to builders: Construct houses with movable interior walls that can allow for fluid room configurations that change with lifestyle shifts.

Jennifer Magee, assistant professor from the University of Cincinnati, reports on this nearly budding trend of new construction houses incorporating home offices: "One model home I toured had a designated home office to the right when you walk in the front door, and in it was this glorious antique desk, but I thought that no one could *possibly* work in this home office with this kind of desk. This is just for show. It was really just a small set-up in which to pay bills, but it wasn't a place where from which to run a home-based business. So builders are incorporating the concept of the home office into new construction, but they are going about it in the wrong way. They haven't thought it through. They treat the home office the same as they do a formal living area and dining room which are simply for show and not for use.

"I was briefly encouraged by two scenarios with potential that I saw in Plano, Texas. I went to see a home show featuring million-dollar-plus homes, and I saw one solution that is good for a home office, but they weren't calling it a "home office." The builders had a separate building that they called a 'guest cabana,' 'grandparents suite,' or 'guest suite,' but no one is calling it a 'home office' because of zoning issues. Home offices aren't supposed to be in a separate building; it's usually illegal according to most zoning policies. So nobody is calling this separate structure a 'home office,' but the salespeople said the space could be used as a home office. There were two of these suites solutions in this one particular home show, which was surprising to me. It's a new thing.

"The only glitch with this is that in my research, people don't want the home office to be separate from the rest of the house. They want to be able to walk to the home office in their pajamas and not have to go outdoors to get to it. They want a separate office, but not a separate building.

"The other solution is more interesting. I saw a model two-story U-shaped home with a pool and a back wing upstairs down a long corridor that took you to the office suite, a series of three rooms. One was a reception area, a step down into another larger space that was clearly designated as a 'conference area,' and a separate room called the 'office' with a bathroom. It was a pretty large designated area. It also had a private back entrance from the driveway that went up the side of the house into the back. Or, you could access it from the house itself. I was excited because it was the first thing I had really seen with a functional home office, designed as if someone would really run a business from there.

"As it turns out, the builder built it because his crew was thinking of working there. He told me they don't get a lot of requests for home offices, and they haven't designed any houses with home offices, but they based the house I saw on their own needs. They were thinking that if the house didn't sell, that would be their next office space. Though the builder had designed it for his business, it was still the best solution I had ever seen for incorporating work into living space. Builders don't see the value yet in doing this for other people, however, because they don't get requests for it."

Zoning and Ordinances for Home Businesses: Is There Hope?

It's no wonder that people are afraid to let the world know they work from home.

In a move that seems archaic and short-sighted in a town full of writers and other work-at-home artists that feed the entertainment industry, Los Angeles has instituted the Los Angeles Home Occupation Ordinance that requires writers and artists, and other at-home businesses, to register and pay a special tax. The Writers Guild of America West, which represents movie and television writers, has filed a suit against the city alleging a violation of First Amendment rights to free speech.

Why is such an ordinance being put upon at-home businesses in Los Angeles? To legitimize previously illegal home businesses and to protect residential neighborhoods from becoming commercialized, say town officials. To qualify for the new zoning category, home office workers must agree to limit client visits to one per hour, and they must limit the number of deliveries made to their home. The tax rates vary depending on the occupation, but for film writers, the rate is a minimum of $106 per year plus 0.6 percent of gross income above $18,000.

Jennifer Magee attended a conference on zoning in 1997, and she observes that cities are still slow to see the value of incorporating home offices in a residential area because too many people think it will disrupt the character of a neighborhood: "People really want to keep their neighborhoods as retreats away from the commercial world, but they want everyone else to separate home and work, as well. It takes a lot of education. Unfortunately, all home offices are lumped into one category, all with the same rules. Zoning officials should try to break the category down into subcategories such as professional offices, service-oriented offices, personal services such as beauticians, and home child care. There are different categories that should be treated with different criteria.

"Fort Collins in Colorado is one city with a new, and encouraging, zoning policy that affects home businesses. Over the past couple of years, they passed an innovative land development guidance system as an experiment in developing more community, bringing people together. For instance, they prohibit "big box" retail in favor of plazas. The zoning allows for mixed-use living, including home offices. For instance, half of the residence can be used for a home-based business whereas typical zoning laws allow for only a quarter of a home to be appropriated to home-based work.

"Can we get people to see the value of mixing residential and commercial? The reality is that home-based workers need a lot more support from their communities. They need a Kinko's and a post office, but people in suburbs don't want to have to drive all over the place all day to get there. The convenience of a smaller community where you can walk to a place of service is appealing to home office workers.

"Community support is important because there is so much isolation when you work at home. If these zoning laws could encourage more home offices, people would stop hiding the fact that they work at home. Hiding your home business is a real shame. If people could come out about it and find it's accepted, people would be able to network more and stop feeling so isolated. Unfortunately zoning officials are pretty slow about responding to this. They just concentrate on bigger issues like suburban sprawl problems.

"People have grown up with home and work being so separate that they have a hard time seeing the potential and the benefits of mixed use. It wouldn't work for everyone, however, but people need to know it's an option." The bottom line, she says, is that more education is essential.

Liberty, Missouri: One Town's Zoning Policy for Home Offices

Liberty, Missouri, is one of the oldest cities in the state of Missouri, and sits 15 miles from downtown Kansas City. Its Web site touts the city's cultural jewels, and surprisingly enough, it includes information on its zoning policy for home-based businesses. Home-based businesses are permitted in residentially zoned districts provided that they operate in full compliance with zoning provisions. Furthermore, they must apply for business and occupational licensing as does any other commercial business. As far as zoning policies for home-based businesses go, this one is quite lenient even though it has numerous limitations to protect the neighboring homes. Here's as summary of that city's zoning policy:

◆ *Employees:* No more than one other employee, in addition to the business owner, is allowed in the home office.

◆ *Conduct:* A home business must be enclosed in the living area of the home or the garage and should be clearly an incidental space in the home. No accessory structures or trailers on the property are allowed to house a home business.

◆ *Parking:* Each residential structure is allowed two off-street parking spaces in addition to driveways, and the operation of a home-based business will not reduce the number of spaces for other neighbors.

◆ *Signs:* Residences are not allowed to have any visible evidence of a home business on the structure including signage and storage outside the dwelling. The only signage allowed is a single nonilluminated wall sign that is no larger than 1 square foot.

◆ *Vehicles:* If the home business has a clearly marked vehicle associated with the business, it must weigh under a ton, and it is not allowed to be parked on the street. Only one vehicle per business is allowed on the premises.

◆ *Equipment:* Commercial kitchens, examination or treatment rooms, oversized kilns, paint booths, oversized plumbing, etc., are prohibited on the property.

◆ *Visitors:* A home business cannot exceed more than two commercial deliveries (other than mail or parcel services) per week. Visitors for the home business must park off the street.

◆ *Customers:* Customers and pupils can visit the home-based business only between the hours of 8:00 a.m. and 8:00 p.m. A retail-type home business cannot exceed the limit of eight business visitors per day. Vehicles associated with the business must be limited to two during any 60-minute period. For classes or instructional home businesses, only 12 students are allowed to come to the premises per day and no more than 4 at a time. Classes must be staggered 30 minutes apart to reduce traffic congestion.

There are more provisions for at-home day-care centers and group homes. To read more, you can visit the Web site at www.ci.liberty.mo.us/develop/homeocc.htm.

Three Lessons about Working at Home

In spite of the dangers of zoning, the potential for grouchy neighbors to complain, the sting of self-employment tax, the insensitive comments the home-based worker has to endure, and the lure of seeing friends and family over work to break the isolation, the home office is still where so many people want to be full-time.

When I started to informally telecommute one day or so a week, I found working at home was a luxury, a treat, something everyone in the world should do! Then, I made the leap…I quit my job to work at home writing full-time. Working at home then became my reality, and I quickly lost sight of its being an everyday treat as it had been when I worked in a corporate setting. The first few months were so difficult, I didn't know whom to turn to or what to think of the new life I had started for myself.

That's why I wrote this book. I hope this book will become a workbook and guide for you while at the same time dispelling the myths about the home office the media continues to stress.

◆ What I found through talking to others is that I had to learn some new thought patterns about my new way of life. Other advice? I had to do three extremely difficult things if I was going to make it working at home: Learn to pamper myself during the day doing things that I would never allow myself to do if I worked in a corporate office. Like take a 20-minute nap at 3:00 p.m., play three hours of tennis with a friend on a Monday morning, or take a walk around the neighborhood at 10:00 a.m. listening to a tape on the Walkman.

◆ I had to learn new thought patterns regarding lifestyle issues. Instead of mentally beating myself up and calling myself "lazy" because I woke up at 8:30 a.m. instead of 7:30 a.m., I had to reframe my thoughts and begin telling myself that this is one of the reasons I chose to work at home, so that I didn't have to get up at an unnatural time and rush into the city for a pointless meeting.

Throughout this book, you'll read about how other people who work at home changed their unhealthy thought patterns, as well.

◆ And most importantly, I had to create a comfortable, livable, and stimulating work space from which I really wanted to make a living. This I found to be terribly difficult due to limited funds, limited time to think creatively, and high expectations. Like a lot of spoiled ex-corporate cogs, I never cared about the cost of supplies, furniture, or technology but always expected them to be handed to me in unlimited amounts. Reality sets in when you begin to work at home, and you'll hear lots of stories from other people who have home offices and home studios about the trials and errors of carving out a special niche in the house.

The Foundation of Your Work-at-Home Experience: The Home Office

Setting up a home work space goes far beyond decorating. I certainly don't consider myself a decorator or interior designer, but I do consider myself an experienced at-home worker who understands how a poorly planned or thoughtfully planned environment can deeply affect your outlook on your work and on your lifestyle in general.

Even the most perfectly appointed corporate office is not enough to motivate employees, so what makes anyone think that a perfectly decorated home office will motivate you to earn your living in the most creative way? Don't feel as though you have to mimic those shelter magazine articles when you plan your home office. Instead of letting highly styled photos dictate your vision, instead, really delve into your psyche to discover what experience you want your home office to offer you and what you can put into your home office experience that will produce a joyful, productive working lifestyle. It's this point that I urge you to take seriously. You'll find more help and a worksheet to fill out in the next chapter.

When you work at home, you have to take a lot of things into consideration that you never, ever had the time or luxury to do when you worked in a corporate office where you had virtually no say as to how it was designed. You now have the chance to really consider what feelings your home work space evokes. You now have the chance to closely listen to your body and decide what makes it most *comfortable* and most *uncomfortable*.

You now have the chance to think about what in your working environment makes you happy, gives you joy, and offers you the energy to get you up and into your office morning after morning to make a living.

So the question remains, *can* you find peace and productivity in a home office? You have to find out on your own in order to dispel the myths and reach the realities of your experience of working from home. But in reading through this book, finding out more about the realities behind the lifestyle of the home office worker, you will be better equipped to make a decision if working at home long term is for you. If you're already working at home and reading this book, you will find glimpses of yourself throughout these pages. You'll know you aren't alone, and perhaps you can learn through the solutions to the dilemmas others have faced, or continue to face, as home-based workers.

What Can't You Live Without in Your Home Office?

Now that you work at home and have the freedom to keep whatever you want in your home office for your comfort and aesthetic pleasure—what *do* you want? Here are some answers from home-based workers:

- ◆ "What I can't live without in my home office is my mini hot plate to keep my coffee warm," says one message on the America Online home office–related bulletin board.

- ◆ "Some people need the physical office to physically focus themselves, but I use music. When I'm doing work, I have to have classical or soft background music to help me focus. It signals to me that it's work time," says Holly Gruske, telecommuter.

- ◆ "I have lots of toys. I have a kaleidoscope, a bell, and frog-shaped hand clicker. I use toys as an outlet when I'm on the phone, or when I need a quick break. It works for me," says journalist Barbara Mayer.

- ◆ "My dog is my office manager," says Stephanie Thompson, a real estate salesperson who frequently works at home. Most home office workers can't work without having their pets share their office with them during the day.

Figure 1-9 Home-based workers relish the company of their pets. Real estate agent Stephanie Thompson says her dog is the general manager of her home office. (*Steve Syarto*)

Figure 1-10 Caught in the act! I find peace and productivity while working at home on my deck. The freedom to choose when, where, and how I work is an unbeatable feeling. (*Steve Syarto*)

Figure 2-1. BEFORE: A typical home office. (*Steve Burns/InHouse*)

Figure 2-2. AFTER : This is what you can have if you hire an interior designer to plan and furnish your home office from scratch. (*Steve Burns/InHouse*)

2

Dilemmas of Planning Your Home Office:
Hire a Professional or Do It Yourself?

"I can't believe I was so stupid…no wonder residential designers are perceived by the average consumer as 'too expensive.' They are! It's not that I can't afford the money, it's that I think I shouldn't have had to pay that much for what was done in my home office. The interior design profession is missing the boat by not figuring out how to market and work with people like me, who are not wealthy but have some discretionary income to spend," says one home-based business owner disappointed in the results of her home office that was planned by what turned out to be an expensive interior designer.

Whether you hire an interior designer or do it yourself, the good news is that home offices are today's most popular home improvement projects.

The bad news is that they are poor paybacks if you are looking for a healthy return in your investment.

Generally speaking, it costs about $8,000 to convert a 12- by 12-foot bedroom into a home office with custom cabinetry, workstation, and rewiring, but the actual resale value would give you a return of just half of your investment.

You have to decide how much you want to improve your home by giving yourself a wonderful home office. But remember that satisfying your own need for an efficient, well-planned work space is more important in the long run than just basing your actions on the return on investment of a home office improvement.

Whether you start from scratch to build a home office or you want to improve your home office, you'll have to decide whether to hire a design or planning professional or do it yourself. There are pros and cons to each way of doing it. Professionals can move your project along quickly, but it will cost more money. Doing it yourself may take three times as long to complete at a quarter of the cost. Then there are issues of quality of workmanship (however, hiring a professional doesn't always guarantee high-quality work). This chapter will explore other questions you may have:

♦ Are there benefits to hiring an interior designer to plan my home office?

♦ How much do interior designers cost, and are services worth the value?

♦ How can a store planner help me design my home office?

◆ What are the realities of planning my office on my own?

◆ If I do this on my own, how do I decide where to put my home office?

There are two levels of interior design services that we'll explore in this chapter:

◆ Interior designers

◆ Retail store staff interior decorators and/or planning services

Then we will discuss the most popular category of home office planners:

◆ The DIYers.

When we think of professionals, we are more apt to think of a contractor. We don't think of interior designers. We block out the notion of interior design services because most of us have misconceptions about what it's like to hire and work with an interior designer. We also harbor lots of delusions about the joys of building things with our own creative mind and hands, in other words, becoming a do-it-yourselfer, also known as a "DIYer."

You can spend money on hiring a designer to help you plan your home office, or you can save money by tackling it on your own. Most of us would happily save money to plan out our home office and buy our own furniture on our own time and terms. In fact, most of us do just that, when sometimes we should be turning to design professionals to help save us from our own worst work spaces.

The problem seems to be time and money. It's hard to find the time to actually choose a designer, much less find a store to go into, look around, meet with a planner and wait for the process to begin and to be completed. At-home publicist Shannon Wilkinson, president of home-based Cultural Communication, has been frustrated with the process of hiring someone to plan and design her home office: "You just don't have time to take the measurements, and you don't have time to wait two months for a planning service like Techline to come in measure, order, and install. It takes time to research, it takes time to buy furniture, it takes time to write the checks, and it takes time for furniture to be delivered. And, you still have to run your business, go to meetings, and train people. I haven't had time to do all the research I should do, but I've done enough to know how long I'd have to wait for these things.

"When you are in business, either you can't imagine having the money to do anything, or when you have the money and income to do things, you just don't have the time.

"A lot of people—designers and store planners—just don't realize what goes on in someone's home office day to day, hour to hour, which makes it difficult to think or plan out these things, much less actually do them," says Wilkinson.

At the same time, we should feel lucky to have the option of hiring a design professional to help us with our home office design dilemmas. When we worked for a large corporation, how many of us had the opportunity to hire a design consultant to help us optimize our cubicle space? Not many of us, I'm sure.

In fact, most of us never had to think about how our corporate work spaces were planned and designed. And we certainly didn't have to pay for any of our furniture.

"People have been used to having their offices furnished automatically by their employer. But then a lot of large companies let people go, and lots of managers were left to start their own businesses, or they wanted to build a home office even if they were still working for the company because they weren't sure how long it was going to last before the next downsizing. But they weren't used to having to pay…for anything!" says Georgine Pijut of her past experiences with selling her home office planning services to new entrepreneurs, a business she has since folded.

In my own experience, I've had a patchwork of people helping me plan my home office. When I first set up my home office in my current home, Herman Miller, a major furniture manufacturer, offered me a brief planning session with the designer of my beta-site furniture. I remember being extremely hesitant about the fact that the designer wanted to plan my space by placing my desk so that my back was to the door. I caved in, and that's how the furniture was installed.

After installation, my office turned dangerously messy. Though productive, I wasn't in love with my set-up. During panel discussions about the home office, I showed slides of my home office space to audiences of interior designers hoping someone would come up with a magic solution to my work-space dilemmas. But after hearing peals of laughter from one too many audience members, I realized I could either hire a designer or fix up my office myself. I chose the former option because although I've been in the design industry for a long time, I still have the perception that interior designers are too expensive for my budget.

So my husband and I became do-it-yourselfers: replanning, repositioning, and reconfiguring my home office ourselves.

And finally, I decided it was a priority to hire a feng shui consultant, rather than an interior designer, to help me figure out the best way to situate my home office. You can read about that experience in Chapter 4, "Why the Ancient Art of Placement Is Important for Your Home Office."

Chances are if you are reading this book, you may not be planning to hire an interior designer to handle your home office. But after reading this chapter, you may feel differently about having a professional designer enter your home. It may not be as expensive and embarrassing to have a designer come to your house as you think it might be! Believe it or not, there are affordable design services you can use to help you with your home office needs.

Perceptions about Interior Designers

Most people say they are intimidated by the world of interior decoration and design, and that's why they buy high-end magazines so they can mimic the look themselves instead of hiring a professional. One of the main problems is that most of us don't know the difference between an *interior decorator* and an *interior designer*.

"People who aren't familiar with the field unfortunately tend to mix up decoration and design. It's two different things. Design is accommodating functionality. Aesthetics are a part of that, as well, but when people hear the word *interior designer*, they think it's a decorator who deals solely with aesthetics. Designers really implement a workable space plan that meets the needs of the person or people that work in that space," says Georgene Pijut, an interior designer who once specialized in home office planning and design.

If you're still intimidated by hiring an interior designer to plan and design your home office, you'll be more intimidated if you read the September 1997 issue of *Architectural Digest*. In that issue, you will find a handful of the country's most prominent interior designers in their own well-appointed home offices and in-home work spaces they've designed for wealthy clients who are art dealers, art and book collectors, and a television producer. One home office is in a castle, so that gives you an idea of the realism involved in the article, but that's what *Architectural Digest* is all about…fantasy.

The most important thing I can say to you is that you *don't* have to hire an interior designer or architect that has been featured in *Architectural Digest*, or any other high-end shelter magazine on the newsstand, for that matter. There are plenty of other down-to-earth, talented and sensitive interior designers who are willing to handle your project. You may have to find them through referrals. Picking a designer from a shelter magazine may not be the best idea. But you can certainly clip the pages of the magazine and show a less-expensive designer what you'd like to achieve within a fraction of the cost.

Cost is perhaps the biggest roadblock when it comes to hiring a designer. Designers are known for their champagne taste, but you no doubt have to settle for a wine-in-the-discount-bin-type budget.

It's rare to find a designer who specializes in the home office as opposed to one who specializes in, say, kitchen and bath design. "Rarely do clients call up and say that they have a home office that they need me to design. It's usually part of a larger scheme if I'm doing over a whole apartment or house," says designer Michael Love. She goes on to say that most people who work at home don't think a professionally designed home office will improve their business. She doesn't encourage other interior designers who want to specialize in the home office to focus on that very small niche. "It's not enough for a designer to build a business on if they rely on the few CEOs that require a newly appointed home office," she says.

Why One Designer Stopped Designing Home Offices

Georgene's Home Office Design, Inc., a firm specializing in home office planning, began in the early 1990s and finally folded in the mid-1990s.

Georgene Pijut, president of the firm, had a host of services to offer the home office worker, from hourly consultations to entire home office makeovers. Her motto: "We will maximize the image, comfort, efficiency of your home office, within your means!"

Unfortunately, people had the attitude that they already worked in the comfort of their homes, so why waste any more time and effort to make their home office more comfortable?

Pijut knew, after just one year of opening her doors, that it wasn't going to be easy catering strictly to home office clients. She had begun her business because she realized the untapped home office could be a growth area for design services.

"I found it difficult to sell space planning for home offices. People thought they could do it themselves. What would happen is that after people tried that and found that they really did need some help, they'd call me because they had heard of me by word of mouth. By then, they had gone through those rigors and had found that it was difficult to work in a small space, and they'd question themselves as to why it wasn't feeling right to them or it was too cramped, or they couldn't fit the kids in.

"First of all, planning out small spaces is a difficult task. You usually don't have much space for a home office, or you are trying to build it into your house as discretely as possible. So you have to put in as much work surface as you possibly can, but storage is always a huge problem. So, how do you maneuver everything in such a small space? You end up with a small, cramped space and a lot of stuff from furniture, storage, lighting, equipment, and kids! There's a lot of stuff that has to go into a small home office.

"But people just assumed that once I walked into a room, I would automatically know the answers to their home office problems. Of course, I had ideas, but to get down to the nitty-gritty details—how everything is going to work in such a tiny space—and that takes time to figure out. If I had clients going into a small space who wanted to use furniture they already had, it was easier to judge their needs right away. But if they were starting over fresh, I had to get every single detail about their work styles in order to rework the space for them, and that takes a lot of time. People didn't think it would take as much time as it really did. When you have a tight space, and in there are two or three window walls, and little space to plug things in the space, the space becomes restrictive, which means you have to get more creative, which takes time. Every little inch is so precious in a home office. Sometimes an inch can make a big difference.

"I found that people were just trying to make do with what they had. Extra bedrooms and basements were popular. Spaces in the main living area weren't very popular with people who had children, so they would work in a spare bedroom or basement.

"I do remember one client who had occupied the top floor of the home. The client was running out of storage and had begun using the shower stall for storage space. The bathroom became one of the storage spaces. I'm sure the files were records that the client didn't have to often refer to. I had a consultation with the client, but the client decided not to move after all, but instead to just make do.

"You can only give people your best advice, but it's their home and their business and their decision," says Pijut.

How to Choose an Interior Designer

Pijut has some practical ideas on how to find a designer who will take on a small home office project. She recommends that you use a contract designer rather than a residential designer. The difference is this: A residential designer has experience in designing houses while a contract designer has experience in designing commercial office space, sometimes millions of square feet of corporate office space Pijut advises:

> **If people work in their space for any more than a couple of hours a day, of course they should consult with a designer. It applies to every other area of the home, why not the home office? The same thing applies to kitchen design. If you are going to remodel a kitchen, wouldn't you hire a kitchen designer?**
>
> **There are a lot of things that don't meet the eye immediately that could be very costly if not addressed by a kitchen designer.**

To find a designer who will plan out a home office, you might call a design firm that specializes in office interiors. Some of the designers might freelance and be happy to take on your home office.

It's unfortunate that there aren't more people in that field to help home office workers. But until people recognize the value of the profession and are willing to pay for it, there won't be more people who specialize in home office design.

Using an Interior Designer: One Designer's Advice

Michael Love, a well-known interior designer in New York City, transformed her bedroom into a home office in her apartment, and she maintained that arrangement for seven years until she just couldn't stand for one more minute having her home taken over by employees and work-related furniture and equipment.

Regardless of her transition into a small office in a nearby design center, Love really knows what she's talking about when she discusses home office design. She has clear opinions about how someone should approach an architect or interior designer when it comes to planning a home office. Here are some of her thoughts on hiring an interior designer for home office planning:

A consumer with a home office wouldn't have to hire a full-service designer. A designer could take two to three hours to evaluate a home office space for about $500.

Most people don't really know how to work in their own home office. They work from habit rather than from knowledge. A designer can make you think about those things.

A consultation with a designer can help in a number of ways. For instance, a designer can help someone out especially if they have tight space and can't figure out where to put a home office.

If the office is going to be on view in the living space and not in a separate room, a designer can show you how to close it off in an easy way so that you don't have to get rid of every piece of paper.

To start this process, find yourself a local designer. Here's what I would do if I were called to consult on a home office space. I'd come to your house, walk through your entire house or apartment, look at how you live, and see where there were pockets of space that could be developed into your home office. Because I'm looking at it differently than you do, I would think more expansively of how and where I could fit in a space for you. I might see a closet that could be transformed into a home office that you didn't see at first. Or I could see another part of a room or a part of an alcove that could be made into a work space. These are kinds of things that the designer sees that a person without training doesn't see.

So at this point I've figured out a few good places for your home office. But the next phase is an interview. I'd interview you to find out what you want in your work space, what your needs are for storage, whether or not you need space for an assistant, plus many other questions. All these things I'll ask you to develop into what I call a "brief." A brief tells us both what you need, how you need it, when you need it, and how many times during the day you need it in your home office. These are all typical questions I ask when I'm doing any office space, but for a home office, it's done on a smaller scale.

Then we finally decide, according to your lifestyle, where the best place to put this home office would be. Just a point here—you can call in a designer at any time for a consultation before you set up a home office, or you can even call someone in if you are already in a home office but feel you are in trouble with your work style. For example, you may feel hopelessly disorganized.

You don't always know yourself *why* something isn't working. Sometimes you don't realize that your phone is on the wrong side of the desk, it can be *that* simple. It can be that the chair you're sitting in is all wrong for your body and the tasks you perform. You say you're tired, but that your chair is comfortable. But it may not be giving your body enough support during the course of the day. Most designers are experts on ergonomics for the office.

I would also get into your filing style. I'd ask you how you handle your paperwork. Quite often, I see the real culprit in poor productivity is in how you're handling your paperwork. The bottom line is that if you have a lousy filing system, you're not working well. Most people feel filing systems are typically done in an "a, b, c" fashion, but it should be set up according to subjects in your business. A lot of people who begin to work at home after working in a corporation are used to having other people file for them.

There are other tips I give people about the home office. I tell people *not* to put their fax machine and copier in the same room in which they are working. Having that equipment in a separate room makes you get up from your desk and walk to another space so you aren't just sitting there all day. I really mean it when I say those two things should be in another room. In an apartment, perhaps the hallway closet is the best place to set up for your fax machine, copier, and stationary supplies so it forces you to move around. I'm a big believer in setting up your home office like that.

I also always tell people to make sure they have a door on their kitchen so they don't walk by and see the refrigerator. I had a screen that hid my kitchen when I worked at home. But if you're going to walk past the kitchen to get to and from the fax machine, that's dangerous.

Interior Designers of the Future: Students Get a Dose of Home Office Reality

It wasn't the typical student interior design project, but it was an eye-opening one at that. When Jennifer Magee, a graduate student at UC at the time, asked 36 University of Cincinnati interior design students to conduct on-site interviews with home office workers, so that they could gather information which they would later use and translate into a live/work environment, students didn't think it would be a difficult project to accomplish. Magee recounts her project:

> **The students had a lot of preconceptions about what a home office should be. They really struggled about where they stood on the issues of integration and segregation of work and living space. Some of the students' parents work at home, but their assignment was to find a person who worked at home and conduct an interview with him or her. It was to be a "client" interview. We thought a lot of students would come back empty-handed, but only 1 person out of 36 didn't know someone who worked at home.**
>
> **They got to know firsthand the problems of someone who worked at home. A lot of them originally thought that home and work needed to be very separate because most of the students are from the suburbs and have mothers and fathers who commuted into the city every day, and they grew up with the notion that work is separate, and they thought they would be designing two separate worlds.**
>
> **The project criterion was such that it wasn't just a home office; the project was to be a space for a full-time home-based business that would receive clients, need a conference area, and need to potentially accommodate a couple of employees in the space.**
>
> **The students really struggled. They struggled to determine how much work and home can overlap. Toward the end of the project, many of them changed their stance from the strong segregated attitude to the feeling that it's useful to have more overlap in a home, that rooms could function for different things, and that a home office doesn't always have to hide behind a huge wall in a room that's not connected whatsoever to the home.**

After the interviews, the students were asked to design a live/work environment in an urban site for a mythical young professional couple with one child. Students were told that they had to take into account the husband's bad back pains and the messy work style of his home-based realty business and the wife's desire for an uncluttered home (though she works outside of the home). Other criteria for the mixed-use space included:

◆ Space for a full-time assistant who works for the husband

◆ Space for a copier, 10 filing cabinets, fax, bookshelves, and other technology

◆ Space for client meetings

◆ An office that is handicapped accessible for clients

◆ A small entertainment area for children

◆ A place for the wife to have late-night strategy sessions with fellow lawyers after the rest of the family has gone to sleep

To display the final 33 vignette projects that depicted various versions of a space taking into account all of the above criteria, Magee picked a site in downtown Cincinnati, an older six-story office building. Her students were to convert 2,500 square feet of raw space into a home and work situation, which can be seen in Figures 2-3 through 2-6.

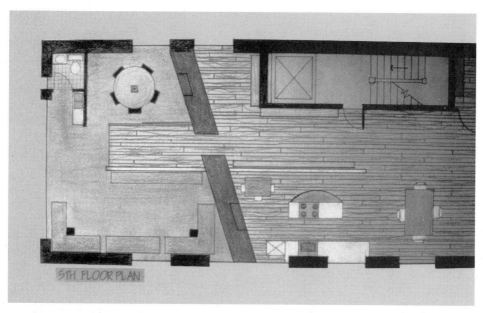

Figure 2-3. Home office designs of the future: Interior design student Abbe Ammann's idea for a mixed-use residential and work-at-home space involves dedicating the left side of the floor plan to an office with lots of work surface and a conferencing area behind a dividing wall. (*Patrick Snadon and Jennifer Magee, University of Cincinnati*)

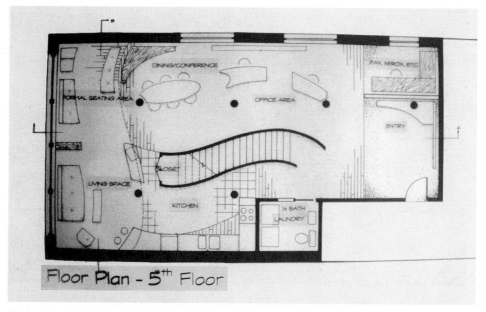

Figure 2-4 Interior design student Sage Harris gives lots of space to the work area and also integrates the work space in the flow of the living area without sectioning it off. (*Patrick Snadon and Jennifer Magee, University of Cincinnati*)

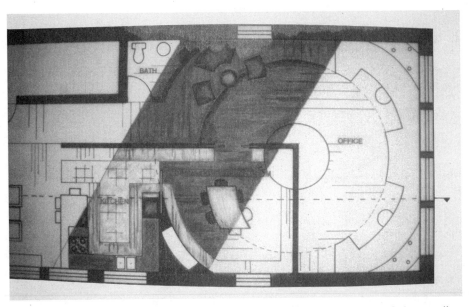

Figure 2-5. Interior design student Heather Fruit's unusual circular floor plan includes an office space with lots of work surface on the curving wall. She includes a large circular bookcase and storage area in back of the desking area. (*Patrick Snadon and Jennifer Magee, University of Cincinnati*)

Figure 2-6. Interior design student Emily Safford's model of a work-live space includes putting the office on a loft upstairs. She includes access to the office through the stairs and from the upstairs hall, or bridge, that leads to sleeping areas. (*Patrick Snadon and Jennifer Magee, University of Cincinnati*)

But the whole project was a challenge to students who still perceive the demarcation between the city, where people work, and the suburbs, where people live, says Magee.

We were making them design something where people would be living and working in a downtown situation. Students weren't used to thinking this way. So some of the students kept living and work space separate; others integrated the two. There was a great range of projects. Some designed a two-story office. Some designed offices on the main floor with private living space upstairs while other students designed the space in the opposite way. Students manipulated the entrances and access to the office space. Some did more open plan and used movable partitions to mark off spaces as needed so that you have the potential for having the office opened up into the family room and the kitchen area, and potential for closing it off. Someone else installed all mobile furniture on casters with the idea that the conferencing area could be expanded when needed, and chairs could be brought in from other rooms of the house.

My hope for them is that now they will see that live/work is a natural extension of interior design. We tried to not give them our preconceptions about work and home. We wanted to see what they came up with.

During the process, I would express apprehension when they designed something where clients would come in to the home office and the first thing that greeted them was the kitchen. That's a problem. We were trying to be flexible, but at the same time express client concerns, getting them to think how it would look to a client working in, or, having a client visiting a home office. It was a fairly limiting space, there wasn't a whole lot of room for extra fluff, and because of this some felt they had to take on a more integrated approach to doubling up the dining room as a conference room. So, many of them ran into problems thinking of where in the living space to position that room in response to the home office. But if you place the dining room close to the kitchen, then does that mean the home office has to be close to the kitchen? I told students that clients don't like to see the kitchen. They struggled with ideas like that.

The same problems happened when students wanted to divide the living room into two spaces, one for work and one for living. Students soon found out that there just wasn't room enough to do that, so they realized that the living room had to double as a space for clients. But then we asked them to think about what happens if the family needs to use the space the same time clients do.

After their original interviews, students wrote up reports, and most of them were really surprised that working at home is such a big issue. When they first got the project, they thought it would be easy since it was focused on a home office. They just didn't think of the home office as being a comprehensive issue in the scope of someone's lifestyle.

They really wrestled with the home office design project, and now they definitely have an appreciation for the home office and the issues surrounding it.

What the Students Discovered about Home Office Design

Students asked interviewees what kinds of problems they had working from home: Are there problems with the location of their home office in relation to the rest of the house? Where do most of the family activities take place, and does that interfere with work? Finally, what would their ideal work space be if they could remodel their office? After visiting the home offices, students got a taste of the home office lifestyle.

One student spoke to a woman on the phone about her work environment, but oddly her description didn't match the reality of the situation. She told the student that her home office was separate and away from family. But when the student visited the interviewee, he found the woman juggling family and work in the same space.

Most students say they saw messy home offices, but then again, they weren't surprised by that. A few photos showed offices that weren't designed in any sense of the word, but were just make-do spaces, mostly set up in spare bedrooms.

Students consistently heard from home office workers that they were quickly running out of space in their current home offices. "The typical 8- by 10-foot spare den or bedroom is constricting in a lot of ways," says Magee. She continues:

> **Students said that many of the workers would prefer to have their home office by the front door but instead had to be secluded in spare bedrooms in the back of the house. One person had an upstairs bedroom home office but decided to move downstairs to a dark and dreary basement. The student couldn't figure out exactly why this worker would do that other than that the person needed more space. The basement had lots of space, but no light, and the student was quite concerned for this home-based worker. It made students realize that people are really struggling in their houses to find adequate space for a home work space, and if they have a spare bedroom, it is probably a little too small for them, so they move to a basement where there's more room, but it's an unpleasant working environment with temperature problems and more.**
>
> **Students realize that houses don't accommodate home-based workers very well, that there were no ideal spaces, only makeshift spaces.**
>
> **Architects and designers haven't really studied home as a workplace as much as we've studied the corporate world. We have the corporate workplace down to a "T" now. Generally people aren't too aware of the productivity they lose in an unergonomic environment, or in even trying to find files when there's not enough storage space to be organized about it, having to go back and forth between rooms because the space isn't big enough to accommodate everything in the same space.**

And that's where an interior designer can help. Perhaps Magee has led a group of enlightened interior design students down an atypical design path on which they will be more sensitive to home office workers' needs in the future.

Taking the Plunge: One Home-Based Worker's Experience with an Interior Designer

Sara Marberry
Sara Marberry Communications
Evanston, Illinois
Publicist and author

Sara Marberry started her business in 1990 after she made her mark in the interior design industry as an editor of *Contract Design,* a trade publication in New York City. When her family moved to Chicago, they rented a small condominium where there wasn't enough space for Marberry to work from, so for two years until they bought a house in Evanston, Marberry rented a small office outside of the home.

Although she never planned on using an interior designer for her house, much less her home office, Marberry was soon a client of Chicago-based interior designer Janet Schirn.

Schirn is well known in the interior design field, so it's no wonder that Marberry initially thought it would be too expensive to hire her for design services.

But here's what Marberry experienced by using an interior designer.

Before: The Home Office Before the Designer's Touch

It's interesting to me to look at the consumer's process of buying a new car. Cars are like $20,000, $30,000! And, it's no big deal to spend that kind of money on a new car. You may grumble a little bit about it, and it's different from the first car you bought for $5,000 used, but that's what cars cost these days.

But when it comes to creating spaces where someone is in every day, people just can't seem to spend the money. We ask ourselves, "Can I really spend $5,000 to make my office a nice place?" That's absurd, I'm here just about every single day! I think it's really important to set up a space that you feel good and comfortable in, and no matter where you move, you can get furniture that is adaptable to that next space.

When I started my business in 1990, I decided not to invest in any good furniture because I wanted to wait and see how the business grew.

Then we moved, and I had the temporary office, and I still didn't want to buy any furniture until I was finally in a place where I thought I'd be for a while. Now, I'm in that place.

There were some issues about whether or not I wanted to spend the money on this, but it became increasingly important to me to set up an office space I really liked. So many times I walk into people's offices or home offices and look at where they work, and these are businesses that are billing a couple hundred thousand dollars a year—and they are working in these spaces that are terrible. A lot of it is the mentality of "well, I'm just starting out my business, it's okay to work on the kitchen table." I know that creating a pleasing home and work environment that is good for you and has familiar elements in it, such as natural light, will make all the difference in the world about how you feel when you are in this space, and hopefully will increase your productivity and your creativity.

For the longest time, I've worked on some pretty terrible furniture (see Figures 2-7 and 2-8). Right now, my office consists of this horrible computer desk I bought at OfficeMax before I even had a home office, an old kitchen table, a couple of filing cabinets, and a tall Parsons table holding my copier. It's all very expendable furniture that will go in the trash.

Figure 2-7. (Before) Sara Marberry realized she owed it to herself to spend money to transform her home office into something she would be proud to call her workplace, so she hired an interior designer to help her achieve her goal. (*Sara Marberry*)

Figure 2-8. (Before) Marberry trashed her old home office furniture once her new desk, chair, and files arrived. (*Sara*

The Process of Using an Interior Designer

During a client meeting in which Janet was involved, I told her that I wished I could afford to use her services. She looked me dead in the eye and said, "But you *can* afford to use my services. I work with people with limited budgets all the time." A little light bulb went off in my head, and I said, that's really true! Why didn't I even think of that? Here I work in the design industry for 15 years and I, too, had this perception that an interior designer cost a lot of money. And while it costs more than just going out and doing it all yourself, there are definite benefits to using an interior designer.

About a month later, I called her. She came to see the temporary office space that I was in, and then the house, and finally the room in our house that I had designated as the office space I wanted to move into.

I told her that my budget for design fees and furniture for my home office would be $5,000. I also had her look at the rest of the house because there are other things I want to do, but we made a deal where I'd start on the office first and we'd do other things in time.

Janet was really excited about working with me because she has a particular interest in home offices. You know how you bring an interior designer into your house and you can be a little embarrassed about the things you have or the way you live. And you expect them to look at you and your home with their nose in the air. But Janet was very gracious and understood my feelings.

Janet loved the house. It's an older house with a lot of light in it. The space I intended to use as a home office has two windows in it and has 12-foot ceilings, so there's lots of light in there, too.

She did pick up right away that I have a storage problem. She could see in the temporary office that although I have files and shelving, piles of paper were still visible, and we both knew that I'd have the same problem in my home office. So the solutions she proposed were based on storage-based solutions using lateral files to provide not only storage but counter space to set things on and to place computer equipment.

I also had to deal with lighting issues. I had fluorescent lights in my temporary office of two years, and I hated them. So for my home office, I was insisting on halogen uplights and a few desk lamps, but Janet said I really had to have better lighting than that. She suggested a suspended lighting system that I may use in the future.

After Janet came to my home that first time, she called three weeks later to tell me she had some design ideas and she wanted me to come down to her office in Chicago to see them. I figured it would only take about half an hour. Two hours later…She had come up with lots of spatial layouts, and several of them had my desk placed in a corner and my back to the door. I was very concerned with not having my back to the door. I really didn't want that. Janet understood my concerns so we took time to go through several different scenarios and talk about how I thought each would work for me.

We finally came up with a good scheme. She proposed I take two walls of lateral files in the office and a desk that came out in the middle of the room.

Figures 2-9 and 2-10. (During process) These sketches, by designer Janet Schirn, represent Marberry's home office solutions. (*Sara Marberry*)

And she said she wanted to put a shelving unit on the wall, which appealed to me because I wanted to put books and art objects up, as well (see Figures 2-9 and 2-10).

The position of my computer is very important to me. I know it is because I sit in front of it so often. I also needed adequate accommodations for keyboard paraphernalia and ergonomically correct positioning. Janet was very much up on that subject.

Most of what drove this layout design was me. But why shouldn't it? Because I have to work in the space. But I am in the design industry and probably have a little more experience in spatial design and layout. I was also the kid who built Lego houses and drawing plans for houses. But there are others who wouldn't know the first thing about doing that and would benefit from an interior designer.

So now Janet knew she wanted to propose some sort of table desk, filing system, wall unit, and chair for me, but at that point she didn't know exactly what product she wanted to specify.

Another three weeks passed after that meeting. Then Janet called and said she had more ideas for my home office and wanted me to come back downtown to see them. She sat me down and said she had three different scenarios—a low-cost, a midcost, and a high-cost scenario. The low and medium were right around the $5,000 mark. The high one was about $7,000 to $8,000 not including her fees.

The furniture Janet proposed for the low-cost scenario included a HON filing system. For the medium to high scenario she proposed a higher-priced Meridian filing system, which I chose to go with because I had a connection with the company and knew I could get a good deal on it.

When I first met with Janet, we talked about my personal style and what I liked. I'm not a traditional person, and even though this house is an older house, it's not traditional. I'm more of a transitional person. I don't like ultra-modern style, but I don't like traditional, either. I told Janet I liked some of the home office furniture out there like Techline, but she had unpleasant things to say about it. Janet has some very strong opinions that there are a lot of furniture manufacturers out there that aren't making high-quality furniture. Her whole idea was to specify regular contract furniture because she feels that is what is going to last the longest and would the most durable. I agreed with her. Certainly if I had been in a different economic status, I would have said that it might be easier to specify Techline. However, I do know a woman who just ordered Techline furniture for her office and she couldn't be happier with it. But I bet she's spending just as much on Techline as I am spending for mine. But of course I have the connections and can get the contract furniture at a discount.

Discounted furniture is really one of the benefits of working with an interior designer. They can get better prices on furniture than you can if you just walked directly into a store or a dealer.

Janet originally proposed for my home office a traditional Baker desk with ball and claw legs. I don't like ball and claw legs. She presented another cleaner style Baker desk, but it was $3,000! Even though I have connections at Baker, I told Janet that it wasn't really my style. The other desk she suggested was a very classic Herman Miller table desk with chrome and wood, which is more to my liking. I also picked an Eames chair to go with it. I know there are lots of next-generation ergonomic office chairs out there on the market, but I just needed a task chair, not some big fancy leather executive chair. I wanted something with arm rests because that's how I work on my computer.

The furniture I'm getting for this space is flexible enough so that if I were to have to move somewhere unexpectedly, I would be able to use this.

The furniture is due early January 1998. I started this process in July 1997! It's frustrating to me because it's taking so long to get designed. Right now there are boxes in the corner, and I'm not going to unpack anything until my file cabinets are here so I can put everything right into them.

I ended up ordering my desk and chair through a dealer, and they have installers, and, Janet has some people she works with to install furniture.

We haven't found an adequate wall unit, so she's designing some shelving units for my wall that she'll have someone come in and install. She's willing to do anything I want her to do. Part of a designer's fee is based on the furniture she sells, but I told Janet I could get the furniture myself and she was fine with that.

I'm going to pay the manufacturer separately, and her fee separately, too. I just received a partial bill from her for $1,400 in design fees. My desk and my chair will come in right around $1,000 and filing system will cost about $1,500 to $2,000. The proposed suspended lighting system will be about another $1,500, but I may wait on that purchase. I have hardwood floors and will probably go out and buy a nice little Oriental rug myself for $500.

I'm going to come in around $5,000, but the quality of furniture I'm getting is pretty high, and I'm not sure someone without my connections could be

Figure 2-11. (After) Marberry's new nearly finished office. (*Sara Marberry*)

able to do it for this amount of money. It wouldn't be that much more, however, because even the prices Janet quoted me were about 20 to 25 percent more than what I'm paying for furniture and filing.

At the same time, my husband doesn't see the benefit of using an interior designer. He thinks what I'm doing for my office is a joke!

My husband looked at the plan after I came home with it, and said "I could have done that!" I said to him, "You don't even know what we went through to get to this point." I believe he just doesn't realize how he's going to feel when he sees the finished product. He doesn't realize that there's no way I could have achieved this result on my own (see Figure 2-11).

After: Lessons Learned from Working with an Interior Designer

If I had to do this all over again, I would use a designer, but I'd start the process earlier. It was a long process. Obviously I'm not Janet's main client, and I never told her I was in any kind of rush. If I had been pushy and said I needed it done quickly, the process would have been finished sooner. But I was surprised at how long it took from one step to the next.

You really have to know your potential problems when working with a designer or else something might get overlooked.

When I moved into the home office from the temporary office, I realized I had a big mess on the floor with all the wires. I told Janet there's a real wire problem here that has to be addressed.

The solution is that the lateral files will have connecting tops on them, and they will clear the wall with an inch or two of space on top so there will be a slot between the file cabinet and the wall to lay wires, but they will be covered by tops.

Also, if you work with an interior designer and they specify the furniture, they will specify several options for you, and you can go out and find the furniture yourself. You can save some money by trying to do that, but the downside of that is in many cases there's no time to do that because time is money.

Points to Consider When Hiring an Interior Designer for Your Home Office

- ◆ Begin the process 4 to 6 months prior to the time you envision the project completed. Design, furniture specification, and procurement of furniture takes time. Furniture has a 6- to 9-week lead time in many cases.

- ◆ Hire an interior designer based on a fee for services, not an hourly rate plus a percentage of the furniture costs. Marberry says she should have negotiated a flat rate with Schirn for design and furniture specification services only. If Marberry found that Schirn wouldn't have done that, she says she would have found a less-experienced, more "hungrier for work" designer for the job.

- ◆ Make sure the design firm sends you monthly bills instead of letting the bills mushroom at the end of a project. Marberry didn't know how much the "meter had run" until it was too late because she wasn't billed on a monthly basis.

- ◆ If you are going to use a designer's full services, make sure you get it in writing that you won't have to pay for the initial consultation. Designers almost always charge for that meeting. "I give complimentary first-time consultations all the time in my business, so why can't interior designers do the same?" asks Marberry.

- ◆ During the first meeting, be *explicit* and *firm* in what you are willing to pay for in terms of design fees and furniture.

"My main motivation in working with an interior designer was mostly to save time and get design ideas that I wouldn't have thought of myself," Marberry summarizes. "Did I save time? Maybe. Did I get design ideas that I wouldn't have thought of myself? Probably not. What I got was confirmation from a design professional that my ideas were on target for my needs, and then direction as to how to fulfill those ideas."

Overhauling a Home Office with the Help of an Interior Designer

Renay Nieto
The Bear's Paw
Corrales, New Mexico
A business dedicated to the artwork of noted New Mexico painter John Nieto

For 20 years, Renay Nieto worked from home managing the art of John Nieto, her husband, for their business called "The Bear's Paw." Before that, she was a banker.

"It was great to quit banking and work at home because I could do my job, raise my boys, and in the middle of the day I'd cook brownies. It was ideal," says Renay.

But what sounds idyllic was actually flawed because Renay worked for 20 years in an office that was such a disaster that she didn't keep a photo of what it looked like.

"My old office was right next to my master bedroom. It was a total disaster. Not organized at all. I had a makeshift shelf for organization, but I'm not a real organizer, so it really didn't help. I would use the floor as my file cabinet. I had a huge desk that was covered with stuff. The office was right next to the master bedroom, which was a problem for my husband because he would work at night and sleep late. I'd get up early and start on the phone, so that would disturb him."

Her daughter-in-law, Lara Nieto, saved the day. Nieto told her mother-in-law about an opportunity for a project where she could have her office of her dreams if she'd allow an interior designer to design a home office using lots of laminate from Wilsonart Plastics. Nieto realized this would be the only way she'd ever get herself organized—with her daughter-in-law's and an interior designer's help.

What everyone realized was that Nieto's home office should be relocated to the 440-square-foot guest house on the property in order to separate the business from the central house. (John Nieto's studio is housed in a separate structure on the property away from the main house and guest house.) No longer did Nieto have to work in a cramped spare bedroom with her storage and materials spread out in closets. Nor did she have to drag bulky crates off into the garage, or have John Nieto sign prints on her dining room table. The business would be contained in the guest house with ample floor space to accommodate all of Nieto's needs:

> **My daughter-in-law worked for me when she was in college, and she's a real organizer. Lara was always telling me to get organized, and she had lots of ideas of how to do it. She came to me and told me about an opportunity to redo my home office with Wilsonart. So she said I could have the office of my dreams! I was so excited because I would have never gotten around to doing it on my own. I would have continued to do everything the hard way!**
>
> **Working with an interior designer, Gay Fly of Houston, was great. Lara helped me work with Gay because she already knew all my needs. She could tell the designer everything I needed—things I would even forget I needed!**

Lara thought of things I never would have thought of doing, such as constructing the light box I now have. I work constantly with 4- by 5-inch color transparencies. In the old office, I would store them in black boxes that are supposed to hold computer disks. I had about 12 boxes stacked everywhere. Then I had this little old light box. Lara helped the designer come up with this wonderful, ideal light box with filing on the side of it (see Figure 2-15). I would have never thought of it! It is my favorite part of the whole office!

In the new office, everything has a place. Lara and the designer had a table built exactly for what we wanted. It's something I always dreamed of instead of using the dining room table. I just told them my needs, and they came up with the idea to design this table that can be used as a regular countertop with bar stools around it. When we need to sign prints, we fold it open to become a huge long table perfect for signing prints. And, there's storage underneath it where we can put prints. You only need a really large space when you are signing prints, that's all. We fold it open and it's at a height where you can comfortably stand and sign prints.

I'd tell anyone who wanted to get organized to get an interior designer into their home office because you just can't do it for yourself. Now, it's just so easy to work in the office, everything is just so perfect. And now my husband isn't disturbed by the fax or the phone.

Figure 2-12. Twenty years after Renay Nieto began to work at home, she was still working in a spare bedroom in the house while the 440-square-foot guest house with kitchen and bath languished, waiting for her to realize what an ideal home office space it could make. (*Wilsonart/Joshua McHugh*)

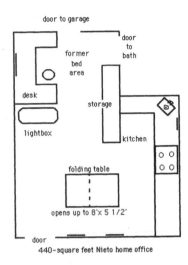

door to garage

former
bed
area

door
to
bath

desk

storage

lightbox

kitchen

folding table

opens up to 8'x 5 1/2'

door

440-square feet Nieto home office

Figure 2-13. (Before) Renay Nieto never liked the guest house's interior until an interior designer transformed the dark space into a professional office. A desk and lightbox replaced the bedroom area, and the folding table replaced the kitchen table and chairs. (*Wilsonart/Joshua McHugh*)

Figure 2-14. (After) Here's a layout of Renay Nieto's guest house turned home office. Custom laminate desking was built in the former bedroom area of the 440-square-foot guest house. The kitchen and bath stayed in place but were updated in laminate. (*MZS*)

Figure 2-15. (After) Renay Nieto's favorite part of her new home office is the custom lightbox with side-drawer storage for transparencies that designer Gay Fly designed for her. The table components, even the legs that look like metal, are wrapped in Wilsonart Laminate. (*Wilsonart/Joshua McHugh*)

Figure 2-16. (After) How does Renay Nieto like living with a laminate-filled home office? The new colors convinced her that the material has come a long way. Carpeting was nixed because large crate deliveries could ruin it, so a laminate floor that looks like wood planking was installed. Here's a shot of the foldout table with storage used for signing prints. (*Wilsonart/Joshua McHugh*)

Figure 2-17. Renay Nieto still keeps prints and other shipping materials neatly stacked on factory-style steel shelves in the garage. (*Wilsonart/Joshua McHugh*)

Making the Decision to Use Retail Planning Services

There are so many retail stores that offer interior design planning services. But you won't get the detailed, therapeutic session that you would if you hired an independent architect or designer to come to your home for a consultation. Obviously, an interior designer on staff at a retail store will try to get you to make all your purchases from that store only. And the process will take nearly double the time than if you went to a store, picked out furniture right then and there, took it home, put it together, and installed it yourself.

Using store planning services is the bridge between using independent interior designers and doing it all yourself. Store planning makes sense if you have a medium-size budget versus doing it yourself with a low budget or hiring a designer if you have a high budget. But remember that sometimes using an interior designer and ordering furniture from a company like Techline can cost you the same amount of money!

In the following section, we'll look at planning services geared toward low- to medium-budget home offices.

Advice from The Container Store's Home Office Planners

The Container Store is a retailer devoted to organizing every area of your home, office, and life (see Figure 2-18). At the same time, they run on a very strong philosophy of being a service-oriented store that provides solutions rather than products.

The store planners report that there's been a substantial increase in the last two years in people coming into the stores or leaving them suggestion cards asking about home office solutions. One trend the store notices: People with home offices need to have room for their children to work in there, as well, especially on the computer. Because of the increase in little hands and eyes roaming around the home office, there's a greater need for organization and storage in the space.

Every buyer and sales associate in The Container Store is trained to be a "professional" space planner. A customer can walk right into the store without as much as exact measurements of the space in which they intend to place a home office, and right then and there, planners will draw a customer's intended home office plan onto graph paper. With this "guestimate" the planner will then be able to estimate the right desk and storage system for their budget. Peggy Doughty, a closet and storage product buyer at The Container Store, describes the service:

> **We develop relationships with customers by talking to them and guiding them to a product that works best for what they need. If it's a kitchen drawer divider that could work as a pencil divider in your home office, that's okay.**
>
> **We all have considerable training in products and in planning. We frequently talk with each other in the store about what types of problems people tend to encounter, and we try to pull in our personal experiences to help each other, which helps us to help customers. Buyers have to work in sales posi-**

Figure 2-18. Many of The Container Store planners have home offices filled with storage and desking solutions, too, and we have to be able to learn the planning process through customer interaction. The process of planning is really developing a relationship and asking questions.

Figure 2-18. Many of The Container Store planners have home offices filled with storage and desking solutions from the store. This home office belongs to Peggy Doughty, buyer of closet and storage products for The Container Store, also a trained space planner. (*The Container Store*)

tions, too, and we have to be able to learn the planning process through customer interaction. The process of planning is really developing a relationship and asking questions.

With home office planning, one of the questions I might ask customers who walked into the store is, how much space do they plan to devote to their home office? So many people don't have a room to devote to a home office and only have a closet, a nook in den, or a wall in the guest bedroom. The first questions we ask are intended to help them determine how much space they can and are willing to devote to the work space.

"One of the pluses of doing the drawings that, rather than just communicating a solution with the customer, we can engage the customer in the process of visualizing the solution, and they take an active part in the process. They will suddenly remember if a husband has a computer he wants to put in the office, and they realize they need a lot more space for two computers.

We then give the drawings to the customer, and that becomes the customer's blueprint in setting up their systems when they get home. They can set up in a matter of hours.

Jill Nance, the home office solutions buyer at The Container Store further clarifies how the store planners can help you with your home office:

The Container Store's employees are not interior designers, but we are considered peers of our customers. Everyone comes from different walks of life—some from teaching, music, and even architecture and design backgrounds—we aren't doing architectural planning here, and we aren't talking about moving walls with customers.

We spend lot of time, effort, and energy training our employees to be space planners. We have a full-time position called the "super-trainer," and it's their responsibility to train employees how to draw elevations whether it's for a home office or closet or other room.

Training is two solid weeks, but it's ongoing training from there with presentations or new projects that are given to us to figure out. Our trainer will say, for instance, that one week our homework problem is to find a solution to a current customer's problem such as this one: What if the customer has an 8-foot wall that happens to be under a staircase and a slanted ceiling above it, how would you get this space planned and functional for their needs? The projects are real-life situations, but they don't happen every day, but when they do happen, we've already thought outside the box on this problem in order to help them in a creative way.

Doing It All Yourself

There is a prevailing stereotype that a do-it-yourselfer, or a DIYer, is some guy with grease and dirt under his nails who doesn't trust anyone else to do the job for him.

The truth is there are levels of do-it-yourselfers that leave room for the hired professional to be involved in the planning and design process, as well. For example, heavy do-it-yourselfers conform to the stereotype—they really like to get into the project by rolling

Figure 2-19. The typical do-it-yourselfer doesn't mind getting down and dirty when it comes to building a home office from scratch. If you plan to become a DIYer, you will need to learn to use a drill to put up loads of shelves in your home office. (*MZS*)

up their sleeves and diving into the dirty work. They will handle every detail from framing, insulating, and sheetrocking a room, to adding outlets, updating the wiring, plumbing, and electrical work, painting the walls, and laying the carpet to finding and finally assembling and painting the furniture. A dedicated, hands-on, but less heavy DIYer will do everything except tackle electrical and plumbing work.

The casual DIYer likes to take control of the simple stuff like painting the walls and picking out a carpet but doesn't want to lay carpet or assemble, install, or paint the furniture. The casual DIYer will most likely not tackle electrical or wiring issues and will hire a professional to handle those projects.

A purely cosmetic DIYer will hit the stores for comfort items to add to their home office such as art objects, executive toys to play with during work hours, plants, flowers, and the like. They will be more likely to hire contractors to handle heavy construction, and rely on store planners to help with furniture and carpet needs.

Most DIYers find that although it costs less than hiring a designer, and the satisfaction of the process is quite high, it may take three times as long as it would if a professional were involved in any aspect of the planning.

The Process of Being a Do-It-Yourselfer

If you choose to be any level of a DIYer, the first step in handling your home office project is to start collecting clips and ideas from magazines about the subject. I'll warn you again not to seek out ideas from fantasy books and magazines because you will only be disappointed in yourself and the office if you don't have the means to achieve the exact look or feel of the featured office. Remember that only a fraction of the work-at-home population works in fantasy home offices created by interior designers and architects.

There are steps to take if you decide to plan or reconfigure your home office as a DIYer. Just remember it doesn't have to be finished or redone in a day or even a few months. Most of us want instant gratification so it will be tempting to throw everything out and run to the superstore to buy everything fresh and new. But in taking that path, you'll no doubt make mistakes that cost money. And, when you're in business for yourself, the last thing you need is to be stressed about spending money on the wrong things for your home office.

So start here with these few steps. Be sure to fill out the next workpage in pencil, because your answers will change over the course of a few weeks or months.

- ◆ Find a place in your home to call your work space.

- ◆ Before buying any furniture, put in some kind of table and chair and work in there for a couple of weeks—this way you are able to begin formulating in your mind's eye what you think would make this office special to work in on a daily basis.

- ◆ Clip articles on *realistic* ideas you wouldn't mind incorporating into your office, but don't let articles and books about fantasy home offices get you down.

- ◆ To get a fresh and inexpensive start, paint the room—but read Chapter 7 first about color issues in the home office.

Finding a Place for Your Home Office

Without the help of an interior designer or architect giving you direction as to where the best place would be to put your home office, you have to figure it out for yourself. Honestly, if it weren't for the advice I received during an in-home consultation with a former designer (current feng shui practitioner), I'd still be working in a cramped spare den while a larger, more inviting room sat languishing down the hall.

Though it's true that the average square footage of homes increased by 20 percent over the last decade and that many floor plans of new construction houses have bonus rooms, great rooms, or built-in home offices, for most of us finding space to fit a functional, professional home office can be a stretch of the imagination.

Most people tend to put their home offices in a spare bedroom or in the basement. I know several people, including myself, who consciously purchased or rented a home or apartment with one extra bedroom that would be specifically dedicated to a home office. But that was because we all knew in advance that we wanted, without a doubt, a dedicated home office.

In the real world, there are those who:

◆ Live in small city apartments but need a home office

◆ Don't plan to move to a larger home any time soon, but do plan to set up a home office

◆ Can find only a crevice, corner, or a closet in which to set up shop

The following section will offer a glimpse of what it's like to work in some types of spaces, shown mostly to give you some help in trying to decide where you should put your home office. Most of the following profiles of home office workers are still going through growing pains. They are prime candidates for the help of a designer or store planner because they haven't figured out exactly how to overcome the problems they face in their work spaces. You will probably see a little of yourself (as I did) in each one of them.

Pros and Cons of Putting Your Home Office in Your Master Bedroom

An enormous amount of people tend to put their home office in the corner of their bedroom. It rankles some people that they literally have to sleep with their work. Others aren't bothered by it one bit—at least consciously.

Sandy Horowitz*, president of a public relations and marketing firm, is one such person that isn't bothered by a bedroom home office. Her home office takes up one full wall of her bedroom, and three quarters of her bed, for that matter (see Figure 2-20). She also has a bookcase on the other side of her bedroom stuffed with work materials. Horowitz is literally surrounded by work even while she sleeps.

Horowitz lives in a one-bedroom apartment in New York City. She doesn't want to put her home office in her living-dining room, for that space is reserved for entertaining.

Horowitz does, however, use her dining room table as a conference table when necessary. But she never takes her work out to the dining table for any length of time:

> **I always had my desk in the bedroom, even before I started working at home full-time. My friend who is a decorator told me to move the desk from one wall to the wall of the window so I can look outside. I never even thought of doing that, but what a simple thing to do, and it made such a difference in my day. I decided to keep it there.**
>
> **When I get up in the morning, I don't look at the desk. I try not to start worrying about what I have to do. I just get up and go to work out at the gym for two hours. I'm not at my desk till 10 or 11 in the morning. Sometimes I'm working out problems in my head at odd hours, but I don't feel the need to sit at my desk till 11:00 at night. So the physical set up and where it is isn't a problem as it might be for other people.**
>
> **I use my bed as a work surface. I have a king-size bed, and I sleep in a sliver of the bed because the rest of it has piles of work on it.**

For Lisa Wendlinger, marketing and communications director for the Beren Group, having her home office in her bedroom is far from ideal, but she had to give up her dedicated home office and turn it into a nursery when she had her baby. She used to work at the dining room table, but as her son got older, she needed to "hide" from him (she was too

Figure 2-20. Putting a home office in a bedroom, like one at-home publicist has done in this New York City apartment, often means your bed will inevitably double as a work surface. (*MZS*)

tempted to play with him all day) and the nanny while she was trying to work, and the bedroom was the only other solution in a two-bedroom New York City apartment.

Wendlinger shrunk her work space to fit in the corner of her bedroom. She's not fond of her furniture or the set-up, and every night, she puts a screen in front of the work space to hide it so she won't see it when she goes to sleep or wakes up in the morning:

> **The fax is in my closet so that in the middle of the night when my European clients fax me at one in the morning, the ringer is turned off, and I don't hear it even when the paper cutter works. Someone will call me and ask if I got the fax, but I don't even know it rang so I have to get up and open the closet door, which squeaks so now people already know I'm going in my closet to check on faxes.**
>
> **Once every two weeks, my cleaning lady comes in and of course, has to clean the bedroom. So I detach my laptop from the docking station, forward my calls to my cell phone, and go to Starbucks for a while.**
>
> **The other problem with having a home office in the bedroom is my husband. He's home getting ready for work between 8:30 and 9:00. I have to tell him to be quiet and get in the shower, then I have to kick him out of the bedroom so I can work, but he understands.**
>
> **My husband is also a slob, which can cause a problem when your home office is in the bedroom. I constantly have to remind him that although I know it's a bedroom and he doesn't have to look at it all day long, I do have to look at it all day long. I work here, I live here, so I shove everything in the closet. He gets home at night wondering where everything is.**

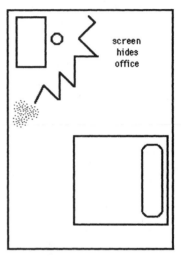

Figure 2-21. Lisa Wendlinger was forced to move her office into her bedroom once her newborn took over her old home office, but she manages to hide it every night with a screen. (*MZS*)

Pros and Cons of Putting Your Home Office in the Basement

Most people who work in the basement didn't want their home office photographed. "My home office is horrible. It's the quintessential, horrible, home office. I have a corner of my basement, and I have to walk through piles of junk to get to it. We have two computers, piles of junk, and stacks of paper all over the place. My washer and my dryer are behind me, and I'm next to a tiny little basement window. Sometimes the washer and dryer are going and I have to stop them to do an interview, and other times, people hear them humming in the background," says Jennifer Busch, executive editor for *Contract Design Magazine* who works from home one to two days a week.

Nevertheless, basements are quite popular for home offices. Georgene Pijut, who used to specialize in home office planning and design, remembers seeing a fair amount of basement home offices.

> **I don't know how people can work in a basement mostly because of the temperature issues. It's damp and cold. Rarely are any basements remodeled to regulate temperature. Aesthetics aside, you have to think that you are working day in and day out in a space that's cold and damp and there's little light, that's not comfortable.**
>
> **"However, one client I had took up the entire basement and ran a sizable business out of her home. This client had an incentive gift business who needed quite a bit of storage area and places to mail and sort plus an office area all in one basement. It was a difficult traffic pattern to accommodate.**

Basement temperature is an issue with telecommuter Brian McGuren, who works out of his basement home office, but he has the problem figured out thanks to the heat of his lights and his computer!:

> **I'm fortunate in that I finished my basement many years ago when I moved into my house. The most difficult part was trying to squeeze my files and equipment into this space. The area I work in now in the basement is 8-feet by 8-feet. I share space with a lot of reading materials and books, which take up**

Figure 2-22. Telecommuter Brian McGuren doesn't mind working in his basement home office even though it's crammed with books and files. Heat emanating from the lights and computer takes the chill off basement temperatures. McGuren works on Steelcase's Turnstone wood desk. (*Brian McGuren*)

all the wall space. I jacked up a desk by sliding two drawer files under it to make it a pedestal desk to give me the room for filing. That helped. I have three two-drawer file cabinets and a four-drawer cabinet in this room, and they are practically all filled. So one of these days I have to clean stuff out. I have a little storage cabinet with my supplies. The room is quite crowded, and everything is almost within a hand's reach so that makes it easy also. If the phone rings, I can just swing around and grab the phone. It's efficient.

Luckily, my basement has three walls open, and the back goes out into a patio, so I'm not completely underground. There's a window, high up, in this room. It's not damp, but it's not a heated basement either. In the winter, I'm probably going to have to plug a heater in here. During the summer it's cool, so I don't need air-conditioning.

I had a problem with the lighting at first. I had a fluorescent bulb in here and changed it to incandescent light. So now I get more light, but it also heats up the room a little bit. Between the computer equipment and the light, the room is much warmer! I may not need a heater after all.

For more information on what it's like to plan and work in a basement home office, turn to Chapter 8 and read about Richard and Elaine Turek's experiences, lessons, and future plans for their basement home office.

Pros and Cons of Converting a Barn into a Home Office

You may be envious that Cathy Barto-Meyer has a great big barn (see Figure 2-23) in which to put a home office, but she has a lot of issues she has to deal with first. It's a tremendous challenge to transform a barn that was once used to slaughter chickens and other farm animals into a stimulating, cozy home office. It just takes vision, a good plumber…and money. Right now Meyer, owner of CBM Communications, a public relations agency in Easton, Connecticut, works out of a spare bedroom. But she has other plans:

I'd like to get into that barn and have a real office instead of having a desk in a bedroom. Having that barn to remodel gives me incentive to grow my business. I'm nervous about spending all the money. Estimates I've gotten are $30 to $35,000 to make the structure into a work space. It needs to be sheetrocked, it needs carpeting, furniture, heat, a bathroom. The electrician needs to sort out the electrical up there. It's wired with lots of plugs. There's no rhyme or reason as to how it's set up. The family that lived here before us owned a restaurant, and they used to slaughter pigs, chickens, sheep, goats, and chickens years ago.

There's running water and electricity over at the barn right now, but no heat. We could do electric heat, but that's too expensive. The house is heated with oil, but one of the rooms in the house uses propane to heat it, so someone told us we can dig a ditch, hook propane up to the barn. It will cost $9,000! I need to get another heating guy out here to figure this one out. I also want to put a bathroom up there. That's another expense. And, it looks like one of the shingles came off the roof in a storm, so that's another problem. So I'm not going to put the sheetrock up and then have the roof go. We talked about doing a checklist of what needs to be done in priority and just get started doing it. The key thing now is to get an electrician out there.

The structure of the barn is fine. It's a garage below and barn up top with stairs leading to the barn. After you go out the door of the house that leads to the barn-garage, there's a little vestibule area that we would turn into a nice sheetrocked area. The stairs go up from the back of the garage right now, but we would turn them around so you come around and go straight up (see Figure 2-24).

The idea is to add a couple windows in the barn and put a bath in the back (see Figure 2-25). Even though it's connected to the house, I don't want employees to go through the house. I want to do this the right way.

I think this could be a fabulous office. I'd put in a couple of cubicles, a conference table over here, and if the business grew more, I'd probably take over the garage downstairs, maybe turn it into a conference area. People who have come into see the structure say that it's fine and doesn't need any more support for an office space.

The view is magnificent from both ends of the barn. Our neighbors keep chickens, and there's a chicken coop around the corner, and in the summer they come down here, they are so cute.

I'm trying to keep junk from piling up in here because if we start doing that, it will just be one more excuse not to renovate the barn.

Figure 2-23. By chance, public relations executive Cathy Barto-Meyer bought a house with a spacious barn on the property. The barn has inspired her to expand her business, remodel the interior, and hire employees. (*MZS*)

Figure 2-24. Barto-Meyer's plans for the barn–home office include turning this staircase around to face an outside door, then building an entranceway so employees don't have to walk through the garage to get to work. (*MZS*)

Figure 2-25. The barn is freezing right now since there's no insulation, no carpeting, and no drywall. It will take between $30,000 and $50,000 to whip the barn into shape. (*MZS*)

Figure 2-26. Barto-Meyer plans to install a small bathroom at the back of the barn so that future employees don't have to trudge down the stairs and through the house to get to the main bath. (*MZS*)

Pros and Cons of Turning Your Sunroom into a Home Office

Though I have not run across anyone working in a sunroom, I imagine that, while at times it could be beautiful, other times the glare from the sun would cause a meltdown in work time, especially during the winter months.

Many home workers convert a basement, guest bedroom, or attic into work space; however, others might opt for brighter, cheerier spaces in unlikely spots such as the backyard and the porch. Enclosing porches and decks with glass and extending a solarium off the house into the backyard is a viable option for those working at home, according to Patio Enclosures, Inc., the nation's largest sunroom manufacturer. Technological advancements in glass and ventilation make these rooms comfortable year round.

A sunroom office also allows workers to economically expand the home's existing living space at about 20 percent. A sunroom office can be created by enclosing an existing porch or deck with glass, or it can be added onto an outside wall of the home. It's also a good way to get a customized fit with your house's existing architecture.

Another benefit of putting your home office in a sunroom is that the vast amount of glass makes even a small office feel expansive. For those home businesses taking deliveries and receiving visitors, the sunroom office provides an outside entrance.

Don't worry about hooking up business electronics in a sunroom office. Companies can custom design sunrooms with the appropriate electrical outlets and computer hookups where needed.

Blinds and shading systems can control light and glare and provide privacy. Insulated glass allows the room to be heated and cooled, which keeps the room comfortable for working year round in any climate.

Figure 2-27. If an attic, basement, or spare bedroom is not your idea of a place to put a home office, try enclosing a porch or adding a sunroom instead. This Atlanta-based home office is actually in an added-on sunroom. Blinds and shading systems control the inevitable glare issue. (*Patio Enclosures*)

Pros and Cons of Turning a Closet into Your Home Office

If you don't have a room you can spare for a home office, maybe you have a closet—with a single door or double doors—that can be turned into a work space.

Perhaps working in a closet seems no better than working in a windowless broom closet in a corporation. What's different about working out of a closet in your home is that you have the freedom to plan it however you want to plan it. And, consider this: You are working from a closet in a room. You have the entire room in which to move around. The only difference is that your work surface is in the space of your former closet. Think of it as a built-in office rather than an office in a closet.

Take a look at the closet that architect Maurice Blanks turned into a good-looking work space (see Figure 2-28). It's as simple as this: Remove the doors of the closet, hang some cabinets from the top of the closet, install a work surface that runs the length of the closet, and then decide whether you want to add something—a curtain, vertical blinds, a sliding door—to hide the space when you aren't working.

If you don't want to go through the measuring and expense of cabinets, install a regular closet system and then add a rolling desk or work surface. This system from The Container Store is simple to install, and the designers can even demonstrate installation methods to you in the store.

Figure 2-28. This closet was easily transformed into a workspace by installing shelves, lighting, and a worksurface that spans the length of the closet. (Maurice Blanks)

Figure 2-29. Another way to make a closet into a work space is to add a simple closet organizer system that doubles as storage. (*The Container Store*)

Worksheet for Planning Your Home Office

On the next few pages you'll find a set of questions I created while commuting by train to and from New York City when I was thinking of working from home on a full-time basis. I realized I had to harness my thoughts, ideas, and dreams of the kind of space I wanted to work in on a daily basis. I wanted to get away from the look of a corporate environment, and therefore, I didn't want my home office to reflect anything from a corporate office other than the equipment I needed to function. I started to jot down these questions and answers while I had the time to myself during my long commute. The questions aren't tedious but fun, quick, and therapeutic.

The answers to these questions evolve over time as your business changes. As you can see here, I've given you examples of the process I went through twice because my goals changed and expanded. I'm sure there will be a phase 3! The third and fourth pages are for you to fill out once, then again in subsequent months or years. As you answer these questions, a picture will start to emerge on just how much money you want to spend on your home office.

Here are some of my initial notes about what I wanted my home office to evolve into that I scrawled down on a pad while commuting. The questions evolved from there into the following work sheets. I admit I did read all the articles on the home office and how to set them up, but found them to be far from my needs and reality, so I relied on my own intuition from which to build my work space. Answering the questions will help you stay *focused* and *organized* with your home office planning.

◆ What did I like about my old corporate office that I *wanted to replicate* in my home office?

My response: I sat next to a huge window so there was lots of natural light coming in. I had a little pretty task light to offset the awful fluorescent lighting. I had lots of cards, letters, and sayings on my bulletin board that I'd look at all the time to boost my self-esteem and confidence. I *loved* having the fax machine near my desk because I relied heavily on that one piece of equipment.

◆ What did I dislike about my old corporate office that I *didn't want to replicate* in my home office?

My response: I sat in a cubicle. I *hate* cubicles. There were no plants. There was no art on the walls. I didn't have a speaker phone. My work surface was so small, it was embarrassing. It was a mess all the time because I never cleaned up and let piles of stuff get out of hand. I rarely filed anything. It was too noisy in the office. Everyone could hear everyone else's phone conversations. The colors of the workstations, carpet, and walls were bland and uninspiring. The windows didn't open. The temperatures were too extreme either way and couldn't be controlled. Supplies were thrown onto any available surface. My space was not truly my own because people would always come over and borrow pens, paper, or other supplies when I wasn't there, which I felt to be an invasion of privacy.

◆ What are my favorite colors?

My response: Yellow and white as a combination, pinks, blues—soft colors. No gray! Tired of gray because of the sea of beige and gray cubicles I see in offices!

◆ What did I think would make me comfortable working in a home office?

My response: Plants and flowers. Baskets. Very feminine, floral things. My lava lamp, which has been sitting unused in a box for months. And an ergonomic chair. Lots of research books at my fingertips. Lots of shelving for piling projects. Having my cat in the office. Having a speaker phone to tape interviews. A clock! A cup warmer. *A blanket if I get cold* (critical!). Windows I could open. A decent rug. A fax machine. A supply closet.

Sample of Work Sheet for Planning the Author's Home Office, Phase 1

Date: May 1997

1. What are the three main things I *hate* about working in a corporate work space?

    I'm tired of all the noise and lack of consideration of other people who are loud when I'm on the phone. I also resent that a facility manager has the right to dictate to me what kind of chair, desk, or bulletin board I can and can't have in my work space. I don't like other people touching items and supplies in my work space. I'm very territorial! I don't like anything about my corporate cubicle!

2. List three goals for my business.

    I want to quit my staff job to work home full-time.
    I want to write more books.
    I want to make 25 to 30 percent more money than I did when I worked on staff.

3. What are three short-term goals for my home office space (two to three months)?

    I want to turn my desk so I'm not sitting with my back to the door.
    I want to clean out my closet for supplies and hide the opening with a curtain or door.
    I need nicer carpeting because the one I have now is dreary.

4. What are three long-term goals for my home office space (six to twelve months)?

    I need a fax machine.
    I need a second phone line installed.
    I need loads of shelves.

5. What do I *love* about my home office as it is now?

    I like the furniture—very warm and inviting.
    I like that I have room for two chairs so my cat can sleep on one while I work.

6. What do I *hate* about my home office as it is now?

    It's a total mess of piles and stacks of paper!
    It's not organized or clean (dust on desk and shelves).
    My back is to the door.
    I hate the carpet.
    I have glare on my computer screen during winter months.
    Again, it's a total mess of paper!
    I am tired of looking at boring beige walls.
    I have cat hairs all over the task chairs!

7. Look at question 1. Will meeting any of those goals impact my work space, requiring me to need anything special?

    Since I want to work at home every day, I need comfort and beauty to surround me. I need to be organized too, but I am not sure how to achieve this.

8. What am I willing to spend on the things I need? What's the priority?

    A second phone line, a fax, painting, shelves, and carpet, in that order! I am not willing to spend money on anything but a fax! I want to buy a fax for under $150. I want long white shelves that my husband will make and install. I want to spend $50 for a carpet remnant. I want to spend under $20 for a gallon of paint. I'll add a couple hanging plants too.

Checklist

✓ **Second phone line:** Called in phone order June 2 for installation date set for June 12.

✓ **Fax:** Spotted clearance sale at Office Depot; bought fax on June 21.

✓ **Paint:** Weekend of July 19.

✓ **Shelving:** Picked out materials June 26; installed them August 9.

✓ **Carpet:** Looked for weeks! Saw sale on remnants September 20; installed September 27.

✓ **Plants:** Found on clearance shelf at garden store for $1 each at end of August.

Sample of Work Sheet for Planning the Author's Home Office, Phase 2

Date: December 1, 1997

1. List my three top goals for my business:

   More large-scale projects
   Diversify book ideas
   Start up craft business again?

2. List three short-term goals for home office (next two to three months):

   Add more work surface (somehow, maybe custom) for piles.
   Put door on closet to finish room.
   Window coverings to soften room.

3. List three long-term goals for home office (next six months)

   Move to larger room down the hall depending on what feng shui consultant
      suggests.
   Get larger, three-drawer lateral file in a bright color.
   Find a way to make fabric-covered panels to put above work surface to take
      place of rarely used bulletin board.

4. What do I *love* about my office right now after working here for six months?

   It's light, bright, and airy. Very happy space. Love the yellow color because it's
   cheerful. It's great to shut the door to the space. The shelves are invaluable.
   I love having plants at the window and on my desk.

5. What do I *hate* about my office right now after being in it for six months?

   The windows are too high, and when I hear a noise, I pop up to see what it is—
   very distracting. I have wasted space under the desk—need some rolling files to
   store underneath? The room is too close to the hub of the house and across from
   the main bathroom. I don't have enough work space. I don't have a conference
   table. The second task chair is in the way. Visitors to my home tend to migrate to
   the office, and there's no room for them to sit down. Bulletin board is useless—too
   hard to get to. I still have a problem with the placement of my mouse and mouse
   pad. It's not ergonomically correct.

6. Look at goals in question 1. Will any of this impact my needs in the office?

   If I want to diversify my book projects, I need more lateral file space so I can be
   organized as I pull proposals together. If I start up my craft business again, I will
   need a bigger office and a standing-height table in a corner of the room to package and store crafts. I'll be able to start my craft business up again only if I can
   move into the larger room down the hall.

7. How much am I willing to spend on all this?

> I don't want to do anything until after I have my feng shui consultation in mid-December 1997. Then, I'll decide if I move to a larger room. If I don't move, I'll need to have my husband look at my desk and see if he can make out of wood an additional work surface that can attach to the desk. During the winter, the closet door and door into the office will be replaced. I still have to determine what window treatments I want on the windows, if any. Rolling files will have to wait until I see a great deal. I don't like any I've seen so far. I still need the answer to my mouse problem—perhaps buy a longer keyboard tray?

Checklist for Immediate Needs:

✓ Add more work surface _____

✓ Put door on closet to finish room _____

✓ Window coverings to soften room _____

✓ Rolling files for underneath desk _____

✓ Figure out ergonomic solution to placement of mouse and mouse pad _____

Update: You can read about my home office in Chapter 4. I subsequently moved down the hall to a larger room. Answering these questions gave me much-needed direction to my own home office planning goals and ideas. Use the next work sheets for your own planning sessions.

Work Sheet for Planning My Home Office

Date_____

PART 1

Answer the questions below if you are planning to work from home. If you are already working from home, skip Part 1 and answer questions in Part 2. (Use a pencil.)

1. What do I *dislike* about the corporate environment in which I work now that I want to avoid in my home office?

   _____

   _____

2. What do I *like* about the corporate environment in which I work now and would like to replicate in my home office?

   _____

   _____

3. Where do I think I want my home office to be in my home?

   _____

   _____

4. Why?

   _____

   _____

PART 2

5. List three top goals for my home business.

   _____

   _____

   _____

6. What do I *love* about my home office now?

   _____

   _____

7. What do I *hate* about my home office now that I want to change?

   _____

   _____

8.   List three short-term goals for my home office (two to three months).

     _____

     _____

     _____

9.   List three long-term goals for my home office (six to twelve months).

     _____

     _____

     _____

10. Look at my business goals in question 5. Does meeting any of my goals impact how my office should be set up or what I have to purchase for my office?

     _____

     _____

11. Checklist of *short-term* goals for home office.

     Goal 1 _____
     Steps to take _____
     Date completed goal _____

     Goal 2 _____
     Steps to take _____
     Date completed goal _____

     Goal 3 _____
     Steps to take _____
     Date completed goal _____

12. Checklist of *long-term* goals for home office.

     Goal 1 _____
     Steps to take _____
     Date completed goal _____

     Goal 2 _____
     Steps to take _____
     Date completed goal _____

Goal 3 _____

Steps to take _____

Date completed goal _____

Additional notes, comments, and plans.

_____
_____
_____
_____
_____
_____
_____
_____
_____
_____
_____
_____
_____
_____
_____
_____
_____
_____
_____
_____
_____
_____
_____
_____
_____
_____
_____
_____
_____

Figure 3-1. Wrist braces are like the aspirin of RSI. But *don't* type or write while wearing the braces because doing so could cause more injury in your elbow and shoulder. Wear them only while you are at rest. (*Steve Syarto*)

3

Avoiding Home Office Hazards That Lead to Physical Pain

What would you do if you couldn't use your hands anymore? Or your back ached so much that you had to fold your home-based business because sitting at the computer was impossible?

Working in a home office can do just these things if you don't take preventative measures or seek help once you're injured.

"People need to think long and hard about what their hands (and their backs) mean to them. If they lose their hands, they will be facing financial ruin, and emotional and psychological consequences. It's a hidden injury so it doesn't show and people can't tell you have it or understand what you are going through. People will think you just want sympathy. Treat your hands like gold. There's no amount of money that will give you back the use of your hands once you've lost them. You'll have a lot of time to think about this if you ignore it now," says Deborah Quilter, author of two books on *repetitive stress injury*, a common injury with computer workers, and that includes home office workers.

Home office workers can be more at risk for certain types of injuries, such as repetitive stress injury (RSI), for a number of reasons:

◆ Because we tend to be intensely focused on our computers for longer hours than corporate office workers

◆ Because we are driven to work longer hours even if our hands and back ache

◆ Because we tend to skimp on buying ourselves the proper chair, desk, light, and keyboard tray

◆ Because we don't take the potential for injury seriously enough to know it can cause us to lose our business and career

"The biggest mistake people who work at home make is that they don't consider a home office an office and they think they are just doing some work at home," says Arlette Loeser, ergonomic consultant and founder of The Ultimate Workspace. "They don't think of or imagine it as an established, permanent place that deserves a thought process of thinking the workspace issue out."

The Impact of Injuries in the Workplace

The American Society of Interior Designers based in Washington, D.C., has struggled as an association for years to convince the public that good design (including ergonomics) can impact productivity and cut down on injuries. For some reason, we choose not to believe in the dangers of a poorly set up work space until discomfort and pain happen to us. Here are some facts that might make you believe in the power of preventative ergonomics a little bit more:

♦ Cumulative trauma disorders, including carpal tunnel syndrome, tendinitis, and other repetitive motion injuries, accounted for about 56 percent of workers' compensation claims reported to the U.S. Bureau of Labor Statistics in 1993. Now that computer usage is up, these numbers have risen at an average annual rate of more than 25 percent.

♦ By the year 2000, one-half of all office workers may suffer symptoms of carpal tunnel disorders (CTDs), according to the National Institute of Occupational Safety and Health.

♦ The average computer user loses 62.5 hours of on-the-job time every year due to eyestrain, according to the Lighting Research Center at Rensselaer Polytechnic Institute in Troy, New York.

♦ More than 10 million people suffer from computer-related injuries to some extent, according to researchers at Purdue University in West Lafayette, Indiana.

Source: The American Society of Interior Designers' professional paper, "Productive Solutions: The Impact of Interior Design on the Bottom Line," 1997, Washington, D.C.

Are Home Office Workers More Prone to Injury Than Corporate Workers?

We might think that corporate workers are lucky because they have a corporation behind them that will "make sure" they are healthy and injury-free. After all, look at all the ergonomically correct furniture companies invest in for their employees. As a home office worker, you may just shrug your shoulders and say, "Hey, I can't afford this preventative stuff so I might as well suffer." You might be surprised to hear that sometimes corporate workers are actually more prone to injury than you, the home office worker!

"In the corporate workplace, employees have less control over their environment, and they may be more prone to injury because they don't want to be considered a troublemaker or complainer. So they stay silent when in pain," says Loeser. "As a home-based worker, you have more control over your environment, and you are more prone to deal with it faster because you know your livelihood is at stake in a much bigger way than the corporate employee. But when you work in isolation, it's hard to compare and get validation of what you're feeling. But even in the corporate workplace, if you get validation, the question is, who's going to come forward and admit it?"

Home office workers have an advantage over corporate workers to handle injury issues in just the simple activities built into a daily routine, according to author Deborah Quilter:

> **Home office workers can have more control over their pacing than their corporate counterparts. Home office workers may work longer hours, but they can choose to take a real lunch and go take a long walk in the middle of the day or work out. That will keep the blood moving, and that break in typing helps you work longer. If a home office worker is pondering a question, he or she can walk over to the window and look out and relax while thinking, and focus on a distant object like a tree. This is a really healthy thing to do. Go to the window, stop, look, breathe. In an office environment, people are often self-conscious about looking like they are drifting off for a moment, even though they are still working. People will say to them, "Get on the ball, get back to work!" People are literally afraid to look away from their terminals at their jobs because they are so worried that someone will think that they aren't working. Home office workers don't have to be concerned with that kind of pressure.**

As a home office worker, we have the opportunity to keep healthier than our corporate counterparts. We just have to be more conscious of what we are doing to and with our bodies when we work at our desks.

The goal of this chapter is to not only introduce you to the potential hazards of your home office that may lead to physical injuries but also to scare you into taking care of yourself while you work in your home office.

Injuries related to computers won't be going away any time soon. "Given all the people who use computers at home and in the office, and given our behavior at the computer, injuries will increase," says Marlene Green, principal of The Comfort Zone, an ergonomic consultancy firm. "The at-home worker is more at risk than a corporate office worker. At a corporate office, you have to get up from the computer to go to lunch, go to meetings, go to the bathroom, or go talk to someone down the hall, but at home, you may not get up as frequently."

The root of the problem with home office workers is that if we worked for corporations, the comfort level of our furniture, desk, and computer accessories was most always taken care of for us. It was up to our facility or office manager to keep us semicomfortable. We didn't have to think about it. We didn't have to learn about it. We didn't really care why we were getting "ergonomic" chairs and articulating keyboard trays installed. We didn't even care what *ergonomics* meant.

Then, as soon as we get home, we don't know how to make ourselves comfortable. We think comfort and luxury mean working ten hours a day in a big, overstuffed chair or working on a kitchen table.

Figure 3-2. This home office is a disaster waiting to happen. The broken chair, keyboard on the desk surface, and monitor angled toward the windows to catch glare are all mistakes most of us make in our home offices. (*MZS*)

Or you think you don't have to bother with comfort, and you'll work on any old spare dining room chair (see Figure 3-2). You don't think twice about putting your keyboard directly on your desk so that you have to raise your arms to type. And you don't care that you can't see your computer screen when the sun is glaring down on you in midafternoon.

"People who work at home are entrepreneurial, they are driven, they are conscientious, very demanding of themselves, and they are more prone to these injuries," says Ellen Kolber, MS, MA, OTR, CHT, ergonomic consultant and occupational therapist, owner of The Ultimate Workspace. "Home office workers have to learn how to take better care of themselves and to take responsibility for themselves. When you work at home, you don't have the resources that you have in the corporate sector to call on to access ergonomic furniture, or personnel available to address worksite problems.

Most of us take more time to research and buy a car than we do to plan and correctly furnish a home office where we spend a good part of our day. This can result in physical consequences. When we hear the warning, we tend to shrug our shoulders, telling ourselves "we'll deal with it if and when we have to."

It's not fun to "deal" with any kind of pain that a poorly planned office and poor working techniques can cause. This chapter will hopefully frighten you into doing something preventative in your home office so you won't have to "deal" with an aching back, neck cramps, eye fatigue, leg cramps, and the worst—wrist, shoulder, and hand pain.

If you have any of the aforementioned physical pains, you may be destroying the very link to your livelihood. For example, when I was typing the manuscript of my first book in a mad rush to meet a deadline, severe pains in my wrists and tingling, and numbness in my fingertips forced me to stop in the middle of the process to go to the doctor who ordered me to immediately go out and buy braces for my hands. But he never told me what to do with them, so I mistakenly wore them while I typed. Typing with braces can cause even more injuries as I found out later from interviews with ergonomic specialists. But most of us lack any kind of knowledge about how to protect ourselves from an injury that can rip away any pursuit of your craft.

It can be as simple as this: "If you have a comfortable chair, adequate lighting, and the keyboard is at the right height, then you will be able to be more effective and work longer without feeling bad," says interior designer Susan Aiello, ASID, principal of Interior Design Solutions and an advocate of educating consumers about ergonomic environments.

What Ergonomics Really Means and What It Can Do for You

What does *ergonomic* really mean? I've always thought that *ergonomics* sounds like a fiscal problem to most people. If not considered, it can very well lead to a fiscal problem in your life.

My simple definition of *ergonomics*? To me, it means being responsible enough to give your body the comfort it requires based on the type of environment in which you work. That isn't the real and academic definition, however. The real definition of ergonomics is this, according to the *Webster's New World Dictionary:* "The study of the problems of people in adjusting to their environment; the science that seeks to adapt work or working conditions to suit the worker."

Whichever definition you prefer doesn't matter. What matters is that you take it seriously, especially if you work at home.

"People hear the word *ergonomic,* but unfortunately most people don't understand what it means," says Georgene Pijut, formerly of Georgene Pijut Home Office Design, a firm that specialized in designing home offices. "When I designed home offices, I found that the people who were most interested in ergonomics already had problems. People rarely look at ergonomics as a preventative measure. People don't believe in ergonomics if their workspace causes them no discomfort. And the people who end up having discomfort as a result of their workspace were not interested in fixing it because they didn't believe in ergonomics."

We hear so much about ergonomics, how we are supposed to buy ergonomic products and how we are supposed to work in ergonomically correct workstations and chairs. The reality is that ergonomics is really a preventative measure. It's primary prevention. You can still make your worksite as ergonomically correct as you possibly can, but that won't help you if you are already injured.

Figure 3-3. Though this home office is aesthetically beautiful, it is an ergonomic nightmare with a hard chair, keyboard on a desk, and lots of light coming down on the screen. Home offices like this, with the ergonomic mistakes, tend to be featured in shelter magazines. Beware. (*Eisenhardt*)

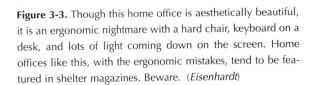

Types of Injuries and Symptoms

An injury can mean a lot of things. Injury doesn't necessarily mean permanent damage, or it doesn't need to mean surgery. Injury can mean *tendinitis* which is an acute temporary inflammation.

"The biggest question to ask yourself is how long you've had it and how much you've reinjured it over time," says Arlette Loeser, ergonomic consultant. "That's what makes a difference in how long healing takes, or if healing can't take place. Injury is as basic as a swelling, tear of the muscle, strain, inflammation of tendons."

The most dangerous injury you can get while working at the computer is *repetitive stress injury,* better known as RSI.

RSI is called *cumulative trauma disorder* (CTD), as well. Most people confuse RSI and CTD with *carpal tunnel syndrome,* which is CTS. Let's clear up the confusion.

RSI, cumulative trauma disorder, or overuse syndrome, are generic names given to injuries that have occurred over periods of time and aren't specific to any structures injured. Carpal tunnel syndrome is a type of overuse injury, but you can get that from a fracture, or even arthritis. It's one type of overuse injury that can occur to this particular region of the wrist. If you have overuse injury, you may have injured your tendons, nerves, your muscles to some extent. When you talk about RSI, it describes more of how the injuries have occurred. Carpal tunnel describes the specific structure that is injured.

Carpal tunnel syndrome is named for the narrow tunnel in the wrist formed by ligament and bone. Tendons that enable the hand to close pass through the carpal tunnel. Overuse of the median nerve of the wrist leads to compression and inflammation. Disorders such as diabetes, hypothyroidism, and rheumatoid arthritis sometimes contribute to the syndrome. However, there are a host of other types of RSIs besides carpal tunnel, all of which can be prevented if you catch the symptoms on time, and then do something about them.

How You Know You're Heading for Trouble

"What do I say to people whose eyes glaze over when I talk about ergonomics? I can't force people to care about their hands," says Deborah Quilter, author of two books on RSI, her latest one *The Repetitive Strain Injury Recovery Book* (Walker and Company Books, 1998). "Those same people whose eyes have glazed over in the past when I tried to help them, listen to every word I say now because they come to realize how valuable their hands are for driving or cooking or even buttoning their shirt. By the time many people are interested in preventing injury, they already have a serious chronic disability. At that point, there isn't an ergonomic gadget on the market that will help them."

I know I still have one ergonomic issue to deal with: mousing. When I mouse, I have to stretch my arm to the desk because the mouse is too high, and that puts pressure on my elbow. I just haven't gotten around to fixing the problem for any number of inexcusable reasons. I should purchase a longer keyboard tray with a fold-up mousing pad (see Figure 3-4). Instead, I strain myself day in and day out, but there is no pain yet, only slight irritation in my elbow and shoulder (uh-oh!) when I type. The lack of serious pain prevents me from doing something about this problem. I know I will pay the price if I don't fix this problem soon.

"Very often people don't feel any pain until the damage is acute. In our society, a little backache or neck tension is considered to be normal. Ask yourself how you feel physically after you

Figure 3-4. This office is half correct. This home office worker sits on the Aeron chair, by Herman Miller, considered one of the best ergonomic chairs. But the keyboard and mouse sit high up on a work surface. She needs to buy an articulating keyboard tray. Note that Aeron is expensive: It costs over $1,000 in some places, but you can get it for $979 through Levenger (see the resources appendix). (*Peggy Doherty*)

come back from vacation. There's minimal tension. Or, how do you feel physically on a Sunday night versus Friday night? Unfortunately, people who work at home tend to work on weekends, too, and rarely take vacations so the pains sneak up on them. It's a gradual loss of range of motion. It's not that all of a sudden, their hands start to hurt," says interior designer Susan Aiello, ASID, who is also an advocate of educating the public on ergonomic environments.

Injuries occur in stages, and they progress. Just before an injury takes place, you feel fatigue and some mild achiness. That should be your signal to suggest that you are overusing the muscles, not that you are injured, but it's a little bit of a wake-up call.

The next thing you will feel from a fatigue or ache is a more pronounced fatigue which becomes discomfort, and then you may feel tingling or numbness that might indicate nerve irritation. Usually the first stage of fatigue happens when they work at a computer. Then as it progresses into an injury, you may feel fatigue or pain while doing any manual activity. During rest, you won't feel it. But as the injury progresses, even after rest, even doing nothing, you may feel shooting pain, which is indication of a nerve injury. You can feel a deep ache while doing nothing.

After a while the injury has a life of its own. If you feel a lot of pain at first while typing, you may feel better after long periods of rest or intensive therapy after you cut down on typing. People let injuries go too far, and they eventually need to change professions or have surgery.

The key is to recognize symptoms of oncoming trouble. The symptoms of carpal tunnel syndrome can be:

◆ Numbness or stiffness of wrist and fingers

◆ Tingling or burning of the thumb, index, middle, and ring finger

◆ Night pain

◆ Pain that travels up the arm and shoulder

◆ Weakness of hands causing difficulty in pinching or grasping of objects

Whatever you may feel in the way of discomfort, don't try to work through any pain. It will worsen the injury resulting in irreversible damage to the nerve that passes through the wrist to the hand.

But what about those of us who work day and night at our computers but never feel any pain? There is a reason for that.

There are a fair amount of people who are more likely to get carpal tunnel syndrome because of genetic predisposition. Perhaps someone has a larger amount of lubrication in the tendons of the wrist protecting it when they flex. Less lubrication may mean you are prone to carpal tunnel problems. But there is no way to determine this kind of predisposition.

"Maybe you know someone who is overweight, does all the wrong things, his technique is wrong, but he doesn't get injured," says author and ergonomic consultant Deborah Quilter. "This is a testament to the durability of the human body. We're not all created equal. We all have different physiologies, different work styles, different anatomies. Someone may seem to be bulletproof, but that person may come down with an injury next year. But why take the chance? It's like smokers who smoke for 80 years and don't get cancer. Great for them, but are you going to take that chance with your life and hope you are like that, too?"

"Also, everyone's case is different. You can't compare your symptoms with someone else's problems. I've seen so many sad cases where they don't take it seriously enough and they lose the use of their hands."

Dumb Things We Do in Our Home Offices That Could Injure Us

Our body tends to react to the irresponsible things we do, or don't do, for ourselves, starting in the home office. For example, we let our computer rule our lives.

"The purchase of ergonomic equipment is as important as the time and money someone puts into buying a computer system. People spend $2,000 or $3,000 on a computer system, and then they want to spend $20 on a chair and just have a table to work on," says Marlene Green, ergonomic consultant. "The information has to get out there about how to set up a workstation properly and take emphasis away from just thinking about how many megahertz you have in your machine or where to surf the Internet."

Many home office workers scrimp and save when pulling together a home office and never consider comfort.

"I've seen things related to the configuration of the work site that are shocking. It usually stems from a lack of knowledge, a space, or a financial consideration," says Ellen Kolber, ergonomic consultant. "But many times their habits are odd. For example, some people put their keyboards on file cabinets. The problem with that is that you can't get your knees under the work surface and that can have horrible effects on your back and your legs.

"The biggest mistake is not putting your keyboard below the level of your desk (see Figures 3-4 and 3-5). A keyboard on a desk is a problem because it's much too high to reach comfortably. The keyboard should be 2 inches lower than the desk surface. The other issue relates to the mouse—some people have the idea that they need to get their keyboard situated correctly, but they don't think about their mouse and we are using our

Figure 3-5. Do you ever feel discomfort in your elbow when you mouse? It's probably because your mouse is on a high surface, like your desk. Your elbow won't hurt if you try a keyboard like this with a mouse tray that slides out at the same height as your keyboard. (*Rubbermaid*)

Figure 3-6. Even makeshift solutions, like putting a mouse on a stool at the same height as your keyboard, is a better answer than putting the mouse high up on the desktop. Preventative ergonomics doesn't have to be expensive to achieve. (*MZS*)

Figure 3-7. To be comfortable and reduce strain on your eyes and body, bring the computer to you. You should never reach out to the computer. An articulating monitor arm brings the screen up or down to a comfortable height and distance. (*ErgoSystems*)

mouses more frequently today with the Windows' programs and graphic design programs. Getting the mouse at the right height would be important, or more important, than getting the keyboard correct (see Figure 3-6).

"It's a major misconception that you have to spend a lot of money to make your work space ergonomically correct. There are many retrofit arrangements to get you in a good position."

Green says that if her clients can't afford to get a monitor arm for $200 (see Figure 3-7), she tells them to use old phone books or reams of paper to increase and prop up the monitor. If you can't afford to buy a footrest, use phone books for that reason, too (see Figure 3-8). Green, an advocate of correct ergonomic seating, also suggests that clients can get back cushions at a medical supply store to support their back without getting a new chair.

Unfortunately, too many people use pillows to help them ease the discomfort they get while sitting in unsafe, downright dangerous chairs rather than purchasing an inexpensive ergonomic desk chair (see Figure 3-9).

One of the biggest mistakes you could make if you have a constant and pronounced backache that you think is from your chair is to go out and purchase a heated ergonomic chair pad. "A heated ergonomic chair pad will make you perspire! Then you will end up getting a chill on your back from the perspiration. And if you use this for a backache, if you sit on a heated pad, you'll turn it into a bigger backache. Heat is not good for backaches," says Susan Aiello, ASID, interior designer and ergonomic advocate.

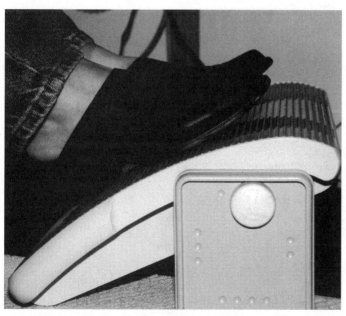

Figure 3-8. If you have a good chair with height adjustability, you may not need a footrest. If your chair seat cuts into your knees and lower thighs (bad for circulation), but you can't afford a new chair, get an inexpensive footrest to relieve your legs. Or just use a thick book instead. (*Steve Syarto*)

Figure 3-9. This home office worker plans on buying a new chair, but it's not a priority. Instead, she puts a Band Aid on this situation by using a pillow to relieve discomfort. (*MZS*)

One Journalist's Nightmare with Carpal Tunnel Syndrome

Barbara Mayer is a well-known design journalist. Her livelihood involves typing and more typing on her computer, which has resulted in some unwelcome pain:

I have all the problems—carpal tunnel in both hands. I wear a brace on my left hand. I used to have problems with my right hand, so I slept with my brace, and the pain went away. I am religious about wearing it seven-eighths of the time. I have one brace in my bedroom and one brace upstairs by my computer.

Six months ago I received an injection of cortisone in my wrists. It worked well. The shot was painful, but since I had it, I'm not waking up in the middle of the night as I used to without any feeling in my wrist. I haven't been wearing the braces as much since I have no symptoms.

Cortisone works for some people for a few months, and for others it doesn't help at all. I think I'll have another shot because lately I get little twinges in my wrists. I don't want surgery—I hear different things about it, that it has to be done again after a few years.

My eyestrain is significant. I also have various shoulder and lower back problems, probably because my chair is not good for me at all. I'm waiting to get a Herman Miller Aeron chair because it's beautiful and ergonomic—it's the most comfortable chair I've ever sat in.

Depending on what I'm writing, my day varies. But I spend most of my time on the phone. The greatest invention I've found for comfort is this head set. I would have a permanent crick in my neck if I didn't have it. I'm cheap, but I spent $175, which is a lot of money, to get good earphones. I find those earphones make all the difference in the world by keeping my hands free and my neck straight. Those earphones are the most important thing in my home office.

Figure 3-10. Mayer has paid dearly for the years she's spent keyboarding while sitting in a dining room chair with her keyboard on the desktop. She also needs an articulating keyboard tray. (*MZS*)

How to Prevent the Aching Before It Begins

Don't panic even if you feel a symptom. It doesn't mean your hands or back will give out tomorrow, but you should be concerned enough to go to a doctor.

Going to a doctor may not mean you need surgery, either. If your doctor tells you surgery is the only answer, always get a second opinion, as in the case of Elaine Turek, home-based business manager for Big Daddy Digital, an imaging specialist company:

> **I had some minor pain in my hands and went to an orthopedic surgeon who gave me cortisone shots under my pinkie and ring fingers. Those shots hurt! And he wanted to give them to me in my wrist. It did relieve the pain, but when I went again for second shots, he told me it was going to get worse if I didn't have surgery immediately.**
>
> **I went to my chiropractor for a second opinion. I love my chiropractor, and I never thought of going to her for a problem like this, but it was a good thing I went to see her. She told me to give her two weeks after which I wouldn't need surgery. So she deeply massaged the area of my hands under my pinkie and ring finger. And I exercised my hands on something called a *Dyna-bee* (see Figure 3-11).**
>
> **I really do think this Dyna-bee worked for me. It's like a little plastic ball with a gyro inside of it. You rotate your wrist one way, and it's spinning the other way for resistance. There's a weight in it that shifts after it's in motion. I bought it from my chiropractor for under $20. It's an exerciser for the wrist to supplement her massage.**
>
> **After two weeks of massaging and some exercising, my hands haven't hurt since. This was nearly two years ago, and now I type more than ever.**

Figure 3-11. This little toylike weighted device helped Turek exercise her once-pain-riddled hands. She's been pain-free for a year since using the Dyna-bee hand exerciser, which she bought through her chiropractor. (*MZS*)

In some cases, furniture could be your first line of defense against an RSI. For example, one graphic designer suffered excruciating pain in her shoulder and wrist. Though her doctor suggested surgery to repair the muscle and tendon damage, she went for a second opinion to the ergonomics center at the University of Connecticut's Health Center in Framington, Connecticut.

The center's doctors told her to hold off on surgery until they observed her work habits. Sure enough, she worked her mouse and keyboard at odd angles because her furniture did not support proper posture. "We got her a well-designed chair, a good desk, and within two months the patient was pain-free without surgery," says Dr. Martin Cherniak, medical director of the center (see Hamilton 1996).

If you think getting the correct furniture can solve your problem, the one thing you shouldn't do is rely on the home offices you see in magazines. They are not the best examples of ergonomics in the home office. In fact, you should look to them if you want to see the worst examples of how a home office should be set up for comfort.

"When I see features in magazines on the home office, I get upset," says designer Susan Aiello. "I've seen granite or highly polished surfaces used in these photo shoots. That's the worst surface for a home office. Even if you don't have a computer on it, you have papers on it, and if you look down, it shows glare, it dazzles your eyes. You often see a home office with lots of windows with light pouring in. You rarely see a keyboard at the right level in a magazine spread. Keyboards always sit on the desk, and you always see laptops on the desk. And they show this as an example of a great office!"

Mark Dutka, owner of InHouse, a San Francisco–based retail-design store that caters to the home office, agrees with Aiello: "The home offices you see today in award-winning magazines are unsound as far as ergonomics. There are keyboards on work surfaces instead of on articulating keyboard trays, and monitors are at an angle from where the person needs to sit because it photographs well. People take their cues from photographs and then wonder why their necks, arms, backs, and shoulders are hurting."

Figure 3-12. This is a beautifully well-appointed home office, the kind you are likely to see in a magazine. The problem? The keyboard is on the desk surface, and the chair is unadjustable. It's fine if you are going to use the computer for a half hour at the most every other day, but not if you're going to run a full-time business. (*Acer*)

So now that you've stopped taking magazine home offices as gospel, what else can you do to prevent aches and pains?

"People who work at home should take more breaks. If you had a choice to have a lousy chair but you had to get up every 15 minutes versus having a great chair that you would never get up out of for 10 hours, I'd say take the lousy chair and get up every 15 minutes. Breaks cost nothing," says Aiello.

In addition, Aiello says that salt is bad for us when we work on a computer. What? "Anything that allows you to retain water is bad because the carpal tunnel area is filled with water so it increases the pressure," says Aiello. "You know how people say the moon affects people? Well, it affects all the water on the earth, and that includes what's in your body. Women have more water in their bodies. Have healthier snacks when you work at home. Walk around a lot."

However, there's some controversy about the salt issue: "There are a lot of theories that exist about salt as a contributor to the onset of injury, and it hasn't been researched," says Ellen Kolber. "Salt causes water retention and may be a contributing factor but probably not a cause."

One of those points you should learn and pay attention to is the technique of your typing. The proper technique can save your hands. "My technique was improper," says Deborah Quilter about the reason she became injured from typing. "To recover, I changed the way I move my hands at the computer."

You may wonder if you need to have a wrist, arm, or palm rest at your computer. "There's a controversy over wrist rests and armrests," says Ellen Kolber. "Some ergonomists tell people not to use wrist or armrests. Well, try holding your arms up over the keyboard for eight hours. It will eventually cause pain in the shoulders. I encourage people to take microbreaks, build them into your typing technique. For example, a writer is at the keyboard for a much greater period of time than you are actually typing because sometimes you are thinking. While you are thinking, take your arms off the keys."

The American Physical Therapy Association recommends several other techniques to prevent or alleviate the symptoms of carpal tunnel syndrome caused by keyboard work:

- Keep wrists relaxed and straight, using only finger movements to strike the keys.

- Press keys with the minimum pressure necessary. Make sure the keyboard is kept clean and in good working order to minimize resistance.

- Move your entire hand to press hard-to-reach keys rather than overextending your fingers. Use two hands if necessary to execute combination keystrokes, such as shifting to uppercase.

Besides technique in typing, consider the pacing of your work. Home office workers are focused so intently on work that they forget to pace themselves. But once again, it can save our bodies.

"The key to pacing is to rest if you're sore or experiencing any symptoms," says Quilter. "To pace yourself so you won't feel discomfort, do the following: Notice how long you were able to work until you felt sore or fatigue. Say you were able to work for 20 minutes until you felt any symptom. Then you subtract 10 minutes from that time. That means you should take a 5- to 10-minute break. I take extra-long breaks as insurance. If I work for 15 minutes, I take a 15-minute break or longer."

Why You Should Think Twice about How You Sit

"Most people won't invest in a good chair. They say they can't afford it. But if they become injured, they could easily spend $100,000 on medical treatment. A good chair costs pennies compared to physical therapy at $90 a shot four times a week," says Quilter.

You probably spend no more than 10 minutes to pick out the things that matter most to your body like a new mattress for your bed or a desk chair. You spend more time in your workstation than you do in your bed. Your body deserves that time and attentiveness spent considering the purchase of a chair and the plan of your work space, says Arlette Loeser.

This woman is clearly heading for trouble."My chair is comfortable (see Figure 3-13). I don't know what the benefits of an ergonomic chair would be for me. But my back is killing me sometimes after I work a day at the computer," says Sandy Horowitz,* a home-based public relations executive.

The act of sitting can itself be a risk factor for many injuries, and sitting improperly makes your risk worse. So, not only do we choose the wrong chairs, we tend to adopt the wrong posture when it comes to sitting in our chairs while working on the computer. "Most people don't use the back of their chairs for support when they use a computer. People might as well sit on stools," says Ellen Kolber. "They are hunched forward, hanging off their ligaments" (see Figure 3-15).

"People need to sit back in their chairs and move their chairs closer to the keyboard and move the keyboard closer to their chair. One of the biggest mistakes people make is that they don't sit back in their chair and they don't sit close enough to the work. The more the person has their arms reaching out away from the body, the more force that will be imposed on the shoulder and back. If you throw your weight out in front of you, your back muscles have to work harder at keeping you erect."

The other issue is that people who sit back in a reclined position tend to bring their head forward to see the monitor, leaving the rest of the body back in the chair, and that creates neck problems.

"I worked with some people who sat on a lawn chair," says Loeser. "It worked for them because it was the only chair they had, they couldn't afford a new one, and there was a space issue. The problem is that when you sit in a lawn chair, you sink into it. So you never use the back. They'd sink into their seat and lean forward. When people sit in too reclined a position, they bring their head forward to compensate, and that creates neck problems.

"It's a similar issue with the big executive chairs. These chairs are designed to consider an executive who is on the phone all day and leaning back into the chair. Don't get this kind of chair if you are keyboarding because you will never be able to lean into the chair while typing. If you use this kind of chair and you lean back into it, you'll say 'ahhhh' but the rest of the time you use the chair, you'll be fighting all the softness all around you in order to stay up and be able to keyboard. You need support. Most people who work at home don't go for those chairs because of space issues" (see Figure 3-16).

Figure 3-13. The woman who sits on this chair often has a backache after working on her computer, but she's not convinced an ergonomic chair will help her feel any better. Luckily, she exercises often, which is strengthening her back, preventing any major injuries while working from this chair. (*MZS*)

Figure 3-14. If you can't afford an expensive ergonomic chair and you sit in a "wrong" chair, at least commit to picking up an inexpensive chair from Global (they also make commercial-grade chairs for offices, so this is your best bet for good quality from a superstore). This particular Global model, called Timberline, has a suggested retail cost of $215. (*Office Star Products*)

Figure 3-15. Here's an example of how most of us sit when working on our computer. We sit on the edge of the chair with our legs in awkward positions. You can see here this man is tensing up his back muscles to stay upright. He should sit all the way back into the chair to save his muscles from straining so hard. (*TBWA/Chiat/Day*)

Figure 3-16. Overstuffed chairs trick your body into getting too comfortable so you hunker down into the cushions, which prevents natural and necessary movement of the body. After sitting here for a few hours, you will have difficulty getting up and you'll feel stiff and fatigued. (*Ziosk*)

Varying posture is a critical activity that people forget about when they are wrapped up in working on the computer.

"I tell people, your parents told you not to fidget—I'm telling you to fidget," says Kolber. She continues:

> **It's good to move, especially for the back. Moving around gets a blood supplies to your back. I don't tell people to twist and turn at the waist, because that's not good, but to move in their chairs and make adjustments to their chairs.**
>
> **If someone is working in a position that experts will say is not so great, and if they are going to work in that position for a few minutes at a time and it feels good to them, they should go with it. You usually can't sustain those strange positions for eight hours anyhow. It's so easy for doctors and ergonomists to tell people that there's one way to sit and work, but most of them don't work at a computer for eight hours a day and don't know what it would be like to sit like a soldier for eight hours. It's impossible, and it's not good to sit like that for eight hours.**
>
> **There's so much dogma out there on this subject. Sometimes it doesn't make sense to tell people the things they do. I can see how frustrating it is to the client to hear this kind of thing from a doctor or a therapist. They will tell me that a therapist told them they had to keep a certain posture that's absolutely perfect, but the client gets tired.**
>
> **What is frustrating is that people get these very expensive chairs, they set them up in one position and they think it's perfect. Well, that's not what that's about. It's good to make subtle adjustments. You need to adjust tilting so some muscle groups can work, then some can rest. Readjust to let the muscle groups that were just working rest, and vice versa. Learn your chair! People are often overwhelmed with things that aren't that complicated, like their chairs, which is about the most low-tech product on the face of the planet!**
>
> **The one best feature you should look for in a chair is that it is height adjustable. The lower back of the chair needs to support the lumbar curve of your back. Height adjustable features are commonplace for chairs today. Even the chairs from five years ago had height-adjustable features—at least you**

could spin it. Now we have levers for height adjustment. In fact, chairs that spin for height adjustments tend to lose their height adjustments. Every time you grab your chair, you spin it slightly, which readjusts the height.

On the bright side, news of lawsuits against computer manufacturers for keyboards that allegedly caused carpal tunnel problems has found its way into the media, which has grabbed the consumer's attention. On the dark side, we are still not willing to spend a lot of money on a good chair.

Most of my clients know what the word *ergonomics* means by now. A lot of my customers are sent here by chiropractors and doctors to find chairs. Plus, there's a lot of publicity on carpal tunnel injuries," says Mark Dutka, owner of InHouse, a retail-design store in San Francisco that caters to home office workers. "The problem is that they see the commercial-grade, high-quality chairs and think they are outrageously priced. I ask them to compare the quality of contract chairs to other less-expensive chairs they have seen out there. When they do that, they are truly amazed at the value of a contract chair. Not only that, if they come here to buy a contract chair, they are enticed with the fabric choices we have that they would never get on a chair from a superstore.

InHouse carries the following lines of commercial seating: Sitag, HAG, Herman Miller's Aeron chair ("our biggest seller," says Mark), Davis, and a lower-priced chair called Sit On It.

How to Buy a Chair

Arlette Loeser suggests:

If you're really strapped for money and still need an ergonomic chair, go to an office supply store, but know which features you need. I tell people when they buy an office chair that they should go in the morning so they can really feel the chair and look at a number of different features. Look at how the lift works and how resilient the foam is. Are the features solid?

When I send someone to a furniture manufacturer's showroom who has furniture that is a little more expensive, these issues aren't even a consideration. But with lower-priced chairs, the quality of the workmanship is not as good as commercial-grade chairs. If you buy a chair for $99, you get a chair for $99. What happens is that a lot of people go out and buy one of these chairs, and one year later, they look at better chairs.

You should also know that if you get a chair in the $200 range, you won't get as many adjustments as you need. For someone who is over 5 foot 6 inches, you won't get enough seat depth because in that price range, manufacturers don't make the seats that big.

If you make an initial investment in a good chair, you will be sparing your body pain.

Figure 3-17. If you find an older desk chair that looks like new, beware. Older, four-castor-base chairs, like this classic Herman Miller chair, are hazardous because they tip over easily. Since the 1980s, manufacturers have been making safer, more stable five-castor-base chairs. *(MZS)*

One of the best bits of advice? Don't buy an older chair that has a four-castor base because it's a potential hazard (see Figure 3-17). Buy a more contemporary chair that has a more stable, balanced five-castor base.

"I have an older chair from one of the office supply superstores, and it has four castors. I was in the middle of a business call the other day, and I fell right over on my back! But I couldn't just stop talking to the person I was on the phone with—he didn't even know I fell over. But I hit the hard cement floor of my basement home office—there's no rug— and thought I had dislocated my shoulder. It was the first time that happened to me, but it really hurt my back." Jerry Stein, president of a micro-brewery start-up company in Fairfield, Connecticut.

There are expensive chairs on the market that most home-based workers hesitate to invest in. "I have two comfortable office chairs picked out and priced. My step-mother chose French Provincial office chairs that are upholstered with blond wood in a leopard-print fabric. But I think they are $1,000 a piece so they are third on my priority list. The chairs I have now are not the most comfortable chairs to sit in. I don't care what I sit in, but I always try to have my assistants' environments very comfortable. To spend $2,000 on chairs when there are other priorities makes me uncomfortable. A copy machine is more of a priority. The unsexy things are priority. My chairs have cushions to soften the feeling of sitting in them all day. But it would also be much easier to have castors," says Shannon Wilkinson, president of home-based Cultural Communications.

Evaluating the Chair That's Right for You: An Evaluation Form

If you've made the decision to abandon working in your home office on your dining room chair or your fold-up lawn chair and are ready to buy a "real" office chair, you'll want to know how to choose that new chair.

Make a copy of this page, and bring it with you when you go to a store, dealer, or showroom to look for a chair. Take your own comments seriously when choosing a chair, and don't rely on just price to make the decision for you. Spend at least 10 to 15 minutes with a chair to get a good feel for it, to understand how the chair functions, to experience how the chair can be adjusted, and to be able to answer the following questions:

Evaluation Form

Store: _____

Manufacturer of chair and model number _____

Choose a number from 1 to 4,   1—poor,   2—passable,   3—good,   4— excellent.

1. How comfortable do you feel in the chair?
        1   2   3   4

2. What kinds of adjustments does this chair feature?
_____

_____

3. Can adjustments be easily made from a seated position?
        1   2   3   4

4. How appropriate is this chair to the kinds of tasks you will do in your home office?
        1   2   3   4

5. Does the chair feel sturdy?
        1   2   3   4

6. Do you feel comfortable with the price of the chair, and does it reflect the value of the chair? $____
        1   2   3   4

7. Do you feel comfortable with the warranty and life cycle that is guaranteed on this chair?
        1   2   3   4

8. Overall score of the chair:
        1   2   3   4

Comments:_____

_____

Total score:_____

Finding Top-Quality Ergonomic Furniture

BP Associates, located at 200 Lexington Avenue in New York City, is not a store but a showroom specializing in ergonomic furniture. They carry Hag seating, Human Factors tables and accessories, Task2 keyboards, Waldmann lighting, Viewtek glare screens, and a number of other lines. President Paul Berglund explains how his showroom works:

> **We have all the ergonomic products on the showroom floor so that, when you come in here, you can pull up a chair you may want to a table you might want too. You can play around to see what you might want your workstation to be like. We call it an "ergonomic playground."**
>
> **Although most of our business is with large companies, we can work with an individual who walks into the showroom from off the street who is looking for ergonomic furniture.**
>
> **We want people to understand that we don't cure people, but what we do is help someone become proactive to either prevent a lot of these injuries or to aid in recovery. There are many times that by getting the proper equipment and**

furniture, you will stop hurting. If you have the beginning of an injury, you can catch it in time, and it will go away. People shouldn't come in here and hope we can take the place of a doctor.

We are critical about what products we choose to carry. We've turned down a great number of ergonomic chair lines. We chose to carry Hag because they are innovators in ergonomic seating. They were the first to have a sliding seat pan. Hag chairs can be adjusted for anyone from 4 feet 10 inches to 6 feet 6 inches. I've even fit a 7-foot man comfortably into a Hag chair. One very tall client is 7 feet 2 inches and 352 pounds, and we found the

Figure 3-18. You can find high-quality ergonomic furniture at showrooms such as BP Associates in New York City. Although they cater to large companies, they are more than willing to work with individuals who need ergonomic furniture that will last for years. (*MZS*)

perfect chair for him. His problem was what would happen to you or me if we were to sit in children's furniture. We wouldn't fit into such small furniture. His old chair wasn't supporting him, and he was starting to have back problems.

We aren't going to just sell people a chair and show them how to adjust it. We are going to talk to them about how they work and what they want to achieve. As it turns out many times, people can make vast improvements by not buying anything at all! But they need to know that buying only furniture is not always going to help them. And sometimes buying the perfect chair to go with an imperfect work surface won't accomplish anything.

We do come up against people who tell us they've seen a $100 chair with all the adjustments in an office supply superstore catalogue. People who don't want to spend money on good furniture for themselves have to look at the life-cycle cost issues. How many years do you want to use this chair? If you are going to use a home office for a half hour a day for next two years, go buy a chair from an office furniture superstore. But if you are going to work in the chair for eight hours a day, it's a different matter.

The difference between us and a superstore is that we sell contract-quality product guaranteed for ten years with pneumatic lifts guaranteed for a lifetime. If you look at materials of cheaper chairs, you see they aren't designed to last. We carry products that are designed to last for years while being used under intensive use.

But if someone still doesn't want to pay the price of a contract-grade ergonomic chair, I will ask them what an injury is worth to them. The difference in price of two chairs is minimal compared to paying the price for carpal tunnel syndrome, any RSI problems, and back or eyestrain.

Voice Recognition Grows in Response to RSI

Voice-recognition technology has come a long way over the years, but there's still more improvement needed. Nevertheless, many people with RSI are turning to this technology to help them continue to work on computers while aiding in their recovery.

"One of my clients got voice recognition because he's a slow typist and because he felt pain from using his mouse. He wanted it as a tool to break up his input activity," says Marlene Green, ergonomic consultant and principal of The Comfort Zone. "I have another client afraid to touch the keyboard because her hands hurt, and she has trained her computer to pick up her voice patterns.

"Voice recognition requires patience, however. But if you do everything by voice, you can lose your voice. You have to have different input devices to break up the activity."

Today's programs, such as *Drag and Dictate,* are more affordable. The programs that used to sell for well over $3,000 in 1996 now sell for about $695.

Keep Children Pain-Free in Your Home Office

"I had a couple ask me to consult with them because their four-year-old son was having wrist problems," says Marlene Green, ergonomic consultant, principal of The Comfort Zone. "They had a huge 17-inch monitor way up on a shelf, and the little boy was sitting on a big chair, and his right arm was abducted with a mouse laid out on the desk. Of course, his wrist and shoulder are going to hurt because everything is too big for him. There's not a lot of ergonomic furniture out there for young children using the computer. Since there are no solutions for this problem, there's nothing to go out and buy. So you either have to prop up the child or lower the computer monitor."

If you have children who share your computer and oftentimes sit at your desk in your chair, be warned. Even the right ergonomic chair for an adult can hurt a child. Ergonomic chairs aren't made for children. And desks for adults are too high for children who often have to reach up high to keyboard, mouse, and see the computer screen at all.

"Today, children's postures tend to look more slumped over, and that bothers me," says interior designer Susan Aiello, ASID. "It's not good to have a little kid sitting on an adult ergonomic chair reaching for a computer. It's like an adult sitting on a bar stool with legs dangling and the computer up above your head, arms up reaching for the keyboard."

What's a parent to do? Put a booster seat on your chair, or buy a height-adjustable table for the computer so that your child can lower it (with supervision) when he or she is using the computer.

Some ergonomists feel, however, that children are by nature active, and they don't sit in any one place for very long, thus decreasing the likelihood of injury.

Figure 3-19. Even ergonomic furniture is too big for kids. Computer furniture for kids is hard to come by. Kinderlink, by Skools, Inc. (see the resources appendix) is a good source of kids' desks that also happen to be designed to hold computers. (*Don Hamerman*)

What Do You Do If You Already Have Pain?

People want a quick fix, but there is no quick fix for RSI, especially if you are already injured. "Seeing a neurologist or orthopedic specialist won't necessarily guarantee that you receive a proper diagnosis because many doctors haven't been trained to handle RSI," says Deborah Quilter. "There is a place for surgery in advanced cases but it can also lead to further problems so it's wise to seek a second opinion."

The reality is that cortisone shots, which are supposed to reduce inflammation of the carpal tunnel, can rupture a tendon.

Ellen Kolber agrees that surgery was the only answer years ago. "Now people are going in a totally different direction by saying surgery isn't helpful, and you do worse after surgery. That's not true either; each person is individual and you have to be open-minded."

Oftentimes wrist or hand braces are recommended for discomfort. But knowing how to use them is key to recovery (see Figure 3-20).

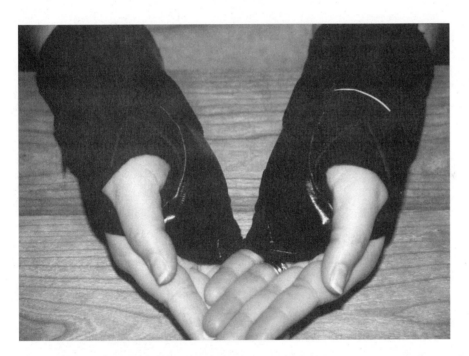

Figure 3-20. Take precautions in your home office so you don't end up adding these carpal tunnel wrist braces to your wardrobe. (*Steve Syarto*)

Most ergonomists feel it's not a good idea to work in wrist braces Kolber continues: Physicians who may not be trained in ergonomics often tell patients to put the braces on and wear them all the time. I don't recommend they use them while they type.

The problem with typing in a brace is that if you think of the arm like a kinetic, moving chain, you stop one of the links in the chain by wearing a brace. And what happens when you stop a link in the chain is that you will make it up by overusing another link in the chain that could cause another type of injury and overuse other structures to compensate for the joint that is immobilized.

Look at it this way. If you've been in a brace for eight weeks, you've done everything right and you've never taken it off, you will have caused your muscles to atrophy since you didn't use the muscle. And, tissues have a tendency to adhere to adhesions.

Moving is physiologically important because it offers lubrication that reduces friction between structures. It's like an engine in a car: You want it to move to lubricate the other parts of the car, and when it's off, it prevents the car from getting the correct lubrication. Moving, contracting muscles are important for blood flow, and that's important to have in an area that needs to be healed.

You might wear a splint or brace at night. That's good for carpal tunnel syndrome because we tend to go into a flexed wrist position at night that tends to put pressure on the nerve. Use it when you are resting or when your arms feel fatigued. You might just want to keep the structures a little quiet and rest them for a bit between typing, for example. Don't wear it during any activity, only during rest.

How to Stop Eyestrain from Interrupting Your Day

Graphic designer, Steve DeMartino talks about his former glare problem:

I discipline myself to get up and stretch often so I'm not sitting here for hours on end. I don't have any wrist or elbow problems. But when I had my home office in the living room, I encountered skylight problems.

I originally thought that it would be great to work with the sun coming down on me. But at certain times of the day, it would reflect off my monitor so much that I had to shut down the office. I couldn't believe it. I would sometimes have to tape a piece of paper to the skylight.

I've since moved to the den where there's no skylight. The den is better for my computer work. It's like a cocoon (see Figure 3-21).

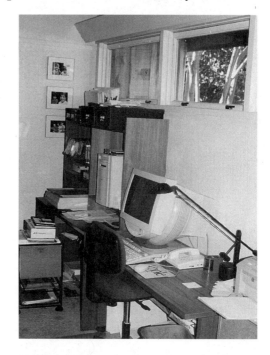

Figure 3-21. Graphic designer Steve DeMartino moved his home office to the "cocoonlike" den with high, narrow windows after constant interruptions from glare that bore down on his computer monitor through a skylight in his living room. (*Steve DeMartino*)

Journalist Barbara Mayer still struggles with her skylights:

One problem that no one really thinks about is the skylight. In the summertime, the glare isn't bad, but in the winter after the leaves are gone, I can't see my screen between 11:30 and 12:30. I tried various things. I would have to stand on a chair, take a piece of paper, and tape it up in front of the skylight, which is really annoying to do.

When I can't see the screen, I do something else from 11:30 to 12:30. That's how I deal with it.

There are better skylights that have a blind encased between top and bottom, but I don't have it. I could replace it, but it would look different from all the other skylights I have in the house, plus it's expensive to do that.

I've never tried a glare screen on my computer. I worked for a large newspaper in an office with huge windows, and there was definitely a glare problem. Employees at the paper asked for glare screens, but found they didn't work.

Unless I'm on a killer deadline, I'll try my sunglasses or squint. It might be easier to wear sunglasses than to do anything else.

Yet another area we ignore is our eyes. The American Optometric Association has coined a name for eye complaints related to computer work: *computer vision syndrome*. The association warns that the following symptoms could occur:

◆ Temporary myopia, or the inability to focus on distant objects after using the computer for a few hours

◆ Dry or watery eyes

◆ Blurred vision

◆ Headaches, neck aches, backaches, or muscle spasms

◆ Heaviness of the eyelids or forehead

As for dry eyes, a Japanese study of how often people blink when using the computer showed the following: We blink on average 22 times a minute; we blink on average 10 times a minute when we read; and we blink on average 7 times a minute when we use a computer. Plus, our eyes are open wider and get dryer when we are looking up at the screen than when we are looking down to read a book, says Dr. James Sheedy, a clinical professor of optometry at the University of California at Berkeley (see Brody 1996).

Glare can cause stress to our eyes. Bright lighting may cause reflections on our computer screens that cause us to bend forward to read the screen. That's dangerous because it can cause stress to the back muscles, resulting in what's called "static loading." Static loading happens when we tense and hold our muscles in a fixed or awkward position for long periods of time.

Glare comes from one source: light. It can be sunlight. It can be a lamp. Whatever the source, fix it. If you don't, you'll find yourself squinting at your screen or at the work on your desk.

"People with home offices often jerry-rig what they have. I would tell people how to use a task light, which most people weren't aware of," says Georgene Pijut, a for-

Figure 3-22. Most of us don't realize why we have such a hard time seeing our work even if we have on a powerful overhead light. Get a task light to put on your desk so that you can spotlight it onto your work surface when you need it. (*Maurice Blanks*)

mer interior designer who specialized in home office planning. "The biggest mistake people make in lighting is that they light the general space; they don't light specific, targeted areas within their space. There's a difference. For example, most people leave the space they work on shaded because there isn't a task light on the desk. Or there is too much glare on the computer because the computer is placed facing a window, which causes eye fatigue. Task lighting is helpful in most situations. I would teach my clients how to light *areas,* not how to light *space.*"

The best solution is to use several small low-intensity light fixtures rather than one large high-intensity light fixture to light a home office. You'll find that's much more comfortable to the eye, but it makes the office more inviting as well.

Designer Susan Aiello, ASID, offers more ideas on lighting the home office the correct way:

Lighting is very important in a home office and can be very cheap. I have torcheres that are uplights that bounce light off the ceiling. But if you have light bouncing off ceiling, that gives you good ambient light. You never want to have any kind of light that's on behind you because it will glare into your screen. Light in the ceiling shouldn't be directly overhead either. In a corporate office, it's designed so that there are two lights on either side of a desk to spill over on to your desk. Mimic that.

Uplights are better than track lighting, but I'd take the cans and face them away from you so they bounce light off to your sides. Another thing people don't realize is that for computer work, they need a lot lower level of light. People think an office should be overlit. Most architectural firms' offices are overlit. Those offices were lit years ago for working with plain paper, not computers. Every office is overlit. Don't worry about getting the level of lighting of your home office up to the levels you're used to in a typical corporate office. You're much better off with having a much lower level of lighting—normal lighting, such as what you'd use in living rooms.

Test yourself to see if you have an overlit office. If you rely on only overhead lighting and you can read a piece of paper on your desk without squinting, it's too bright in there. Always use a task light to be able to read the papers on your desk.

Your work surface should be a medium color, not a sexy black lacquer because it can cause glare on the surface and a pure white surface is also glaring. If you don't want to spend much money, your work surface can be made out of almost anything—even plywood on sawhorses!

In addition, it's best to use a flat, satin, or matte finish on any work surface.

Shop Smart: Cures for Cold Feet

Anything that contributes to our warmth and comfort is good for us. For those of us who work in our home offices during the winter in our slippers and don't want to crank the heat up through the whole house to keep from freezing—one solution is a heated footrest!

The footrest under my desk collected dust for years so I finally relegated it to the basement only to take it out once more for good use. Though mine isn't heated, I found one that is. This footrest not only contributes to better posture by taking the strain off of the lower back while sitting, it radiates safe, even heat at 100 watts and 120 volts. It's U.L. listed and C.S.A. approved. It's potentially a lot safer than a space heater, which can tip over and start a fire. But 100 watts is a lot, comparable to a toaster oven, so don't plug it in to the same power strip your computer is plugged into.

You can buy the heated footrest for $49.99 from *Penny-wise Office Products* at 1-800-942-3311 (stock number MCG-10601).

One note: If you are enticed by this product but feel that having something electrified under your feet will make you feel slightly uncomfortable or unsafe, don't consider buying this footrest.

A Different Kind of Ergonomics...for the Brain

Here's an unusual twist on ergonomics, but it does make sense, although it's related to organizing your home office. Some say if we don't organize our office in a certain way, we are hurting our work-related cognitive behaviors. So not only do we have to worry about physical pain but we have to worry about mental anguish in the home office as well!

Various degrees of mental anguish comes from the distractions that we all face. And even though at-home workers don't face the distractions often found in the corporate office (meetings, loud voices, interruptions by coworkers, coffee breaks, extra-long lunches, gossip, etc.), the home office has its own brand of distractions, some of which can be right under our noses. The question is, how do we get a grasp on what's really distracting us and our capacity to concentrate in our home office, and then how do we fix it?

Most of us—whether we work in a corporate setting or at home—end up in a state of "cognitive dissonance," which is a condition of conflict between our cognitive processes and our surrounding work environment. This causes us to work in a situation where distractions prevent concentration to finish our task at hand. In other words, we may get too messy to accomplish anything.

Why do we let ourselves get so messy, creating the circumstances to trip up our efforts to be productive and complete projects? When we make a mess, it's our brain's way of trying to purge information into tangible and visible forms in and around our office and desk so that we don't forget to finish a related task. A piece of paper strewn on our desk or pinned up on a cork board should be our visual cue to help us remember a task (see Figure 3-23). Unfortunately, this backfires on us half of the time because our unorganized, cluttered surroundings don't support our brain purges.

Our physical environment acts as an external storage device for our thoughts, but we have a limited capacity for recall (five to seven thoughts in short-term memory) and that demands that our work spaces are organized in such a way to help us to retain those thoughts and more thoughts. Haworth, a furniture company, has created a number of prototype products inspired by this new discipline, and additional research and testing are ongoing (see Figures 3-24 and 3-25).

"Your mind is like a bucket of water, and the goal of your office should be to help preserve that water for important, intellectual tasks and avoid wasting it on energy-sapping distractions," says Jay Brand, an organizational behaviorist at office furniture manufacturer Haworth, Inc.

Haworth is studying something they term "cognitive ergonomics," or the relation of your working behavior to your work environment. One of Haworth's research and development groups, called Ideation, focuses on cognitive ergonomics, the aim of which is to maximize intellectual assets by creating ergonomic work environments that help people think.

A key principle of cognitive ergonomics is that a person's thoughts are consciously and unconsciously translated into a physical manifestation in their office and on their desk. Haworth calls these physical manifestations "cognitive artifacts." These artifacts in essence make a person's work space an extension of their mind.

(continued on page 128)

Figure 3-23. We use corkboards to subconsciously help us handle cognitive ergonomics. It works well if the cork board is easily reachable. (*MZS*)

Figure 3-24. Haworth experiments with designs for cognitive ergonomics. The irregular shapes of the shelving units of this storage structure, called Flo, help us to remember which shaped cell holds which pile of information. (*Haworth*)

Figure 3-25. Eddy is a tiered work space to display reference materials that usually end up hidden in stacks of paper. According to the principles of cognitive ergonomics, the entire scope of our current work needs to be exposed, creating an arrangement that resembles our brain, which helps us to work more efficiently. (*Haworth*)

(continued from page 126)

Jeff Reuschel, manager of officing research at Haworth, equates the stripping away of cognitive artifacts—promoted by telecommuting and hoteling programs and clean-desk policies in the corporate office—as "environmental lobotomies." If you're too clean and neat in your home office, the lack of visual cues can also deter your productivity.

"With each move or cleaning of the desk at day's end, people lose the cognitive artifacts and embedded cues that a more steady environment provides. Workers in such environments can sometimes feel as though they spend more time getting organized each day than working on actual projects," adds Reuschel. According to Reuschel, we barely give any attention to finding ways to support and improve our thinking in our work space, which translates to poor cognitive ergonomics.

So how do we achieve the correct cognitive ergonomics? You can reduce the visual noise in your office to help you concentrate better. But that doesn't mean completely cleaning out your office so there's nothing left of your work. It's a matter of becoming clear in your work patterns, your projects, and where you need to put your groups of information in order to attend to them in a timely and orderly fashion.

Reuschel suggests that we do "chunking," or, consolidating related subject matter into fewer but larger, overarching groups of information, thereby reducing visual noise in the work space; paper piles, often viewed as a mess or lack of storage space, are visible signs of chunking.

You can also "churn" your work. That means you need to remember to constantly purge, absorb, create, and relocate artifacts (e.g., file folders, reports, Post-it notes) as they become more or less relevant, ensuring that the exposed work and work space reflects the most important and current tasks and projects.

Now that you know about cognitive ergonomics and physical ergonomics, your body should be at its optimum comfort inside and out.

A Last Word on Ergonomics, Comfort, and Risk of Injury in Your Home Office

When you get to the point where you are injured and you are going to the doctor to get shots or thinking about surgery, it affects your whole work life. It affects your family life, your relationships with your spouse. It becomes a dominant presence in your life.

We take our computers and the way we work at them for granted. We need to learn to be more careful with our bodies and our behaviors when we work.

Next time you sit down in your home office to work on the computer, don't just sit down and start working. Take a few seconds to notice how your head is positioned, how your wrists are positioned on the keyboard, how your back feels in your chair, and how far back in your chair you are sitting. Take an inventory from top to bottom, and get comfortable before you get into your work.

When you are working, notice any fatigue or tingling sensations in your fingers, wrists, or arms. Make a note to take time out in your day to find a doctor who can guide you in prevention or treatment of these symptoms.

You owe it to yourself, to your family, and to your business.

Safety Checklist for Home Office Workers

To work safely at your computer in your home office, note these points of concern:

- ◆ If you are squinting at the computer, eliminate glare or bring the monitor closer to you.

- ◆ If you are squinting while reading paper on your desk, you don't have enough light in the room, so get a task light.

- ◆ If your hands, fingers, wrists, or forearms start to hurt when typing, **stop.**

- ◆ If your keyboard is located on your desktop, buy an articulating keyboard right away.

- ◆ If your mouse is located on your desktop, buy an articulating keyboard with a sliding mouse tray, or, if you have a shorter tray already in place, put a stool with books on it until the mouse is the same height as your keyboard tray.

- ◆ If you are stiff when you get up from your chair, take more frequent breaks to increase circulation.

- ◆ If you have an overstuffed chair and you work at the computer, consider an ergonomic chair.

- ◆ If you work on a dining, kitchen, lawn, or other type of chair, consider an ergonomic chair immediately.

- ◆ Watch to see if your child reaches up to use a keyboard on your desk and strains his or her neck to see the monitor.

- ◆ For most average adults, the keyboard should be 24 to 25 inches above the floor.*

- ◆ For most average adults, the bottom of the monitor should be about 34 to 35 inches from the floor.*

- ◆ For an average child, everything should be 8 to 9 inches lower than for the average adult.*

Source: Susan Aiello, ASID, president of Interior Design Solutions, New York City.

Figure 3-26. The SoHo Chair from Knoll is one of the best little ergonomic home office chairs available. It's small, colorful, and affordable for a contract-grade ergonomic chair (See Resources). (*Knoll*)

Figure 4-1. The location of your office and the position of the furniture within are very important to your well-being *(Steve Syarto).*

4

Why the Ancient Art of Placement Is Important for Your Home Office

You must be wondering why a book about practical home offices would include a chapter about something as seemingly ethereal as the ancient art of placement, known as Chinese *feng shui.*

The Chinese believe that everything, even inanimate objects and buildings, are surrounded by energy fields. Ask yourself this question: Have you ever walked into a building, a house, an apartment, or a room and felt instantly comfortable, warm, and welcome? Or have you walked into a place, only to suddenly feel afraid and depressed for no apparent reason?

There is a reason for these kinds of feelings that you get when you step into a building or a room. It has to do with the way the unseen energies flow throughout the space. If these unseen energies are flowing, you feel good and energetic. If the energy in a space is stagnant and stuck, you will feel bad or apathetic. You'll definitely want to make the energy flow in your home office.

The Chinese have believed in the flow of energy for thousands of years. To enhance the energy flow in their homes, offices, and properties, the Chinese have relied on feng shui, or the ancient art of placement, to assure that their lives will be filled with abundance in wealth and in love.

What does feng shui mean? *Feng shui* (pronounced fung schway) means "wind and water." The term *feng shui* comes directly from a simple, yet ancient Chinese poem, according to master Edgar Sung:

> The wind is mild
>
> The sun is warm
>
> The water is clear
>
> The vegetation, lush.

This popular poem described the ideal environment from a feng shui perspective. And as time passed, the poem was referred to as "feng shui."

What is feng shui? It's an ancient Chinese art of arranging your physical environment so that you can live your life as harmoniously and as balanced as possible. Feng shui practitioners say that by making certain that your living environment is harmonious, you will attract good luck and prosperity in all areas of your life.

So who *wouldn't* want to apply feng shui in their home office?

"I have a waterfall on the wealth corner of my desk. Right after I installed my waterfall, I did receive many calls for new business," says interior designer Susan Aiello, ASID, principal of Interior Design Solutions. "But my husband scoffed at feng shui. We went to an event that had a drawing for prizes. He said, 'okay, if feng shui really works, then you should win one of these prizes.' Well, I won!"

Feng shui is based partly in intuition and partly in practicality. Though I've personally witnessed the power of practicing this art, I do not profess to be a feng shui expert. But I want to communicate as best and as safely as I can to you the benefits of feng shui.

There are many fantastic books that explain feng shui in depth, for it's quite a complex, yet fascinating subject that takes nearly a lifetime to fully comprehend. This chapter will discuss the practical nature of feng shui and all the applications that make sense for a home work space.

I'd like to share with you in this chapter the basic principles and experiences I've learned about through my curiosity, to a degree from my own feng shui consultation, and from my own belief in the practice so that you can begin to safely apply them to your own home office where the art of placement is critical to your success.

Figure 4-2. Place a trickling desktop waterfall on the wealth corner of your desk for prosperity. Moving water moves energy. Therapist Mimi Akins placed this waterfall in the wealth corner of her office-therapy room. (*MZS*)

More importantly, I hope you might find the value in consulting a feng shui practitioner for your own home and home office, and I invite you to consult the resource appendix on how to start your research.

But first consider this: You're already thought by feng shui experts to be lucky if you have enough room in your home for a study or home office.

One Interior Designer's Thoughts on Feng Shui

Most of feng shui is common sense. People say it's a bunch of baloney and that it works because you took action in your life to make things happen anyway. But that's not the issue. The issue is that if it works, it works! Any application of feng shui is going to make you feel better, and if you feel good, you'll work better. I will say that if you don't believe in it, it won't work for you. That's where we get into the psychological debate of which came first, the egg or the chicken. Which came first: your taking action to create a specific outcome or the feng shui cure? But why not believe in it—everyone is seeking as much luck as they can get anyhow!

In feng shui, how you place your desk is important—well, no one wants to sit with their back to the corridor. When I worked for Banker's Trust years ago, one of my first projects was to look at one particular floor where everyone complained that they didn't work well, they were uncomfortable, and didn't like the space. I walked in there and took one look—all the secretaries sat with their back to the corridor. I suggested they turn the secretaries' desks around! They balked because they said all the desks already fit the floor plate, and they'd have to redo the whole floor. But I told them that people don't like to work with their back to the door or corridor! They still didn't understand why they needed to turn those desks around. So to simplify it, I told them that the uncomfortable feeling of vulnerability goes back to prehistoric days when people watched their backs so they wouldn't be attacked by wild animals." (Michael Love, interior designer, principal of Interior Options)

Basic Feng Shui Principle 1: Ch'i

The basis of feng shui has to do with something called *ch'i*. Loosely translated, ch'i is the unseen, yet vital energy that surrounds us and that is within us. What's important is how we use and enhance the ch'i that circulates around and in our bodies so we can improve our life.

Feng shui master Edgar Sung says that few of us truly see or sense ch'i because as westerners, we are taught to consider the energy that surrounds us as merely "space."

Remember that Albert Einstein devoted his entire life to the idea that empty space is filled with energy. According to feng shui principles, ch'i is a force that is palpable and gives way to physical manifestations when it flows freely or hinders physical manifestations when it is blocked.

Blocked ch'i can create discomfort and discord in a room, in a house, building, or a piece of land. Have you ever walked into a home or office that was designed, planned, and decorated to perfection, yet the space didn't feel right in some way? But you couldn't pinpoint *why* you felt uneasy or uncomfortable? Or, have you walked into a home or office that was designed, planned, and decorated in an imperfect way, yet it felt inviting, warm, exciting, and you couldn't explain exactly why you are drawn into the room? More than any decorating scheme, it's the invisible flow of energy in those spaces that directly affects how you feel when you step into a room.

"I had a feng shui master come in and look at my house because I always had a feeling that something wasn't quite right with the house from the moment I stepped foot inside," says Maxi Cohen, a film and video producer. A feng shui master gave Cohen cures for her own home office, one of which was to move out of it because it wasn't located in the right section of the house.

To harness and direct ch'i, we must understand how objects in our environment affect the flow of ch'i around our property, in our homes, and in our work spaces. To improve ch'i, feng shui offers many cures—or therapeutic techniques—for your environment once you can pinpoint an area of poor or blocked circulation of ch'i. This can be tricky, which is why a consultation with a practitioner is critical if you're going to implement feng shui in the correct way.

Figure 4-3. Ch'i is invisible energy that flows throughout the atmosphere. Water, a vital cure in feng shui, carries ch'i, but the speed at which water moves is critical. Meandering running water moves ch'i in a smooth way. Rapid running water moves ch'i too fast. (*Steve Syarto*)

Basic Fen̲ ̲ciple 2: The Bagua

The next ̲ inciple of feng shui is the *bagua* (some call it a *pakua*). What is a ba̲ ̲pe that is considered extremely lucky. In feng shui, it's a basic ̲ ̲pects of your life. In it's most stripped down definition, a ̲ ̲se on just about any desktop or hor- ̲ ̲e floor plan of your home office, in ̲ ̲to the appropriate symbol. ̲ ̲t of your life:

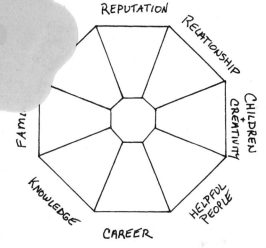

Geriatrics
GRAB A GROWING MARKET

◆ Wealth, abundance, ̲̲

◆ Fame

Good feng shui is activated when these eight specific areas are activated using the correct colors, symbols, or arrangements.

Believe it or not, a bagua can be laid over your desk, the front of it always the place where you sit. Although it's hard to keep your home office desk neat, you might want to try this: Put a healthy plant or crystal bowl in the upper left corner, the wealth, abundance, blessings area, to assure prosperity; put family photos in the upper right corner, the marriage and relationship area, to ensure a happy emotional life. You'll find more cures for your home office throughout the chapter. But I *strongly* urge you to find a feng shui practitioner to get the most from this ancient art.

Figure 4-4. Place the bagua over the layout of your home office to determine what areas to empower. The career section of the bagua is always placed on the main door to a room or house. *(MZS)*

Basic Feng Shui Principle 3: Understanding Cures

If you've ever rearranged the furniture in your house and suddenly felt better, without even knowing it, you've installed what is called a *cure*.

In the art of feng shui, a cure is a change you make in your environment to bring balance and harmony into the space, and thus, into the lives of the occupants. When the flow of ch'i, or energy, is blocked or stagnant, a feng shui cure can move energy around quicker to create change. The body of feng shui cures comes from centuries of experience and teachings of feng shui masters. But the essence of most any cure is practical. For example, a basic feng shui cure is to clear physical clutter in your home or office, and that will begin to clear away certain problems in your life. In feng shui, the internal and external worlds reflect each other so when you eliminate clutter in your home, you eliminate clutter in your mind, and in your life.

However, in the Black Hat (a most common sect of practice) art of feng shui, there are mystical cures, as well. A logical, more practical cure is called *ru-shr*. A ru-shr cure makes sense to us (like elimination of clutter) because it is within the realm of our experience in the world. A mystical cure is called a *chu-shr* because it seems illogical to us. Practitioners should be the ones to offer chu-shr cures to clients because they can be complex and must be used in the correct way.

There are endless lists of both ru-shr and chu-shr cures. You can obtain some of the items for cures in a Chinese gift shop (see Figure 4-5). For instance, you will notice that near the register in many Chinese restaurants or specialty stores the owner has placed one or two large gold or white cats with raised paws. A cat with its right paw raised is a symbol of prosperity. A cat with its left paw raised symbolizes incoming business. You'll also notice other objects, such as bagua-shaped mirrors, plants, pictures of flowers, and other symbols as decoration to symbolize prosperity and good luck. These are basic cures you can install in your own home and home office.

Figure 4-5. Basic items, such as red horses, cats with raised paws, and crystal objects can bring good luck to the occupants of the house. If you hear or read about a complex cure that you'd like to install, please consult a practitioner first to see if it's right for you. (*Steve Syarto*)

Basic Feng Shui Principle for the Home Office: Desk Placement

The most important element of your home office is your work surface. Most of us arbitrarily place it where it best fits in the space. But perhaps we should take a bit more care in placing our home office desk.

When Richard Webster, author of *Feng Shui for Beginners,* began writing his second book, he had just moved into a new house. He placed his desk under a window with a great view to the garden. Webster would sit at the desk and think about writing his book, but he never actually began the process.

"Then, in 1977, I changed the layout of my office, and placed my desk against another wall at a 90-degree angle to where it had been before," says Webster, "I immediately started writing seriously again." Webster thought it was just coincidence that his creative juices finally began to flow again.

But at the same time, he became aware of the subject of feng shui. He analyzed his home office and discovered that he had unknowingly moved his desk from a negative position to a highly favorable one (see Webster 1997).

Webster says in his book that desks should always be placed against a wall, and never put in the center of the room, or else the worker will lose power and authority. A desk in the middle of the room is considered to be "floating," which also symbolizes to the Chinese the position in which they used to place coffins in the temple's yard while waiting for burial.

Don't place your desk so your back is against a full wall of windows either, because you might feel there's nothing solid backing you up.

Feng shui experts say that if you place a desk so that your back is to the door, you will always feel that you are being stabbed in the back.

I once worked at a magazine where the publisher reconfigured his large office so that his back was to the door. He also reduced his desk from an oversized executive desk to a mid-size U-shaped workstation. Most of the staff tried to discourage him from sitting like that because of feng shui principles. Though he didn't heed our warning, and he began to look rather vulnerable sitting in his office at a small workstation with his back to the door.

If you absolutely have to sit with your back to the door, place an adequately sized mirror in front of you or angled above your desk (this can be awkward, but it is a cure) to see anyone walking into the room.

Why even consider the placement of your desk? It's simple, and practical: If you sit with your back to the door, you may feel unbalanced, as though you're going to be caught doing something you shouldn't be doing. You'll be jumpy, easily startled, and distracted because you never know who's behind you (see Figure 4-6).

When I was an editor at a magazine, I worked with my back to the corridor, and all too often my very quiet boss would come up behind me, place her hands on my shoulders, and I'd jump sky-high from being so startled! People used to say, "Boy, you're jumpy today." In truth, I wasn't jumpy at all but rather concentrating deeply on my work. A disruption like that wouldn't have been so jarring if I could have just sensed that my boss was walking toward me. I never realized it was this particular feng shui principle at work.

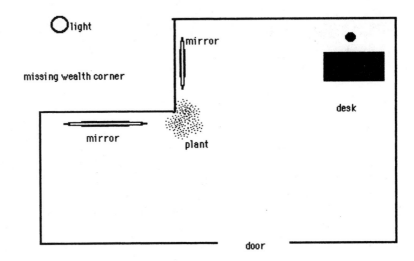

Figure 4-6. A house or room should really be square or rectangular. The problem with this home office is that it's missing its wealth corner (upper left area). To "fill in" the wealth area, place mirrors on the inner walls of the missing spaces, and if possible, place a light to fill in the missing part of the square. Also, place a plant in front of the corner that juts into the room. (*MZS*)

Unfortunately, there was nowhere else to move to in that particular row of cubicles because they were all set up the same way.

When my desk in my first home office was set up so that my back was to the door, my husband would come into the room and shock me without meaning to do so. Now, my desk is placed so that I can immediately see who's coming into the room, and I'm never startled anymore.

Webster says that a desk should be the right size to reflect your status. Although this may mean more in a corporate setting where you are always on display, you might want to think about this for your home office because you will feel better psychologically about your work if the work surface is meaningful and spacious.

Cures for Structural Elements

Exposed beams in a home office symbolize something heavy hanging over your head. They create stress, tension, and headaches, all leading to ill will and bad luck.

Although a successful film producer, Maxi Cohen loves the open, airy feeling of her home office, but she does have a problem with overhead beams.

> **A feng shui master told me what's wrong with my home office. He said there are beams running across the ceiling. The beams really look great—they are painted white—but they are right over my head. However, I do feel oppressive a lot of the time when I'm in this office. But the beams are there for structural reasons. So the feng shui master suggested that we put back the drop ceiling, but I didn't do that because I really like the height of the ceiling.**

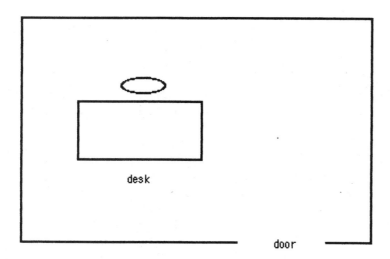

Figure 4-7. If you can, place your desk so it faces the doorway. Never sit with your back to the door. If you must sit like this, place a large mirror on the wall in front of you so that you can always see who is coming through the door and what's happening behind your back. (*MZS*)

"A friend of mine used to suffer from constant headaches caused by a beam over his desk," says author Webster. "Once he changed the layout of his office, the headaches completely disappeared."

Using Color As a Feng Shui Cure

Susan Aiello, an interior designer who has studied feng shui, tells a story about a writer who worked in the wrong color office for her profession.

> **I know a woman writing a serious book, and she was having lots of trouble getting the book done. She showed me her home office that was already set up and painted by the previous owner. The whole room was red. I told her that it wasn't any wonder why she wasn't getting anything done in that office! It was impossible to concentrate in there!**
>
> **Based on the nature of what she was doing, I suggested she paint the office a robin's egg blue—between a blue and a green—which is soothing, but creative. I really felt the color change would help her.**
>
> **The color red made perfect sense for the previous owner. He was in the music business. Music executives never need to concentrate on anything for more than three minutes! These guys make snap decisions, or else they blow opportunities and deals! It also wasn't his primary work space. When he was there, he was on the phone making deals. Red is good for deal makers and for people that entertain. Red is an aggressive color. And for someone writing a book, it doesn't make sense.**

Aiello also tells the story about someone she knew who lived in a house, part of which was decorated with a brown tiled floor and a lowered brown wood ceiling. "When you walked into this room, you felt as though you were literally walking into a vise. The color of the two surfaces was too confining for comfort," Aiello explains.

The best color for a home office, according to Denise Linn, an interior realignment specialist and author of *Sacred Space* (1995, Ballantine), is yellow. "Yellow is excellent for any home office because it stimulates thought, creativity, and mental activity. Color research shows that people have more clarity of thought when working in yellow environments," she says. It also promotes discipline, which we all need when working in a home office!

I decided to paint my home office yellow after reading Linn's book. She said to use yellow "in any room where you want to feel mentally uplifted," and that's exactly what I wanted my home office to be for me—a place where I would always find joy and a space in which I would always feel my most positive self. At times when the sunlight streams in, the whole office lights up and makes me feel a bliss I rarely if ever experienced in a corporate setting. I'm convinced it's the yellow tint that evokes that joyful feeling inside of me.

Publicist Shannon Wilkinson painted her entire home office yellow. "An interior designer recommended that I keep all the furniture light in color, even the walls and the curtains. She said that everything should have a feeling of lightness so when you come in to the office, you don't feel depressed," says Wilkinson of her apartment-home office.

Linn also says that oranges and other warm desert colors stimulate socialization and collaboration. She warns about using red as a dominant color in a home office: It stimulates the appetite.

Don't paint your ceilings a dark color or else you'll feel like there's a dark cloud over your head all the time you're working.

An Interview with Deborah Meyer, Feng Shui Practitioner

Deborah Meyer, president of Cinnabar, first became interested in feng shui when she was a commercial interior designer and had to learn about it while working with clients in Hong Kong. The more she learned about it, the more convinced she was that studying and practicing feng shui was the path on which she was to walk down in life. Her goal today is to help people and bring more of an awareness of the art of feng shui into not only our homes but into our commercial office buildings, as well.

Deborah came to my house to give my husband and me a feng shui consultation. What follows are portions of our dialogue regarding the home office and feng shui principles:

What I learned most about feng shui is that everyone is struggling. You don't have to be struggling. You chose this house for a reason to work out different things in your life. But now you can fix them and move forward.

Feng shui is really about moving energy. I'm a healer, and I'm an energy mover. I can tell a lot about people from their offices and their closets.

The first thing you have to look at is the location of the home office. You want the home office to be in the front of the house because the energy comes

into the front of the house easier. If you're in the back, it's tougher to receive any energy. So anyone who starts a home office, assuming he or she is trying to actually work and make money, should put it in the front of the house. Other people who set up home offices to do a little side business can put their home office anywhere. But if you are trying to get a business going and you need to be connected to the outside world, your office needs to be in front of house. If you want to add a separate entrance to your home office, you should put it at the front of the house.

The biggest mistake people make is that they have the wrong mindset about their home office. Most people think that because they don't see their office, it really doesn't matter where it is or what it looks like. That's a giant mistake because it's their energy they are playing with. It's not what other people see and think of them or their home office, it's the energy they are telling themselves they are going to put into this place every day. Working in a home office you don't care about is not going to energetically support them.

A lot of this kind of thinking stems from people having a lack of respect for themselves. People don't want to spend the money on a decent home office because they are just starting up. But if people would only realize that money and energy are the same thing, that money is just another form of energy—it's just in paper format—but it's a symbol of energy, they'd take better care of setting up a home office. If people would set their offices up with the same kind of intention they have in their heart and in their mind to make their business grow, the office will support them and they will succeed a lot faster and a lot easier.

Your intention of how much energy you plan to put into your business is reflected in where you choose to set up your home office. Many people have a lack of space in which to fit a home office. So if that's the case, and you can set up an office only in your living room, do it with great intention and arrange it so you are sitting at your desk facing the door with your back against the wall.

Basement offices are not a great idea. Offices in the basement makes it more difficult to get energy down there, but it does depend on the basement. If you like to work in a basement, then that means there's a part of you that wants to shut down and hide. You're kind of thinking to yourself, "Okay, I want to succeed, but I don't *really* want to succeed."

Attic home offices are better for people because they are upstairs. There's different energy in the different floors of the house, and the best energy is up on higher floors. But there's a danger to that, too. Some attics have sloping ceilings. If you are in a sloping ceiling environment, you need to implement a variety of cures to make the room a complete box or cube that will make it a more balanced, harmonious place to work.

Bedroom home offices are not great because people will either sleep a lot when they are trying to work or they have a hard time sleeping because they are too wired up and feel the constant need to work. An office in a bedroom means that there are two totally different energies, which is why it's so important to keep them separate so that you won't be confused about which energy should be circulating in that room.

It gets more complicated if two people share a home office. Energetically, it makes a difference. You have to see if the two people planning to work together have the same energy. If someone is the quiet thinker and the other one is on the phone all the time, then there will be two opposing energies in the same room.

People also have to take greater care about what they put into their home office. You need to put objects in the right corners of the office and of the desk based on your intentions. If you never put anything anywhere with any intention, nothing much will happen, but more energy is brought to that part of your life if you empower the objects when you place them in your office.

Most people have too much stuff in their offices, which means they are clogging themselves up. If you have junk in your wealth corner, then it means you are junking up your wealth corner, as simple as that.

It's good for people to put their fax machines in the areas of helpful people or fame. Where you put your phone can be really powerful. You have to have a mindfullness of where you are putting things. A lot of times I can look at the space and I can tell what kinds of issues are there before we talk. I can see what's cracked, what's missing.

Pay attention to the quality of things you put into your office. You get what you pay for. If you energetically put a $5 plant in the office, you get more from it than you would from a half-dead $1 plant. It's a mirror of how you view your worthiness.

Sometimes putting a home office together on a shoestring isn't the best way to do it. It takes money to make money. So if you are giving out the energy that you are making money and you are acting as though you are making more money, then more money will come to you. People may or may not be able to read it, but it's still going out there as energy.

Practical Guidelines from Feng Shui

Don't discount these feng shui guidelines even though they may sound superficial to you. Why? "People don't understand, it's three thousand years of common sense. There's also an art, a form, and a reason to the way it's done. It's practical and pragmatic—not just happenstance, with some crazy decorator coming in and shoving around furniture," says William S. Doyle, executive with a New York advertising agency who enlisted the help of a feng shui expert for his 16,000-square-foot offices (see Rossbach 1987).

Here are more ideas of things you can do in your home office to bring good energy into your work space. A feng shui practitioner will offer more in-depth counseling with more complex, and many times more mystical, cures.

◆ Red flowers placed in the upper left quadrant of your office or desk can bring financial success.

- If you don't have a view outside from where you sit at your desk, hang a plant or a picture of a plant in your line of view to bring the outdoors inside. It will calm you down.

- Yellow is the best color for the home office because it is peaceful and cheerful.

- Keep only healthy plants in your home office. Get rid of dying plants because it symbolizes that your business is also dying.

- If your desk sits on the other side of a bathroom wall, block any energy from the bathroom by hanging a thick, decorative fabric on that particular wall.

- Round-edged furniture stimulates creativity; squared-off edges promote killer negotiations.

- If your home office has a tall piece of furniture that your eye can easily see when you sit at your desk, move it. You might feel as though it's looming over you and cause you stress.

- If your office is at the end of a hallway, put a 100-watt bulb in the hallway light to illuminate the pathway to your office. It will make you and anyone else approaching your office feel secure and comfortable.

My Own Experience with Feng Shui

I was first introduced to feng shui in the early 1990s when I stumbled into a seminar on the subject at an interior design conference. I was fascinated with the idea of feng shui from the start even though the speaker at the conference, William Spear, a well-known Connecticut-based feng shui master, told me to immediately move out of the apartment I was living in at the time because it had terrible feng shui problems! Since I met Spear, he has written one of the best and clearly understandable books on the subject, *Feng Shui Made Easy* (1995, Harper Collins).

When I moved out of that ill-fated apartment and into a house, I decided to try some of feng shui principles in the small room I chose to be my home office. However, since Herman Miller was using me as a beta site for its home office furniture, they would provide some planning assistance to design the space. When I told the planner that I didn't want to place the desk so that my back was to the door, he asked why. I told him I was concerned about feng shui, but he thought I was crazy. I let him proceed with planning my office in the way he first envisioned—with my back to the door.

So for a few years, I sat uncomfortably with my back to the door of my home office, always jumping when I heard the slightest sound (which was usually my cat walking down the hall), especially when I worked in the house alone.

In spite of sitting with my back to the door, I was extremely productive in the old set-up of my home office.

When I decided to work from home full-time, I rearranged my desk in that same room. For six months I sat in a slightly better position, yet my back was still facing the door most of the time. Then I realized my home office was caving in on me. I had too much stuff, not enough room, and no matter how much I tried to straighten up and organize myself, I wasn't making any headway, and I had no idea why.

Then fate stepped in and through a series of fits and starts, feelings of hesitancy and finally the feeling of an eagerness I found hard to contain, my husband and I were scheduled for a feng shui consultation with Deborah Meyer, a feng shui practitioner (see resources appendix).

My consultation was magical, and at the same time, my husband and I felt it was one of the wisest and affordable investments we've ever made for ourselves. Meyer's consultation was quite literally a wake-up call for us, and my husband and I found an energy within ourselves we never knew existed, enough to literally move mountains in our lives that we never thought we could or ever would budge.

Meyer gave us a full house and property consultation, and then she spent some time discussing feng shui in the home office. I can tell you that as a result of our consultation, I moved my home office to a larger space because Meyer sensed that I had outgrown my old home office and no longer felt comfortable working in there (no wonder I kept hitting my head on the furniture).

I asked her why I felt so productive and comfortable in there at one time, and she said it was because when I had a staff position and a cubicle, my home office wasn't the primary work environment.

So in the later part of December, literally one month before my manuscript for this book was due, I made the commitment to dismantle my home office, clean out four years' worth of junk that had landed in the room down the hall to which I was to move, paint that room yellow, and move completely in there by New Year's weekend, 1998. And that I did.

What Was Wrong with my First Home Office

As I mentioned above, my first home office was a small 8- by 10-foot room next to the living room and across from the main bathroom (see Figure 4-8).

Of course, my back was always facing the door. But there were other problems, which I've briefly described below:

◆ My husband installed three shelves to span the entire length of an 8-foot wall under which I placed my desk. Bad move. For sitting directly under shelving is bad feng shui, and the occupant subconsciously feels an oppressive mass above his or her head that looks ready to fall down. I will admit that I became increasingly agitated whenever I looked up at the shelves from my desk because they were getting overcrowded with heavy magazines and books (see Figure 4-9).

◆ My top shelf, to make matters worse, was filled with little gifts, toys, and art (questionable) that I had accumulated over the years and that I didn't know what to do with when I got them home after leaving my staff job. The art was given to me by a dear friend, which prevented me out of guilt from giving it away or burying it in the basement. Meyer pointed out that I should have only those things in my office (and the rest of the house, of course) that I love.

"Do you really love that little green wheelbarrow up there on the shelf?" she asked. Of course, the wheelbarrow was cute, but it meant nothing to me whatsoever. I ended up bringing into my new office only one toy—a doll from Japan—which means a great deal to me, so I've placed it on my desk.

♦ In addition, I placed a crystal in the window of my old home office because I thought it would bring me great energy and good luck. During my consultation I found out that a crystal doesn't attract anything unless it's hung on a 9-inch red ribbon. It must be hung in an auspicious place in a room, placed there with intention, not just placed there in an arbitrary manner. And, you must *like* the crystal for if you feel it looks funny or out of place, you will resent its presence, and it won't help much.

♦ In one corner of my old office, my *wealth* corner was "dead," according to Meyer (see Figure 4-10). There was a basket in the corner (its contents pure junk). The wealth corner is the most important part of your home office—and your desk—and you can find out how to find it by referring to the *bagua*. I've taken great care of my wealth corner in my new home office!

♦ I was constantly hitting my head on various corners of furniture in my old home office. Whenever I'd have to go into a file cabinet that was in the closet, I'd always hit my head on the corner of my wooden file cabinet. When I would go under the desk to adjust the wiring, I'd hit my head on the edge of my desk. I felt as though every time I entered that office, I was going into some sort of battlefield that I couldn't control.

♦ My office was a mess! In feng shui terms, disorderly surroundings reflect internal chaos. If I was going to achieve any type of harmony with myself, I'd have to work in orderly surroundings so that I could concentrate fully on my work.

♦ I placed a deep blue lava lamp on top of my file cabinet, which was also piled with a mess of papers and folders. But Meyer said never to put anything blue in the fame and reputation quadrant of the office or desk. That's exactly where my blue lava lamp was sitting (see Figure 4-11).

Figure 4-8. During my feng shui consultation, practitioner Deborah Meyer sensed that I felt crowded out of my home office because it was cluttered and the room was too small to accommodate my needs. (*MZS*)

Figure 4-9. Meyer also noted that I should not have placed my main desk underneath the three shelves. When you sit under shelves, you tend to feel as though you have the weight of the world on your shoulders, or that something might fall on your head. (*MZS*)

Figure 4-10. Meyer noted that the wealth area of my old home office was empty except for a basket filled with junk. She said I was "junking up" my wealth corner. (*MZS*)

Figure 4-11. Another problem: I placed a blue lava lamp on a cluttered file cabinet located in my reputation area. Never place anything blue in your reputation area because you will be "killing and drowning" your fame. Always put something red in the fame area.

What's Right with My Second Home Office

The new, larger office felt uncomfortable to me for the first two days I was in there. I didn't want to go into the office. Instead, I'd walk into the room where my old home office was located and sit in there. I avoided my new home office for a couple of days until my husband insisted that I "bond" with the space. Now that I've bonded with my new office, I've never been so efficient in my life. After all, there's space in which to move! What a necessity for a home business. Here's what I tried to do right this time in relation to feng shui principles:

Furniture and Object Placement in the Room

- ◆ I put my desk in a position where I face the door (see Figure 4-12).

- ◆ I put my blue lava lamp in the wealth corner of the office along with a mock-up of my first book cover to ensure good luck. I put the lava light on as much as possible to create movement in my wealth corner.

- ◆ I put my fax in the helpful people corner of my office (so helpful people can easily communicate with me).

- ◆ I put my file cabinet in the relationship corner of the office, but on top of it I put a healthy plant, lamp (which I keep on most of the time), and photos of my husband to ensure a healthy relationship.

- ◆ I'm only putting fresh, new supplies in my closet, which is the "new beginnings" quadrant of my office. I will resolve not to put junk into the closet (although *this* is tough to follow through on).

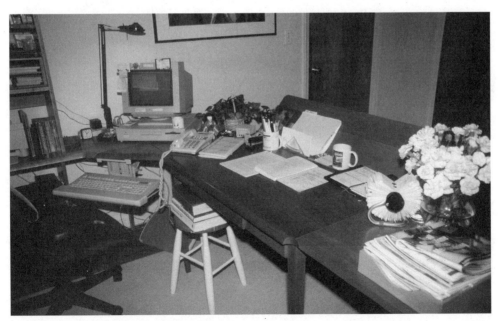

Figure 4-12. Meyer suggested I move my office out of the tiny office into a bigger room. Now my desk is set up so that I am facing the door. (*Steve Syarto*)

Figure 4-13. I placed carnations in a crystal bowl in my relationship area of my desk. My computer is on the wealth corner of my desk. I've added healthy plants and silk plants everywhere I can to add a sense of life and growth to the home office. (*Steve Syarto*)

Object Placement on My Desk

◆ My computer is the wealth corner of my desk to stir up energy in that department and to ensure that my writing will bring me wealth.

◆ Next to my computer is a red object (an auspicious color) that means a great deal to me and reminds me that my writings could very well be financially fruitful. I also have a photo of two roses in my wealth corner signifying to me that my wealth will blossom.

◆ In my fame and reputation area I placed my business cards on a crystal dish for respect.

◆ In my relationship corner I have a crystal heart-shaped paperweight next to a wedding photo along with a crystal bowl filled with pink and white flowers (see Figure 4-13).

◆ I vow only to place objects that I love into my work space.

Five Home Office Problems and Minor Feng Shui Cures

Here are five hypothetical home office problems and basic feng shui cures to help you get started in moving energy in the right direction in your home office.

1. **Your home office has no window.**

Paint it yellow, put in lots of bright bulbs, and put up pictures of outdoor scenes. Add lots of silk flowers. Never use dried flowers because they are "dead" flowers.

2. **Your home office is located in the basement.**

Paint the ceilings and the walls bright white. Put up bright bulbs and pictures of outdoor scenes. To get energy moving, install a small fan in the basement that blows on something to create movement. Add an electric wind chime (rings without a breeze) at the base of the basement stairs to create more energy flow. In addition, mirror one wall so that the lower ceilings won't make you feel constricted.

3. **You find your phone isn't ringing that much with new business and you're getting worried.**

Put your phone on the wealth section of your desk (upper right section) or helpful people part of your desk (lower left section). Hang a small leaded crystal from the ceiling above the phone, but you must hang it on a 9-inch red ribbon. Place the phone and the crystal with intention, always praying, meditating, and visualizing what you want to happen over the phone once you place it in its spot (see Figure 4-14).

Figure 4-14. Here's a crystal hanging on a recommended 9-inch-long red ribbon. This particular crystal is placed in front of a corner jutting out into the room. It's a cure to "cut killing ch'i" that corners create. Corners are like arrows pointing into a room. (*Steve Syarto*)

4. Your home office is in your bedroom.

Move the desk so you are facing the door and take great care to place the bagua on your bedroom, then on your work surface. Place objects accordingly and with intention. Place a screen over the home office at night so that you don't mix energies when you are trying to go to sleep (see Figure 4-15).

Figure 4-15. If your home office is in your bedroom, you are mixing conflicting energies into the room. One solution, a logical cure, would be to place a screen in front of your desk area every night so you don't go to sleep or wake up looking at work. (*MZS*)

5. **You and your spouse work in the same home office.**

The way you place your desks is important. Note the wrong position of the home office where husband and wife both work. Both of them sit with their backs to the door of the room so neither of them are in a leadership position (see Figure 4-16). If there is enough room, place your desks in a semibagua position (see Figure 4-17).

Figure 4-16. Meyer pointed out the problem with this home office shared by husband and wife: Both of their backs are to the door to the office and to each other. No one is seated in a power position. (*MZS*)

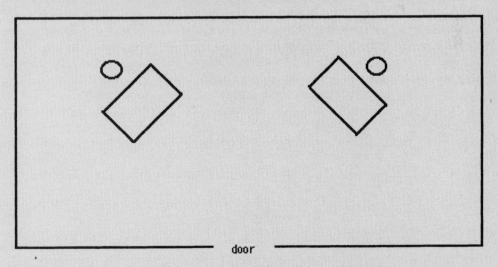

Figure 4-17. The correct set-up for a two-person home office is to both face the door. If there's room, place desks in a semibagua position for good luck, as indicated in this drawing. (*MZS*)

Finding a Feng Shui Practitioner and What to Expect During a Consultation

Since feng shui is becoming more accepted in the West, many more people are studying the art. Many people that take three-day seminars on the subject hang a shingle out and call themselves "feng shui practitioners." It's best to investigate or get a practitioner's name by word of mouth just as you would any other professional. You can find helpful information in the resources appendix section at the back of the book that can tell you where to begin your search for a practitioner.

Feng shui readings can cost around a few hundred dollars up to $1,000 for a site, and many practitioners come from a school in Berkeley, California, where The Yun Lin Temple is located. Each master has a different way of assessing a structure's feng shui. Some use a directional compass called a *luopan*; some use crystals; some use mirrors; some simply meditate. Much of the emphasis is placed on enhancing the amount of sunlight and flow of air through a building.

Every practitioner has his or her own unique way of consulting with clients. A feng shui consultant will typically come to your home and first assess your plot, then your house, then the rooms in your house. The bedrooms are the most important part of the consultation, so expect to spend a lot of time talking about those rooms.

Based on the practitioner's knowledge, he or she will offer you cures that you should implement as quickly as possible in order to begin moving the energy flow around your home. I suggest taping the consultation because there can be complex cures and explanations that you will want to refer back to.

If you have been given a cure that seems difficult to implement, don't start it and then abandon it in the middle if you can't find a specific part of a cure. That is bad luck. Part of the process of moving energy to flow in more beneficial ways is in finding and completing the cure. Your practitioner can lead you in the right direction in finding a cure.

After your consultation, don't tell too many people about the cures you were told to install. It will dilute the power of the cures. If anyone asks you why you have a crystal hanging from your window, just tell them it means Chinese good luck!

wealth (purple, red, blue)	reputation (red)	relationship (pink, white, red)
family (green)	health (yellow)	creativity (white)
knowledge (blue)	career (black)	helpful people (gray)

chair

Figure 4-18. Your desk is a bagua. Place meaningful objects in the area of your life that you'd like to enrich. For example, place a healthy plant in the wealth and relationship areas of your desk. Try to put the color object that best pertains to a certain area. Put red flowers in your wealth or reputation area, for example. *(MZS)*

Figure 5-1. Beautiful traditional-style furniture like the desk pictured here won't accommodate today's desktop computer. The desk lacks a place for an articulating keyboard unless the top drawer is eliminated. Putting the computer on the desk leaves little if any work surface, and there's nowhere to put a vertical hard-drive tower. (*Acer*)

5

A Bargain-Hunter's Guide to Buying Home Office Furnishings

"I've seen home office workers set up rickety card tables with computers on them," says Arlette Loeser, ergonomic consultant, occupational therapist, and owner of The Ultimate Workspace, a company that assesses corporate and home office work spaces. "They scrape by and function until the card table collapses. A lot of people like two file cabinets with the door on top as a desk. Although it provides lots of work surface and filing space, the height is usually too high for comfort."

When we set up a home office, we tend to use existing furniture that we turn into a patchwork home office. The trouble is, most of the older styles of furniture, like a rolltop desk, won't accommodate the computer user's needs. Since most work-at-home workers use computers, make sure you aren't romanced into buying a great old piece of furniture that can't be retrofitted with a computer keyboard (for examples, see Figures 5-1 and 5-2).

The biggest problem, however, is the lack of home office furniture solutions on the market. It's not for their lack of creativity. For example, for just under $1,000 retail, you could buy a Maxim recliner from La-Z-Boy that includes a speakerphone with a digital answering machine and laptop hookup built into its arm. Obviously this product isn't meant for the full-time home office worker, but for the corporate worker who occasionally brings home work. But for the full-time home office worker, there aren't too many more options other than the traditional desk or workstation. Although residential and contract furniture manufacturers feel they have the problem licked, they really don't if you talk to equipment-intensive graphic designer Steve DeMartino. His home office is located in the den in view of family, where it is especially intriguing to his toddler, Rob, who loves playing with computers:

> At one point, I thought about enclosing all of my technology and work in an armoire so Rob wouldn't be able to get to it and so it would look contained when other people are in the den. But we looked around for one, and we realized that none of them on the market would hold all the stuff I have.
>
> Then I thought about custom cabinetry, which can run about $5,000 for my needs. That costs too much. Then I thought a rolltop desk might work, but they aren't built to hold technology at all.

Figure 5-2. This desk represents the problem most of us have when we pull together our home offices. We tend to use furniture that doesn't accommodate our needs because we don't want to spend money on new furniture. This home office worker had to add a piece of wood on brackets to lengthen the desk to accommodate a large computer. (*MZS*)

Figure 5-3. Affordable, durable, and mobile furniture for computer-intensive home offices is difficult to find. Graphics specialist Richard Turek's solution was to add castors onto the bottom of long, heavy-duty utility tables. When his computers go down, he can roll the tables away from the wall. (*MZS*)

> **The problem is that I have too much stuff that I need in order to do my job! In addition to technology, I still need work space to lay projects, comps, and layouts out on a work surface. I desperately need a work surface, and I don't know what the solution is out there for me.**

Richard Turek, coowner of Big Daddy Digital, home-based imaging specialists, also has lots of technology that traditional furniture can't contain, and furniture designed to hold technology can be more expensive than home-made solutions:

> **We looked at Anthro furniture, but for a desk and cart, it would cost $600. It looked nice and sleek, but I went to Home Depot and bought $78 worth of materials to make my own computer stand. I also put castors from Staples on the legs of the tables so I can get to the back of the machines (see Figure 5-3). I put 3/4-inch wooden dowels into the table's hollow legs and drilled little holes in them for the castors. When the machine crashes, I pull the whole table out to fix the equipment, but the weight of the table is ridiculous. It also made the tables rise 3 inches, which throws off the height a little. But I'm 6-foot, so the height is not a problem for me.**

Or maybe you don't have as much "stuff" as a graphic designer, but you've decided to clear the room of time-worn furniture, and you're ready for a new, more efficient look. But perhaps you've decided against using a professional to help you pull your home office

Figure 5-4. This is the perfect home office we're used to seeing in shelter magazines. Although it's a beautiful, luxurious home office, do you have $10,000, or even $5,000 to spend on furnishings right now for your home office? An efficient home office can be furnished on a shoestring if you know where to look. (*Manes Street*)

together. Then it's good to know that furnishing a good-looking, well-functioning home office can be done on a shoestring budget. Sometimes we don't even bother to find decent-looking furniture for our home office because we have been brainwashed to expect that our home offices should look like the ones featured in upscale shelter magazines (see Figure 5-4).

"Most of the home offices in books and magazines must have $200,000 worth of furniture in them. Now, who do you know with $200,000 would spend it on office furniture? Some people, perhaps like Steven Spielberg or someone in high tech with lots of money. It's an ego trip to spend that kind of money on home office furniture," says interior designer Michael Love, principal of Interior Options in New York City.

If you don't feel that your office has to be perfect, perhaps you just don't have time to scout out cheap furniture. You don't have time to put together the ready-to-assemble (RTA) furniture. Maybe you have already purchased RTA (ready-to-assemble, also known as *knock-down*, or KD) furniture, and it's still sitting unassembled in a box in the basement. Perhaps you don't know if RTA is right for you or whether used office furniture is a better route to take.

This chapter looks at a number of scenarios including:

◆ Why you haven't found the perfect furniture solution for your home office

◆ Why home office experts turn their nose up at superstore-quality furniture

◆ The realities of ready-to-assemble furniture

◆ Why commercial-grade furniture is so expensive and hard to buy

◆ Why liquidators and secondhand shops are a good bet for home office furniture

◆ How to find catalogs with good-looking home office furniture

◆ How to find cheap storage, avoid carpeting mistakes, and find low-cost paint

What's Right and Wrong with Today's Home Office Furniture?

Most of us haven't found the perfect furniture solution to our home office needs: "If I were to design a workstation myself, I'd design one where I could stand up or sit by the push of a button or the tap of a foot. Everything would raise along with me because I prefer to stand when I work," says Deborah Quilter, ergonomic consultant and author of *The Repetitive Strain Injury Recovery Book* (Walker & Company, 1998) and *Repetitive Strain Injury: A Computer User's Guide* (John Wiley, 1994).

You would think that because the home office is a fastest-growing market that furniture and product manufacturers would be bending over backward to offer top-quality, low-cost furniture solutions to us. Unfortunately, that's not the case, but why?

There are a number of reasons that both manufacturers of residential furniture and commercial-grade furniture don't cater to the home office worker. They have made the effort, but the home office is not an easy market to grasp in terms of research, design, selling, price, and delivery issues. When furniture companies sense frustration, they tend to throw up their hands and return to focusing on their core businesses.

Mark Dutka, owner of InHouse, a retail-design store that caters exclusively to the home office worker, knows the problems associated with home office furniture. Since he opened his store in 1995, he has developed a criteria system for choosing the lines of home office furniture he sells on his floor (see Figure 5-5). He explains why we have such a hard time finding the perfect home office solution:

> **Home offices were very much in the news, and I knew what was on the market and how frustrating it was to shop for home office furniture. When I first thought about opening the store, I knew about the typical oak systems and pressboard systems on the market—that they are very rectilinear, very bulky, and nothing aesthetically pleasing. I could sense that no one would look at any of these pieces and say they wanted to work on them for the long term. No one would be proud to work with these types of office systems for the home office.**
>
> **So I decided to open a store where people would have access to off-the-shelf manufacturer's goods that I would identify by meeting certain criteria. My criteria has evolved since I've become more knowledgeable in the field and unearthed all the problems with home office furniture manufacturers.**
>
> **Manufacturers think they are taking the home office market's needs seriously, but when it becomes too much of a headache, they back off.**
>
> **First of all, there's no place for a consumer to walk in to buy new commercial-grade office furniture. Contract furniture dealers used to be excited about developing a new opportunity like the home office market, but it turns out they weren't equipped to handle individual consumer orders, they only service large corporate orders. They realized that customer service was equally or more arduous for one or two units as it was for 500 units of furniture for a company order. They could not respond to the consumers' needs. And they don't want to sell their furniture to consumers through retail outlets because they don't want to upset the traditional network of contract furniture dealers that cater to corporations at different price points.**

Then there is the retail side of the equation. Stores typically sell desks from residential furniture manufacturers but nothing more. The salespeople don't understand ergonomics or wire management or electronics. They offer great aesthetic packages, but they don't understand why the more expensive Accuride glides are so important for heavily used drawers and file cabinets. They don't realize that desks are used for something more these days than just filling out checkbooks. They need to understand that furniture has to serve computers, faxes, monitors, and printers.

Selling home office furniture on the residential furniture store floor is a problem. Distribution networks are typically retail outlets that aren't equipped to handle home offices. The employees need to be trained, but there's hesitancy on the part of the retailers to retrain or to set aside certain square footages for home office furniture. All the markets are realizing this is a growing market, and they want to be part of it. But they have to overcome all these obstacles.

Quality is also an issue of home office furniture made by some of the well-respected names in residential furniture. One residential manufacturer had a cabinet that was supposed to hold a minitower, but it didn't fit the minitower!

In addition, the hardware that comes on residential furniture lines is inadequate. Manufacturers don't understand that the drawers are opened and closed continuously all day. I'm not just talking about RTA, I'm talking about residential casegoods.

Figure 5-5. InHouse owner Mark Dutka has a difficult time finding home office furniture to sell in his upscale home office specialty retail store that fits his strict criteria. He wishes more manufacturers would take the time to better research the true needs of home office workers. Some of his offerings are shown here. (*InHouse*)

RTA manufacturers also have several problems. Their prices are better because they've done retail for so long they know the ratios. But the quality isn't there for a desk system. However, RTA is getting a little higher end.

Then there are shipping problems. Contract furniture manufacturers pack their products amazingly well. But we've had lots of problems with residential manufacturers with damaged furniture.

It's frustrating that we do so much custom work but there aren't a lot of well-designed, compartmentalized casegoods with appropriate storage and wire management for the home office.

What Most of Us Buy: Ready-to-Assemble Furniture

One of the most popular forms of furniture for the home office is sold unassembled, also known as ready-to-assemble (RTA), because it can be purchased immediately with no waiting for delivery.

RTA manufacturers say their goods are as stylish without being as expensive as traditional preassembled furniture and that people are typically creative and find the assembly process gratifying.

One thing you must understand about RTA furniture is that it's usually made of not-so-durable particleboard composition and small dowels (that might split when hammered for assembly). Not only that, the RTA hardware used to assemble furniture is not usually top quality. Why? To keep costs down.

If you are still thinking of buying RTA furniture, read the following insights by Atlanta-based commercial furniture designer Manfred Petri, in order to make a more informed purchase:

> RTA furniture manufacturers have the manufacturing expertise for a palatable price for the consumer. But when you look at the product from a functional standpoint, these manufacturers don't have any experience with computer issues that the contract (commercial) furniture manufacturers have had in making office furniture.
>
> Contract manufacturers have had 10 years of experience with questions like "Where do I put my wires, and where do I put my computer monitor?" But the RTA product rarely addresses these issues.
>
> It's disastrous if you've seen any RTA furniture set up in a home office as I've had. None of the functional issues have been addressed like wire management and monitor placement. There's usually some silly little shelf that is much too deep for the monitor, so the user puts the monitor elsewhere. Now all the wires get dragged across the work surface, and the work surfaces are way too shallow anyhow, plus they are too thin for weight of heavy computers and printers.
>
> My guess is that people buy those things once and don't buy them again. RTA does the job for a couple of years, but after that, consumers of RTA probably look for something more substantial.

The reality is, however, that discount office supply retailers, such as OfficeMax and Staples, remain the most popular source to purchase home office furniture, particularly files and chairs, according to a survey on home office trends conducted by Wirthlin Worldwide, a research firm. Wirthlin polled 1,627 consumers to gather information on the latest trends in home officing.

RTA is attractive to the retailer, as well. There is only one line that is more profitable than RTA furniture, and that is bedding. RTA furniture—home office or otherwise—provide retailers with good margins, rare returns of goods, no delivery expenses, no installation expenses, and quick turnover.

Many retailers have a thriving home office RTA business. Ikea's home office furniture sales volume has more than doubled in the last three years, according to a report in *Home Furnishings News,* a weekly trade paper on the furniture industry (see Gilbert, 1997).

Ikea has brought more flair, design, and style to RTA products than almost any other company so far. The Swedish company has a reputation for keeping prices low and style high (see Figure 5-6). Ikea introduced its Business Furniture line for the home office and small office in 1997 and has published a separate catalog from their main one that is dedicated to home office furniture.

"I love Ikea, and I love their home office furniture," says design writer and home office worker Barbara Mayer. "Ikea talks to well-educated people who don't have a lot of money."

Figure 5-6. Ikea's new target audience is the home office worker. The retailer came out with a new catalog, called *Business Ikea*. The furniture is good looking and extremely affordable, but be forewarned that you have to assemble it yourself or hire the store to do it for you. (*Ikea*)

That may be true, but no matter how well educated you are, Ikea's RTA furniture can be slightly difficult to assemble. Ikea does offer assembly assistance for a "moderate" charge, but most of us want to tackle it ourselves as soon as we get it in the door.

Home Office Computing Magazine, bible to home office workers, set out to test RTA furniture to see how long it would take to put together a piece of furniture. Former editor-in-chief Bernadette Grey and business manager Steve Palm agreed to participate in the RTA marathon. Both admitted to having limited construction skills, like most people who purchase RTA furniture (see Syarto, 1996).

The test included Anthro, Ikea, O'Sullivan, and Rubbermaid. Out of the four, Rubbermaid's SnapEase Desk was the easiest, least time-consuming RTA furniture to assemble (see Figure 5-7). It took 30 minutes and no tools to build the desk. Anthro was second best, taking only one hour to assemble with a custom-designed screwdriver included in the package (see Figure 5-8).

Figure 5-7. If you don't mind plastic furniture, Snapease home office furniture is the most durable (very kid-proof) and easiest ready-to-assemble furniture on the market, confirmed by a test taken by *Home Office Computing Magazine* editors. (*Newell Office Products*)

Figure 5-8. Anthro computer carts and furniture also won top points with *Home Office Computing* for its easy-to-read furniture assembly instructions. Besides, it's good looking and mobile. (*Anthro*)

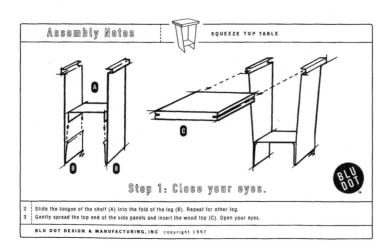

Assembly Notes

SQUEEZE TOP TABLE

Step 1: Close your eyes.

2 Slide the tongue of the shelf (A) into the fold of the leg (B). Repeat for other leg.
3 Gently spread the top end of the side panels and insert the wood top (C). Open your eyes.

BLU DOT DESIGN & MANUFACTURING, INC copyright 1997

Figure 5-9. Blu Dot's assembly notes are written in a most user-friendly way. The founders of the RTA manufacturing company know how daunting assembly can be. (*Blu Dot*)

The news wasn't as good for Ikea and O'Sullivan. Ikea's Kurs desk and hutch took well over two hours to assemble, in part due to the confusing instructions that show only pictures of how to put furniture together, with no words for explanation. O'Sullivan's desk and hutch took close to three hours to assemble, the photographers and assisting editors pitched in to help, but there were just too many parts to keep track of. For the photo, the editors ended up taping components together because they couldn't figure out how to complete the desk.

To take the fear out of RTA furniture assembly instructions, a new furniture company called Blu Dot makes its "assembly notes" super simple (see Figure 5-9). More important, Blu Dot designs its furniture so that it's easy to put together.

"We put humor in the directions," says Maurice Blanks, an architect and part owner of Blu Dot. "We call them 'assembly notes,' not 'instructions.' 'Instructions' seemed too condescending. There's a line on one of the notes that says, 'Take a deep breath,' then it says 'Rejoice' at the end. We wanted people to understand that *we* understand that it's frustrating to put this stuff together. We didn't want to have bad black and white copies of text, which conveys to the buyer, 'Here's the piece of furniture you want, now you have it, and I don't care what happens to you now.'"

Although Blanks doesn't use his home office as his primary work space (he has a small architectural firm with an office away from his home), he uses his home office as an experimental area for Blu Dot furniture. Blanks transformed his own home office from bland to Blu Dot, and he put together all the furniture in minutes, he said (see Figures 5-10, 5-11, 5-12, and 5-13):

The room the home office is in is just an extra room in which all the stuff we didn't know what to do with went. I have an old 1950s 60-inch-wide drafting table with green board and Luxo lamp that I put in there because I didn't know where else to put it. We also threw into the room white melamine bookshelves we had from college, an old black 30-inch lateral file two-drawer file, a knock-down type of armoire I've had since college, and an old dining room table of my wife's. It became a catchall room. Surprisingly, it worked because there were so many surfaces. I also put my fax machine on a tall box an old

Mac came in. It was just a junk room, and whenever anyone would come over, we'd shut the door. People would always wonder what was behind the door.

I started my firm a year and a half after we moved into this house. I never worked at home that much before that. I used to segregate home and work. Once you start your own business, that distinction starts to blur. I saw the need to have a reasonable work space in the home that was fairly comfortable and visually calming.

Every time I'd go into that room, though, I'd think, "ugh," this is a mess, I have to clean it up, but I have to take a whole weekend to fix it up!

When the opportunity to work with Blu Dot came along, it looked like a good time to do make that room into a decent home office and move the junk down to the basement, clean, and plan it better.

What I realized is that you can't really spend a lot of money on a home office. There are people out there who spend $30,000 on furniture for a home office, but that's the exception, not the rule. To go out and buy a nice desk and bookshelf adds up to a few thousand dollars pretty quickly. It also frustrates me to furnish a room a little at a time, that drags on for months. I wanted to take everything out of that room, start fresh, and complete it quickly.

I debated getting rid of the drafting table, but I just can't. We don't have any drafting tables in the office, and I really like working on it for schematic work. It's really the only piece that ended up staying in the room! The bookshelves were replaced with Chicago 8 Box, and we replaced the lateral with stackable files (see Figure 5-13).

I will admit the laminate shelves were the inspiration for the design of the Chicago 8 Box. Surprisingly enough, the laminate shelves never fell apart, and they are famous for bending badly. But every time I saw them, I said "ugh." It was a starting point for the Chicago 8 Box in that it was an affordable system that you could stack everything on without worrying that it would fall down.

Figure 5-10. Before: Maurice Blanks, architect and designer of Blu Dot furniture, had the typical spare bedroom home office filled with cast-off furniture and other junk, making it an uninviting, unorganized place to work. (*Maurice Blanks*)

Figure 5-11. Before: Blanks and his wife kept furniture from college days in the home office, including these two laminate shelving units that surprisingly never sagged under the weight of magazines. (*Maurice Blanks*)

Figure 5-12. Blanks's home office after: The laminate shelves went to the basement and were replaced with the Chicago 8 Box Wall Unit by Blu Dot. The wall unit retails for about $1,500 and comes in cherry or maple veneer with tubular steel legs. Blanks promises it's easy to assemble. (*Maurice Blanks*)

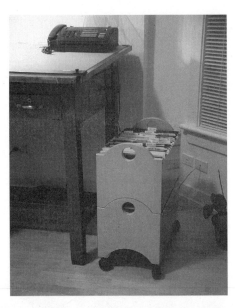

Figure 5-13. Mobile filing never looked so good, and is an upgrade for Blanks's office. The stackable filing units from Blu Dot come in 1-inch-thick Russian birch and steel side panels with a silver finish, retailing for about $70 a unit (castors are a little more). (*Maurice Blanks*)

Figure 5-14. The Container Store caters to consumers who don't mind taking on affordable do-it-yourself furniture projects. Plus, it's a haven for storage solutions. (*The Container Store*)

Another RTA furniture line that's reasonably easy to put together comes from The Container Store. The Container Store offers everything from a desk component system to brightly colored storage bins shown in Figure 5-14.

"There's a significant increase since 1996 in the number of people coming in to our stores asking about home offices," says Jill Nance, buyer for the national chain. "We get suggestion cards from clients and our own employees on what needs people have, and they are geared more than ever before toward home office solutions."

Part of the attraction of The Container Store is how easy it is to put together their RTA furniture. Peggy Doughty, buyer of shelving and closet products, explains:

> **Our customer comment cards say they just can't believe how quickly everything was assembled. That's gratifying to hear because we especially look for products that are easy to assemble and install. We give customers extensive directions in the store, as well. We give them detailed directions to take home, but if customers come in who have never put an anchor and screw into a dry wall, we will show them how to do it in the store. We make sure they are comfortable with doing that in their home before they leave the store. We don't have assembly services, it hasn't been necessary.**

What does Nance see for the next generation of RTA home office furniture?

"I used to see lots of home office product that was purely functional, and honestly, quite ugly," she says. "If people are putting in a home office in a quarter of their den, or in their kitchen or guest bedroom, they need good-looking products that are of good quality and blend in with the rest of the home. We are looking for products that have more design to them. We aren't looking for decorative products, but we are looking for more well-designed, functional, but generic looks that fit a number of household styles. We aren't looking for putty or gray plastic letter trays, for example."

I will admit that on a recent visit to my local Caldor store, I was surprised to see some decent styles of RTA from Sauder, O'Sullivan, and Bush! RTA manufacturers have veered away from medium, bland oak looks and have introduced darker fruitwood and cherrywood finishes in Shaker and Mission styles. Styling for RTA looks cleaner now, but not too utilitarian. It's worth a look.

Figure 5-15. This home office is furnished entirely of The Container Store products, including the chair. The store guarantees that this RTA furniture takes no sweat to assemble, and they can even demonstrate how to do it in the store. (*The Container Store*)

The Hype about Computer Armoires

Computer armoires became popular during the mid-1990s when everyone fell in love with the way they integrated so well into a living space. You usually buy an armoire when you don't have any room to put a dedicated home office. But the problem with a computer armoire is that you really can't run a full-time business from a piece of furniture like this. There's virtually no work surface, no place to spread out. And how many of us who are working on projects want to put them away every night so that we can close up the armoire doors? It's not a very efficient way of working.

"It's an idea borrowed from another 1980s classic, the armoire as entertainment center, which helped us hide the messy accouterments of enjoyment—TV, stereo, videotapes— behind an elegant facade," says Maura Sheehy in an article she wrote on computer armoires (see Sheehy, 1997). "Now the armoire has been dispatched to help us integrate the clutter of office life seamlessly into our home life."

The problem is that the clutter of office life for most of us running businesses from our home can't possibly be seamlessly integrated into our home life.

"The computer armoire is the home office solution for a small apartment. The computer armoire works only if you put it behind a dining room table or something that will work as a real work surface. It looks good when it's closed, but you can't work on that little 18-inch-wide desk. All you have to do is close those doors and it looks like you have a breakfront in the living room or dining room. If you don't have a dining area, if you have a good-sized console table behind a sofa, then put the armoire on the back wall so the table is in front of it—incorporate it with another piece of furniture so it will be your real work surface," says Michael Love, interior designer.

Figure 5-16. The Monarch armoire from Sauder, closed. (*Sauder*)

Figure 5-17. The Monarch armoire from Sauder, open. This RTA armoire typically retails for $399.99, on sale, at mass merchandisers. It is 71 inches high, 56 inches wide, and 51 inches deep. (*Sauder*)

There are three worthy alternatives to the typical residential computer armoires designed over the past few years. One of the armoires, designed by Manfred Petri, president of Frogbench, a furniture design studio he runs from his own home office, originated from a request by IBM:

> When we started Frogbench, we realized there was this big gap in the marketplace for home office furniture as a solution for younger, 25- to 35-year-old people just out of college being hired by big corporations in large cities. These new hires are given a laptop, cell phone, and fax machine and then are told to go home and work because there's no space in the office for them. The problem is that they live in New York City, Chicago, and Los Angeles in small apartments. So we designed Frogbench specifically for this group of people (see Figure 5-18 and Figure 5-19).
>
> We showed Frogbench to IBM, Peat Marwick and Ernst & Young, and they all expressed interest in it for their employees. The liability issue has reared its head. A company is worried about the employee working from a kitchen table who trips over their fax line as they reach for the phone. So corporations give their employees $2,500 to purchase home office furniture, therefore waiving their responsibility toward liability problems.
>
> Other companies take the second step and make a furniture recommendation. Most people grab the $1,500, and that's the end of that, and you won't hear from them even if they do trip over a wire!
>
> If you analyze Frogbench, it's a sophisticated secretary-armoire. Our approach with the laptop unit is that it all folds out, and it functions as workpiece, but when someone is done with work on Friday night and they happen to live in this small apartment, then the armoire just folds away and is unobtrusive.

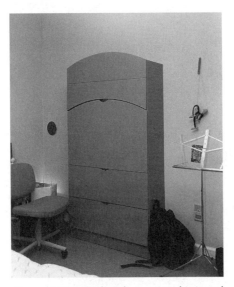

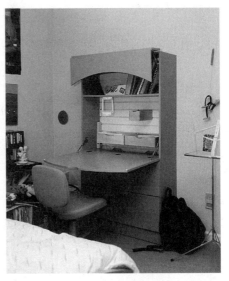

Figure 5-18. Frogbench is a sophisticated armoire-style office used by top corporations for on- and off-site employees. Here's a Frogbench prototype in the closed position that designer Manfred Petri's daughter uses in her bedroom for her own home office. (*Manfred Petri*)

Figure 5-19. Here's the Frogbench open. Filing cabinets are below the work surface. The work surface is deep and roomy. (*Manfred Petri*)

The second sophisticated armoire is called The Office (see Figure 5-20). When The Office workstation won top prize during Neocon's Home Office Product Competition in 1996, sponsored by the Merchandise Mart in Chicago and *Interiors Magazine* in New York City, judges cited this piece of furniture for its ability to be a self-contained, full-service work module that actually integrated itself well into most home decors.

The patent-pending unit is designed and engineered by the Summerland Group. Made from marine plywood, it looks like an armoire on the outside and opens up to reveal a fully equipped workstation with an ergonomic chair that fits inside when doors are closed.

The Office comes in five models, each with different standard and optional equipment: The CEO (the largest model measuring 28 inches deep, 72 inches wide, and 77 inches high), The Professional (48 inches wide), The Manager, The Whizzzard (in white laminate only), and The Office Traveler (for hotel rooms).

Standard equipment for The CEO, for example, includes prewired–cable-ready access for electric, phone, fax, modem, and TV/VCR; desktop lighting; a monitor lift and conceal; a wall-mounted speakerphone; cooling and exhaust controls; a desk accessory tool bar; a bulletin and white board; and an ergonomic task chair that folds and closes up inside the unit. Each unit is mobile by way of a proprietary built-in lift-and-roll mechanism. Finishes for most models include whitewashed oak and mahogany. The CEO costs about $7,000, and other models are less.

The Office was designed by Floridians Robert and Cynthia Gurin, who were "unable to find any decent home office furniture on the market." The team's design objective was to create a home office that is practical, attractive, nonintrusive, computer-oriented, ergonomically responsible, user-friendly, rugged, and mobile. When the Gurins accidentally dropped a unit down a flight of stairs, it suffered only a small repairable crack in the exterior wood veneer, and they knew they had the perfect product for the serious telecommuter.

New to the U.S. market is LinkWorks' ConSole home office, designed by Canadian industrial designer Chris Wright. For an armoire-style home office, it has more work surface than any other piece of folding furniture on the market (see Figures 5-21 and 5-22).

ConSole is recognized by corporations endorsing telecommuting; The Bank of Montreal and Sony Music Canada selected ConSole for their recently launched Telework Programs.

What makes ConSole unique is the fold-up work surface. Inside there's also a pull-out keyboard–work surface and mobile peds with handles for movement so that they can be stored inside or outside the unit. There's also lots of book storage located on the doors, and there's a top cabinet for extra storage. ConSole's dimensions come 48 inches wide closed, and open to 96 inches. The main cabinet is 26 inches deep, and the top storage hutch is 18 inches deep. Total height is 70 1/4 inches high.

As you might expect, ConSole is not for the low-budget home office, but it's not that expensive compared to other armoires with less interior room. ConSole comes in a laminate maple finish for a suggested retail price of $1,600, an MDF model for $2,100, and a solid and veneer cherry wood version for $3,100. The value of this product is worth the price.

"We've designed the unit using a 1-inch-thick work surface where RTA furniture uses 1/4- to 1/2-inch-thick tops," says Gary Hierlihy, LinkWorks' president. "The doors are 6 inches in depth to handle filing, disk storage, books, and the pull-down work surface."

ConSole is also available through some of Canada's largest commercial furniture retailers such as Eaton's, and in the U.S., Linkworks is talking to the likes of Macy's and other retailers (see resources appendix).

Figure 5-20. This armoire-style office, called The Office, has won a number of awards for its forward-thinking design that addresses the serious home office worker's needs. The details of The Office are shown here. (*The Office*)

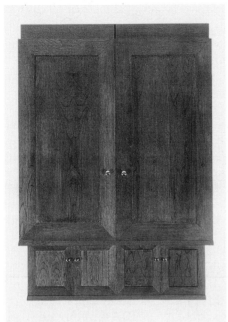

Figure 5-21. The ConSole closed. (*ConSole*)

Figure 5-22. The ConSole, open, revealing an enormous amount of pull-down work surface for an armoire-style home office product. This Canadian product is new to the United States. (*ConSole*)

Some Unusual Home Office Solutions from Sligh

Sligh is recognized for its creative approaches to solving the work-at-home dilemma when it comes to furniture. Just know that Sligh is also not for the budget-conscious home office worker (it's pine home office armoire with a self-storing folding chair was on sale for $1,699 at Macy's in 1997, for example), but again, there's lots of value for the money.

Jack Kelley, an independent furniture designer who has worked with Sligh Furniture Company for over a decade (and has worked with Herman Miller to develop contract furniture, as well), feels that for over a century, manufacturers have been "toying" with ways to help people work at home.

Sligh launched its own research and development program on the home office in 1986 because it believed that merely drilling a hole into desks to accommodate technology and wire management was not enough.

Its first home office offerings came out in 1989. It wasn't until 1995, though, that it introduced its File-A-Way Desk Bed (see Figures 5-23 and 5-24), which really caught the consumer's attention. What Sligh did for consumers was to think out of the box.

Figure 5-23. What looks like a traditional desk has a few surprises inside. (*Sligh*)

Figure 5-24. Inside the Sligh File-A-Way desk is a bed. Although it may seem like a strange idea, it's a well-thought-out solution for people who have to combine a home office and a guest room into one space. (*Sligh*)

The company kept hearing about home office workers who had to move their home offices into the guest room but couldn't fit a bed and desk in the same space. So Sligh introduced this hard-working desk that hides a folding sleeper sofa bed inside.

"The home office must respond to complex needs," says Kelley. "We're not just dealing with desks anymore, but complete work environments designed around ever-changing technology and room constraints (see Figure 5-25)."

Sligh's newest product is a modular home office called C-2 (see Figures 5-26 and 5-27). C-2 is made to solve the fundamental problem of home offices: Home offices come in all shapes and sizes, but most home office furniture doesn't. The group comes with 19 components that can be mixed and matched to create configurations for any room regardless of shape or size.

Figure 5-25. Sligh should be applauded for it's one of the more innovative solution seekers for work-at-home dilemmas. The company sells a coffee table with a built-in, lift-up desk for people who have to combine their living room and office space. (*Sligh*)

Figure 5-26. Sligh's newest research showed that home office workers want modular furniture. Its C-2 Modular Walls units may not be inexpensive, but they are flexible. Here the computer armoire is closed while the work surface remains untouched. (*Sligh*)

Figure 5-27. Here's the C-2 Modular Wall unit open, but notice the chair is folded and tucked inside the unit so that it doesn't have to take up any more room than it has to. (*Sligh*)

Is Techline a Good Home Office Product?

Techline developed its line of cabinetry and furniture in 1977. In 1979, Techline realized the potential in office furniture and introduced Techline Studio to focus on that market. Today there are Techline Studios in 59 cities across the United States and Mexico who are major distributors of Techline furniture and cabinetry. In addition to the Studios, over 200 retailers (including chains such as Storehouse and Room and Board) sell Techline's office lines.

A Techline Studio can give you space-planning services for your home office. The product line is made from laminate that now comes in wood looks as well, but traditionally the company has focused on neutral laminate colors such as white, antique white, black, and platinum gray.

The beauty of Techline is that there are over 300 components made for the home office that make up furniture and cabinetry systems. That means you can continuously add on to your Techline home office suite, like Linda Shea, president of The Shea Company in Dallas, Texas, did over the past decade in her home office:

> One way to have others, and myself, take this business seriously was to have my office properly outfitted. It's taken me two years to get to the point where I'm comfortable with the way my office looks because I came from a company that furnished its offices, including mine, with custom-made furniture.
>
> A lot of the furniture I had in my old home office I simply gave away. The only thing I didn't give away was a very classic, clean, piece of laminate furniture from Techline that I built upon—I had the desk, now I have the return; I added on another three-drawer file and a ped. My latest and greatest addition is the hutch. Before I added my hutch, things were falling behind my line of view, and I was simply losing stuff.
>
> I bought my Techline stuff from a furniture store in Dallas called Euroworks. I didn't need them to come here, but they would have done so if I needed help in measuring and planning my office. I already knew what kind of space I had, so they sat down with me and told me some of my options.
>
> I found out that the colors at Techline were changing, however. When I first bought my Techline furniture, I bought a neutral gray like my equipment so that everything would go together. Now, Techline has white and black laminate, and that's it besides its new wood looks (see Figure 5-29). Maybe they got rid of the gray because it reminded people of the 1980s. But I like this color because I think it's neutral. I wanted something I could have for a good long time and something I could live with, and that's the risk you run of buying something trendy and colorful because you might end up despising it six months after buying it.
>
> The beauty of Techline furniture is that you can buy it now and convert it to something else in the future.

Figure 5-28. Here's a real-life home office built from Techline furniture. Web site designer Linda Shea started purchasing Techline years ago, and she slowly built up to a complete office, including her favorite piece, the hutch. (*Linda Shea*)

Figure 5-29. Techline has expanded its laminate finishes to include wood veneers like the cherry wood shown here. The company also offers updated contemporary design options, such as the rounded desk shown here in the Atelier unit. (*Techline*)

Why You Should Consider Commercial Office Furniture for the Home Office

Interior designer Michael Love has a lot to say about home office furniture. She understands the needs first because she's a former work-at-home entrepreneur (she has a commercial office outside of her apartment today) and second, because she's an interior designer who has designed both commercial and residential spaces:

> **Contract furniture manufacturers should *not* get into home office furniture. Most people furnish their home office to blend in with the rest of their house. The average entrepreneur is *not* going to invest his or her capital into expensive commercial-grade furniture. They want technology, they want marketing materials, stationery—what they want is the simplest possible furniture at the lowest price. And rightly so. Because if they are successful, then they can throw it out, not worry about the investment, and then invest in the future in a big, beautiful desk.**
>
> **What I do see missing is well designed, moderate-priced furniture that goes beyond the typical box made out of laminate or melamine like furniture is sold at the Door Store and other similar retailers. Go look at the furniture at Ikea— it's *good looking*. It's hard to put together, but you can hire home assembly for $100 or so, to put it together. I would tell anybody to do this. What are people going to do—go out and pay $8,000 to $10,000 to furnish a home office? *No*. If they do, that person will never be successful in business because he would be putting his money in the wrong place!**
>
> **That's why I think it's wrong that contract furniture manufacturers are so gung ho to do home office furniture. I know for a fact that a furniture salesperson who is working at Crate & Barrel on commission or gets a bonus can't afford to spend the time with consumers to educate them about RTA, only to have them leave, have them come back, come back again, etc. They don't have patience.**
>
> **I tell the commercial furniture manufacturers if they make it furniture too complex, the consumer won't understand it; if it comes in too many sizes, they won't know how to put it together, and who's going to sell it?**

Nevertheless, sometimes commercial-grade furniture is the best value for your money. It will last for years, not months like some lower-quality products on the market. And the commercial furniture industry has decades of research to back up the design of their furniture whereas the residential market is just realizing the needs of home office workers. Commercial furniture manufacturers know how to hide wires, they know how to build a desk so it's the right height for computer work, they know how strong a desk has to be to hold all the heavy computer work, and they understand how much work surface you need in order to be productive.

The trick is how to find and purchase it.

Some commercial furniture dealer showrooms are slowly agreeing to cater to the individual who walks in the door looking for home office furniture. But beware, dealerships are not retail stores, and they aren't set up to help you as would a traditional furniture store. These dealerships cater to mid-size to larger corporations who need furniture by the truckfull. Nor are they set up for consumer pricing. There are no price tags on the furniture, so don't faint when you hear the prices they are quoting to sell furniture to you. However, it doesn't hurt to try if you find a dealer near you. Just call and ask.

For information on finding a showroom that specializes in ergonomic furniture, see Chapter 3, "Avoiding Home Office Hazards," especially the section called "Finding Top-Quality Ergonomic Furniture."

How to Find Commercial Office Furniture through Liquidators

Office furniture liquidators are a long-kept secret of office managers. Liquidators buy furniture from corporations that are either downsizing, going out of business, or purchasing new office furniture. Because commercial furniture holds up so well, most of the pieces you will find at a liquidator are in great shape for one quarter of the original price.

One liquidator, Office Furniture Heaven in New York City, is a prime outlet for used, high-quality office furniture. The one-floor shop is crammed with office furniture from lounge, desk, and guest chairs to executive desks, panel systems, and the highest-quality file cabinets you can find for the price. Usually liquidators deliver furniture to your home for a fee.

Figure 5-30. Office Furniture Heaven, a secondhand office furniture store in New York City, has top-quality products for one-quarter to one-half the original cost. You can find a liquidator or secondhand office furniture store in any part of the country. (*MZS*)

Figure 5-31. Liquidators, such as Office Furniture Heaven, sell furniture in one of three ways: unaltered "as is," touched up refurbished, or completely refinished remanufactured. These ergonomic Steelcase Sensor chairs sell for $200 and $300. As-is chairs can sell for $100 depending on the manufacturer. (*MZS*)

Figure 5-32. Office liquidators, like Office Furniture Heaven, are great sources for superior-quality file cabinets. Shown here: A five-drawer Office Specialty file cabinet with some dings for $300 and a Steelcase five-drawer for $350 in good shape. Half of Office Furniture Heaven's store is filled with file cabinets. (*MZS*)

Telecommuter Holly Gruske chose to use a liquidator to furnish her home office. She realized that her old home office was inadequate, impractical, and uncomfortable for the amount of work she wanted to do at home (see Figure 5-33). Gruske knows commercial furniture well because she once worked in the facility planning industry, and she knew she wanted to buy a simple, good-looking, high-quality workstation to outfit what she calls a "serious work space":

> I called a liquidator, explained to her what I was looking for, and she sent me these photos of possible units I could buy (see Figure 5-34). The Steelcase workstation I bought costs brand new $1,500, and I bought it for about $650 (see Figure 5-35).
>
> This workstation is one year old. A few of these workstations were pulled out of a law firm to make way for new furniture. They are beautiful. I decided to put it in this den because workstations like this wouldn't work well on an upstairs floor of a house since they are so heavy. The other issue is that I didn't want to damage the walls by bringing a huge piece of furniture upstairs.
>
> The liquidators will deliver the workstation for about $150, but I think that's a lot of money.
>
> You could go to Staples to buy furniture, but for practically the same money, I don't see any reason that you can't get the quality instead. To me, Staples doesn't offer *real* office furniture. It's not sized well, and there isn't enough work space with that kind of furniture as there is with commercial-grade desks. This is a *real* workstation that will last for 20 years. For $650, it's quite a value.
>
> I also bought a used lateral Steelcase file cabinet from the liquidator for $150. Chairs run $125 to $150, and that's a great price for good-quality ergonomic seating. To pick out my chair, I will go to the warehouse in Brooklyn and sit in each and every one till I find the best chair for my bad back.
>
> It's easier to buy a chair from Staples, but a workstation, and even files, are a different story when it comes to quality.

Figure 5-33. When telecommuter Holly Gruske moved into her new husband's house and saw his home office, she knew she'd have to buy the correct furniture and move it into the den for a more professional home office. (*MZS*)

Figure 5-34. Gruske contacted two liquidators who promptly sent her pictures of commercial furniture they had available for resale. (*MZS*)

Figure 5-35. Gruske's new (actually it was used in a law firm) Steelcase panel system arrived, along with the chair she had picked out, directly from the liquidator's warehouse. Though she paid a slightly higher price for this furniture than she would have paid for RTA, this ensemble will last her over 20 years because it's heavy-duty commercial grade. (*MZS*)

Finding Home Office Efficiency in a Secondhand Store

Lesley Goddin, owner of Lesley Goddin Writing, Editing & Publicity Services, came from the lap of corporate luxury. After a long-time career at BASF, the major fiber company with offices in New York City, Lesley and her husband moved to Albuquerque, New Mexico, to begin a new life away from the rat race of a crowded and dirty urban environment.

Lesley knew for years that she wanted to become a freelancer. It was just a matter of when and where. When the couple moved into their three-bedroom condominium, Goddin already knew which bedroom would become her home office. Then, it was just a matter of furnishing it on a shoestring.

Although Goddin worked in a well-appointed private office at BASF, she never believed that new furniture was the key to productivity:

One window of my home office looks west over the city and the mesa, and out the other window I look up at the foothills. So no matter where I look up, I have this great view of the world.

This is the room we chose to be my office since this is where I'm spending most of my life. We purposely bought a three-bedroom condo so that one of

the rooms could be my home office. I did have a home office in the second bedroom in the apartment we lived in before moving here, but I always felt I was crammed into the corner. Now I have a dedicated home office full of furniture I bought from an office furniture liquidator in Albuquerque (see Figure 5-36).

I shopped around for a desk, and I found a huge wooden one. I picked this desk because it has a lot of space, and I have a lot of junk, so I need space when I work. I definitely was looking for something that had a filing cabinet drawer in it, too. This desk is a little older, it's a little beat up, but I'm the only one looking at it. I don't have clients come up so it's not much of a problem.

The thing I really love about the desk is the pull-out shelves. They give me a little more room. Just when I think I've run out of room, I remember I have these two surfaces to pull out (see Figure 5-37). It's 60 inches wide by 29.5 inches deep. The two pull-out shelves are 13.25 by 16 inches deep.

I bought my desk chair from Office Depot in January, 1996. It was about $100 and I don't know the brand name. It has armrests, which I read are important to have. Dave, my husband, bought his no-brand chair at the liquidator's for about $80. The cats love them both.

I work on a laptop and don't have an articulating keyboard tray. My wrists don't hurt, however. I thoroughly researched my laptop and bought one that has a built-in ergonomic wrist rest, which is completely comfortable. My notebook is the Winbook XP, purchased in 1993 or 1994.

The desk cost $80, and the store delivered it for a little more. At the same time we bought my desk, my husband's desk, and his chair, and the whole bill came to under $200. My desk was probably worth about $500 when it was new. I'd love to refinish it, but truth be told I don't have the time or inclination. It's a nice idea, but I'm already behind in painting projects in my home. Plus, I'd have to take everything out of the desk, and I don't want to do that, either. So I have this great desk, and then we went to an unpainted-furniture place and bought a bookshelf. I completed my needs with two good-quality five-drawer vertical HON file cabinets for $99 each.

Eventually, I'd like to buy myself a new desk that doesn't have nicks or scratches. It would be great to have floor-to-ceiling shelves and new filing cabinets. The office is totally functional and doesn't look shabby at all. Other than that, I don't have many more needs.

Secondhand stores and liquidators are great sources for home office furniture. But beware because sometimes you'll buy used furniture for the same price as it came new. For example, the same Fournier corner computer workstation that retails for $89.99 in a Caldor store sale flyer was found listed in a *Bargain News* (like a *Penny Saver*) listed for $85!

As with any product or piece of furniture, do your homework first before you make a purchase.

Figure 5-36. Except for the views and the cats, this home office could be mistaken for a "regular" corporate office. Goddin has filled her office with good-quality, durable, secondhand furniture. Although she wouldn't mind a new desk without any dings or scratches, she is content and says her office is totally functional and doesn't look shabby at all. (*Lesley Goddin*)

Figure 5-37. Goddin loves her desk because it has additional work surfaces that she can pull out when needed, which keeps her organized. She doesn't think she would have been able to find a desk this big with all the extra work surface for the affordable price of $80 unless she shopped secondhand. (*Lesley Goddin*)

Warning: Chair Castors Can Ruin Your Floor

When I first put together my home office in 1994, I went to Home Depot to pick out a carpet from their remnant selection. I figured Home Depot would be the best place to pick up some inexpensive commercial-grade carpeting. I bought a 6 by 9 carpet for $39. We put it down without a pad, and eventually, all of the edges began to unravel after two years of use, and each time I'd vacuum my carpet, it would suck up the already unraveled carpet fibers, creating more fraying. It was clearly time to get a new carpet after only three years of use.

We took up the carpet to find a disaster. Since we didn't put down a cushion, three years of rolling around on the carpet with a task chair on castors destroyed the carpet backing, crushing it down into sand. The sand then ate away the wood finish of my floor and made a horrible mess to clean up (see Figure 5-38). We vowed to get a better-grade carpet and put a pad down no matter what it cost.

The lesson here is twofold: Remember to buy a low-pile carpet for your home office so that you can easily move your desk chair.

Second, be aware of what kind of carpet pad you're buying. When you buy a carpet for your home office, oftentimes you receive a free pad with installation or with the purchase of a bound remnant. The pad will most likely be a thick marbled foam pad. This type of pad is great for living rooms and bedrooms where you want deep plush carpeting, but that kind of backing is completely the wrong type for a home office. It's too thick for office chairs, and your castors will sink into the carpet. Putting a plastic chairmat on the floor will help a little bit, but it will begin to sink down, too. Your bottom file drawer may not even open easily with a thick pad.

Your best bet is low-pile carpeting over a thin pad. You need to buy some type of pad so the carpet backing won't disintegrate and sand your floors after months of rolling around in your office chair, so I suggest you purchase the Mighty Gripper Non-Slip Rug

Figure 5-38. This mess is the result of laying down a low-quality commercial-grade carpet over bare wood floors, then rolling around on an office chair with castors for three years. The fibers disintegrated into a sandy substance, which wore away the finish of the wood floor. (*Steve Syarto*)

Figure 5-39. When buying carpeting for your home office, you have to consider the fact that you will most likely be rolling around in a chair with castors. Don't get the traditional foam padding (left) because your chair will sink down into the pad. Buy a thin pad (right), which will hold your carpet in place and allows your chair to roll. (*Steve Syarto*)

Cushion (a 3' x 5' costs $7.50 and a 4' x 6' costs $16.00). I purchased mine at The Home Depot after installing my carpet over this thick pad and realizing I couldn't shut my door or move my chair. It's an ultrathin pad that costs about $20 for a 6 by 9 size, which lets me close my door and move my chair, but I'll still buy a small chairmat to protect the rug.

Storage: How to Pull It out of Thin Air

Wish all you want, but there is not—and never will be—such a thing as the paperless office (see Figure 5-40).

No doubt, electronic media usage is on the rise, but that doesn't mean paper usage is in decline. A survey conducted by Sorkin-Enenstein Research Service for the Printing Industries of America revealed that although two-thirds of consumers they interviewed anticipate an upswing in their use of electronic media, they also anticipate an increase in using print media as well. Other findings of the survey say that despite the fact that younger consumers (under 35) are prominent computer users, this age group also anticipates increased paper usage, which runs counter to the traditional view that young adults prefer electronic media over print media.

So, it doesn't matter how many computers you have, how old you are, or how big or small your home office is; the number 1 design dilemma of a home office is still storage. Most of us start off our home office with enough empty file drawers, shelves, and if we are lucky, a closet, until weeks later when each storage area is filled to the brim with projects, paper, and research. We either have too much incoming paper, or we have a business that demands inventory for a variety of objects, products, supplies, and boxes.

> ◆ **I represent a book publisher who sends me cartons of books that are piling up with nowhere to store them. (Shannon Wilkinson, publicist, New York City)**

> ◆ **Storage is always an issue. The one thing I spent money on were lateral files. I know I need to find another solution because I have much too much stuff. I think the best thing to do is to figure out a way to find a place for every-**

Figure 5-40. The paperless office is a fantasy. It's estimated by paper suppliers that by 1998, the amount of fax paper used will rise to nearly 300,000 tons, up from 175,000 tons in 1996! (*MZS*)

thing so that you don't have to take so much time to figure out where things go. I waste a lot of time just trying to clean up because I can't work when my space is a mess. Another problem is that I have a desk without drawers. (Maxi Cohen, independent film producer, Los Angeles) (see Figures 5-41 and 5-42)

I don't know where to put the boxes the computer came in. They don't fold, and there's no room under my bed. there's no room anywhere, and I don't know where to stash them. I was told to keep them as packing boxes for at least a year in case I had to send the computer back to the manufacturer. I have even more boxes in the front hall closet. Not only that, where do I keep FedEx boxes? They send a pack of 20 at a time when I order them. (Sandy Horowitz,* publicist, New York City) see Figures (5-43 and 5-44).

* Names have been changed at request.

We all need help finding more storage. Some ideas are so obvious we tend to overlook them entirely. Here are some storage tricks taken from real-life home offices that you'll learn in this next section:

- Unearthing storage space in a home office that you didn't know you had
- Where to find inexpensive file cabinets
- Comparing costs of new and used file cabinets
- How to buy inexpensive shelves that are ready to assemble or already made
- How to make inexpensive shelving
- How to spot creative and affordable storage solutions

Figure 5-41. Film editor Maxi Cohen has a drawless desk, so she puts these rolling carts to great use. They are inexpensive, too. Carts similar to this run from $24 (plastic at Staples) to $99 for a heavy-duty Taboret caddy found at Office Max or in art supply stores. (*Maxi Cohen*)

Figure 5-42. Maxi also stores each finished project in these heavy-duty jumbo filing boxes that she neatly stacks by a wall. They run about $8.99 each at Staples. (*Maxie Cohen*)

Figures 5-43 and 5-44. Storage of computer boxes that should be saved for a few months to ship back equipment to manufacturers is a problem if you don't have a garage or basement. There's nowhere else to store these boxes in this New York City apartment except in the hall closet and in the bedroom! (*MZS*)

Finding Storage Space You Never Knew You Had

Some of us complain that we don't have enough storage space when all that's needed is some organization and clean-up! Remember when you worked in the corporate office how much unnecessary paraphernalia you would stash into any available drawer, under-desk, or closet area? When I worked at the magazine, every year we would have a manda-tory corporate-wide designated "clean-up day," which inevitably fell on the busiest days. So I never had a chance to clean under or around my workstation, clean out my file draw-ers, or go through the dusty piles of paper, magazines, and who-knows-what languishing on the heater. But when I did manage to do a cleaning, I filled up dumpsters of garbage.

But when you work in a home office, you:

- ◆ Can't rely on a cleaning crew to come in after hours to vacuum and empty the waste-baskets or dumpsters

- ◆ Don't have the time or support help to give your office a thorough cleaning or straightening-up

- ◆ Tend to retain the same bad packrat habits you had when you had unlimited space when you worked at the corporate office

If you subscribe to the last two points, then inevitably your work space will spread out and unnecessarily so. Just clean up, and you will find more viable storage and work space.

Quick Tip: Help for the Disorganized

If you are in dire need of a professional organizer to come in and help you find storage space, contact the National Association of Professional Organizers at 512-206-0151 or visit their Web site at www.ccsi.com/ asmi/GROUPS/NAPO/napo.htm.

Take a lesson from Bernadette Grey, formerly of *Home Office Computing* magazine, who says she did something "embarrassingly luxurious" by hiring a professional organizer for a day: "I paid a woman $300 for less than five hours of filing," she says in the September 1997 issue. It might be well worth the money to buy a box of garbage bags for $2 and dig in yourself.

Finding Inexpensive File Cabinets

In NYC I bought used file cabinets on Canal Street and in Los Angeles I bought some used from Materials for the Arts which donates materials to artists. (Maxi Cohen, film producer)

It doesn't matter where you buy your file cabinets as long as they do the job. Most designers and architects, and anyone in the contract furniture market, will tell you not to buy your file cabinets (or any other type of furniture, for that matter) at an office superstore because they are of poor quality. Having written about high-end contract-grade file cabinets, I will admit it would be a great luxury if everyone in a home office could afford a brand new Steelcase file cabinet for a few hundred dollars each. If we're lucky, we'll find a used version. But it's not a crime to buy a file cabinet (or almost—*almost*—any other type of furniture) from an office superstore if it's what you can afford and it holds your files.

When I realized I needed file cabinets for my home office, I knew I could get a great deal on some commercial-quality products from one of the major furniture manufacturers. But I also realized I couldn't wait two months for them to be delivered. Plus, it's not so easy for an individual to just call up a dealer to order one file cabinet, then have it delivered. I also didn't like any of the file cabinets I saw at OfficeMax or Staples because they were overpriced for my budget.

So I decided to hunt in our local *Bargain News* paper for used file cabinets. There were lots of ads (it seems many offices were dismantling at the time), but everything was either sold as soon as we called or still overpriced for my budget.

What I wanted was relatively simple: a two-drawer lateral file in white for $50. What I ended up with was a HON two-drawer lateral file in black with minimal dings and scratches for $22 from the Westport, Connecticut, Goodwill store. We pulled up to Goodwill *just* as the file cabinet was being carried into the door to be tagged, so it was a lucky break. It took two cans of white spray paint, but I ended up with a budget file cabinet set up in my office one week after purchase (see Figure 5-45).

Figure 5-45. This secondhand file cabinet cost $22 at the Salvation Army. The staff didn't even have time to attach a price tag before it was snapped up. Lateral file cabinets are in big demand in the secondhand market. (*Steve Syarto*)

Comparing Costs of New Versus Used File Cabinets

Let me tell you the differences between a contract-quality file cabinet and less-expensive file cabinets you find in superstores or mass merchandisers. Do note that you can buy what I call a "semi-commercial-grade-quality file" at a superstore. Usually it will be manufactured by HON or M&M, which aren't bad purchases for home offices.

But the premier file cabinets (Steelcase, Office Specialty, Haworth, and Allsteel, for example) will never, ever fall apart because they are made for corporate office environments where they may be moved frequently and used by a multitude of people, which means drawers will open and close constantly and they will inevitably be overstuffed.

If you are determined to pay small potatoes for your files ($30 for a two-drawer vertical file is really very cheap), you should be warned of the following differences of cheap versus more expensive files. Remember, in this case, you get what you pay for:

◆ Inexpensive files are lightweight, are flimsy because the steel is thin, and bend easily; contract files are heavy-duty, heavyweight, and made of thicker steel.

◆ Inexpensive files are difficult to open because the drawer handles can be shallow and inexpensively made; contract file cabinets have deeper drawer pulls.

◆ Inexpensive file cabinets may not be weighted correctly, meaning that they can tip over easily; contract files are correctly counterbalanced so they won't tip over.

♦ Cheaper files don't have a safety interlock system, that means that you can open two or more drawers at the same time, which is quite dangerous; contract files have a safety interlock system that allows you to open only one drawer at a time so that there's no chance that the cabinet will fall over on you (or for that matter, your child).

♦ Cheaper files might not have the heavy-duty ball-bearing suspension drawer systems that contract files have and that allow for an easy glide even if the drawers are packed and heavy.

♦ Cheaper files rarely have hanging rails and they must be purchased separately!

Here's some eye-opening price comparisons on file cabinets made in 1998:

Vertical Files, Four and Five Drawers

♦ The *Reliable Home Office Catalogue* (brands undisclosed): $189 for an oak veneer traditional-style, four-drawer, 51-inch-high, 17-inch-deep, vertical file cabinet

♦ *Bargain News* (Penny Saver type paper for used goods): $125 for five-drawer vertical, no manufacturer listed, which means you must have the seller identify the brand to make a judgment on quality and value for the quoted price

♦ Office Max: $99 for a conventional steel HON four-drawer 52-inch-high, 25-inch-deep, vertical file cabinet

Vertical Files, Two Drawers

♦ *Reliable Home Office:* $159.95 for a Queen Anne-style wood finish two-drawer, 32-inch-high, 17-inch-deep, vertical file cabinet

♦ Office Max: $89.99 for a two-drawer steel file cabinet 26-inches deep with high-sided drawers

♦ Caldor: On sale, $24.88 for a two-drawer steel file cabinet with lock, 18 inches deep

♦ K-Mart: On sale, $17.99 for a two-drawer steel file cabinet with lock, hanging file frame separate for $3.99 on sale

Lateral Files, Four and Five Drawers

♦ Office Furniture Heaven, used: Premium Steelcase five-drawer lateral, 30 inches deep, in gray for $350, good shape

♦ Office Max: $319.99 for a conventional steel HON four-drawer lateral file

♦ Office Furniture Heaven, used: Premium Office Specialty five-drawer lateral, 36 inches deep, in beige $300 with some dings

♦ *Bargain News* (Penny Saver type paper for used items): $150 for premium Steelcase five-drawer lateral

Lateral File Two Drawers

◆ *Reliable Home Office:* $229.95 for a two-drawer lateral file in Norwegian alder finish for a wood look

◆ Office Furniture Heaven, used: Premium Steelcase two-drawer lateral in gray for $200, great condition

◆ Office Max: $199.99 for a conventional steel HON two-drawer lateral file with ball-bearing slide suspension, lock, and "drawer extension restraint"

◆ *Reliable Home Office:* $199.95 for a conventional melamine two-drawer lateral file

◆ Salvation Army: $22.00 for a conventional steel HON two-drawer lateral file with ball-bearing slide suspension, internal safety interlocking system, and lock (see Figure 5-45)

Buying Inexpensive Ready-to-Assemble or Prebuilt Shelving Units

Purchasing inexpensive RTA or prebuilt shelving is relatively easy to do. However, one of the problems with ready-to-assemble products such as shelving is that they aren't built to take heavy loads (see Figure 5-46). The shelves of a typical melamine or particle-board shelving unit can sag in the middle over time because there is usually little support under each shelf to adequately hold the weight of books or other heavy material.

RTA shelves are typically supported by little plastic tabs on each end, which causes a lot of the weight in the middle of a shelf to go unsupported. One way to overcome this kind of potential sag is to mount a 1-inch by 2-inch strip of wood along the front edge of each shelf as a support by either gluing it or screwing it in place (use hard wood such as maple or oak).

Figure 5-46. Laminate RTA shelving can buckle under the weight of books. Luckily this shelving unit isn't stressed by weight...yet. As human beings, we tend to overstuff our shelves. (*MZS*)

Making Inexpensive Shelves

If you plan to build shelves in your home office, you have many choices for materials including wood, melamine, wire, and medium-density fiberboard (MDF). I didn't want wire shelving for my home office, and I was sure I wanted the look of white melamine shelving. I didn't want wood shelving because it was too expensive for my budget and too much work to first prime the surface, then paint it white.

I wanted three 10-foot-long melamine shelves on one of my walls over my desk. But when I got to The Home Depot to choose my shelving materials, I found that laminate pieces didn't come in 10-foot-long lengths. So, I looked at 8-foot lengths of wood for $9.26 a board and 12-foot lengths of wood, which ran $12.95 each board (plus primer and paint). Eight-foot melamine boards (most of which were already chipped) ran $9.45 each board.

However, there was a pile of 8-foot-long MDF boards with beautifully finished bull-nose edges for a palatable $4.85 each! MDF needs primer, then paint, so you have to treat it a little bit like wood, but it's still much cheaper, and when installed, it looks like wood.

Remember, melamine doesn't need any painting. But I loved the bull-nosed edge of MDF and opted for three boards. Note that it only took less than a week to prime and paint the MDF boards (it doesn't soak up paint as wood does). For the price and ease of cutting, MDF is a great choice for shelving.

One thing you need to know before buying any shelving materials is the load rule. Every 3/4-inch-thick, 10-inch-wide piece of particleboard shelf will support a load of 30 pounds per linear foot as long as there are supports for the shelf every 24 inches. In other words, these shelves can safely handle one row of medium-weight hardcover books across the span of the shelf. Just don't overstuff shelves with *two* rows of hardcover text-books and art books.

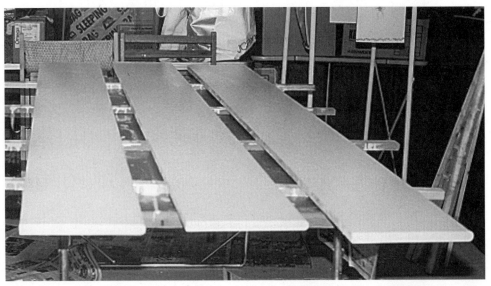

Figure 5-47. I bought three 8-foot-long, bull-nose-edged MDF boards at The Home Depot for under $5.00 each, and I painted them glossy white. The same-length melamine board costs $9.45 each. It took a gallon of white paint and almost a week to complete the paint job. (*MZS*)

Figure 5-48. Two critical tools for hanging shelves the correct way: A level and a $2 magnetized stud finder. If you hang shelves and want them to bear weight, always screw the strips of metal that hold the shelves into studs. (*Steve Syarto*)

No-Budget Creative Storage Solutions

If you have absolutely no money, go into the housewares section of your local discount store for next-to-nothing storage ideas:

- ◆ Free: Drawers from old bureaus to stack stuff under a desk or table

- ◆ (Great product!!) $9.99 at OfficeMax: For one collapsible crate in great colors—stackable, stores flat, and opens to full-size crate

- ◆ $10 at Staples: Pack of 10 knock-down Stor-Al plain cardboard boxes with covers found in office superstores—not great-looking, but does the job

- ◆ $8.99 at K-Mart: White melamine stackable shoe organizer two-shelf unit from closet organizer product collections, which can be used for desktop storage, too

- ◆ $3.85 from Harriet Carter's catalog: Corner shelf unit with three or more shelves for stacking chinaware, pans, lids, and canned goods in rust-proof white vinyl-coated steel, measures 10- by 10- by 8-inches, purchased in a discount store for stacking stationery and magazines

- ◆ $19.98 from Harriet Carter's catalog: An overdoor rack to put on the back of the door to your home office. (Overdoor racks screw onto the door and are typically made to hold videos, spices, or household products, but you can use them to hold home office supplies and light books.)

- ◆ $1.19 at Walgreen's Drug Store: 12-quart dishpans (I hide mine in the closet)

- ◆ 99 cents at Walgreen's Drug Store: Standard or underbed storage boxes, which are sold in assorted designs

Figures 5-49 and 5-50. There are so many inexpensive storage tools that keep a home office organized. These little baskets can be found for a couple of dollars each in the laundry and bath area of any mass merchandiser. Heavy-duty, yet inexpensive flip-top file crates with handles are another idea if you don't want to place files in flimsy boxes. (*MZS*)

Kitchen Cabinets

"Ikea kitchen cabinets are inexpensive, and you can get them from Home Depot. It takes away from having to have custom-made things, and I got a lot of storage out of those kitchen cabinets. Those upper cabinets cost me $800, and I had a lot of them that went around the whole room. And I moved them here to my office, and they are perfectly fine. Ikea has a closet group section that you can get a closet cabinet from. File cabinets came from Workbench," says interior designer Michael Love.

When she worked at home, Love outfitted her home office with simple, great-looking kitchen cabinets. They looked beautiful! However, before I started to do research on the subject of home office design, I was under the impression that installing kitchen cabinets in a home office would be an inexpensive way to create a good-looking home office. But when you look at the costs of remodeling a kitchen, cabinets tend to take the largest chunk of money regardless of the level of quality you choose! It was a surprise to me, but in reality, choosing to furnish your home office with kitchen, or even bathroom cabinets, is nothing less than creating a custom home office.

Construction of Kitchen Cabinets

So what's the best cabinet construction you can get for your money? If you choose to outfit your home office with kitchen cabinets, there are some pointers you should know about the levels of quality of cabinetry construction.

Figure 5-51. Love used kitchen cabinets from Ikea in her former home office. She swears by kitchen cabinets. She tells all home-based workers that kitchen cabinets are the best use of wall space for storage in a home office and a fraction of the cost of custom cabinetry that upscale home offices often have installed. (*MZS*)

Check out *Consumer Reports*, the May 1997 issue, for their tests of kitchen cabinets. The magazine built a contraption to open and close drawers filled with gravel and doors 30,000 times, then used sandbags and metal weights to see how the doors, floors, and shelves held up when hit hard. Here are some tips:

- ◆ Solid wood may be more prone to warp, so choose cabinets of wood veneer.
- ◆ Thermofoil (polyvinyl chloride sheets heated and molded to form a sculpted surface) may stain and scratch easily.
- ◆ Melamine chips easily.
- ◆ Doors with dovetailed joints are more durable than doors with stapled joints.
- ◆ Check to see if drawer bottoms hold up when you press your weight down on them.
- ◆ Look for metal or wood clips to support shelves, and stay away from lightweight plastic clips that bend under any weight.

Low-end $150 or less per cabinet: Expect lots of particleboard, plastic supports, and stapled hinges with thin hardboard drawer bottoms.

Midpriced $150 to $200 per cabinet: Expect some particleboard with thicker drawer bottoms and doweled joints and metal or wood shelf supports.

Higher-priced, over $200 per cabinet: Expect some particleboard and plywood, solid wood drawer sides and front, dowel or dovetail joints, and metal supports for shelves. It's rare to find a solid wood cabinet even at this price range.

Shop Smart: Cheap Paint

If you must paint your office, you don't have to pay top dollar for paint. Visit your local paint store, and ask if they sell cans of paint that have been returned or are mislabeled.

Usually, to get rid of this kind of paint, stores pile cans in a corner with a sign that says "reduced for clearance." I never knew this until I began redesigning my office with a limited budget. Paint that gets returned or rejected is perfectly good paint: it's just that the color didn't mix to the buyer's exact expectations, or the recipe for the color was wrong on the computer chart and the buyer didn't want it. The real color in the can is dabbed on the can cover, so you will always know which color you're buying.

These paints are great deals for small spaces. I spent $2 for a can of premium paint that retails for $24. I found the same "reduced for clearance" area at The Home Depot where I saw rejected (and originally high-priced) cans of Martha Stewart and Ralph Lauren premium paints that run from $29.94 and up reduced to $5.00 to $10.00 each can.

Figure 5-52. An example of an inexpensive, better-styled, ready-to-assemble home office desk, called the Command Center, from Studio RTA. This manufacturer offers home office furniture like this from $99 to $199 retail. (*Studio RTA*)

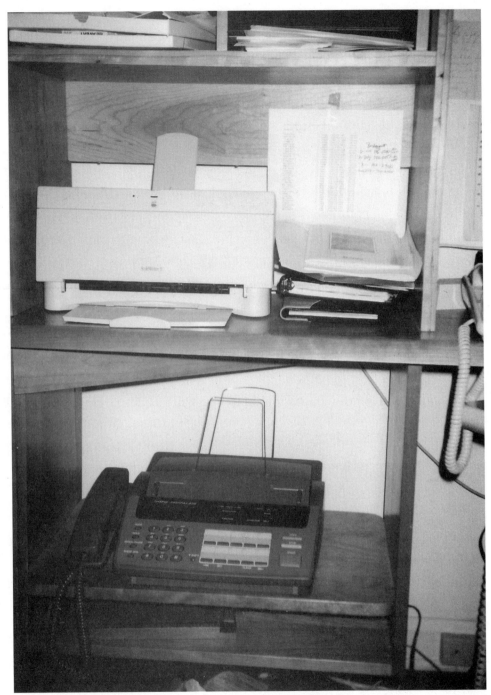

Figure 6-1. What does the typical home office worker have in their workspaces? A fax is a key piece of equipment, along with the computer and printer. By the way, you don't have to get a plain paper fax to have good quality paper faxes: Brother's older IntelliFas models use plain paperlike fax paper. It's hard to tell the difference. *(MZS)*

6

Real-Life Home Office Technology Needs

What kinds of technology do real-life home office workers have in their work spaces? This chapter will give you a glimpse into the kinds of practical technology it takes to run a home office. You'll learn what you can live without, as well. This chapter is not meant to take the place of the invaluable computer magazines on the newsstand, it's just meant to relax your expectations of what it takes to run a business at home.

Chances are you have, or will have, an average home or apartment office with average technology. If you're not a graphic designer, you will most likely have the basic elements: a computer, printer, modem, and fax machine and possibly a scanner, cell phone, and beeper. If you're a graphic designer, you'll have more:

"I use several major programs to do my work, like Adobe. I am a Macintosh user. I have a CPU, a scanner, a 17-inch monitor, an external hard drive, a Jazz drive, a Zip drive, a CD ROM external unit, a Syquest unit, and oh yes, a phone," says graphic designer Steve DeMartino.

You may be lucky enough to live in an area that offers you high-speed access to the Internet, such as a T1 line. Although T1 lines are common in corporate offices, there are a few apartment buildings—called *cyberbuildings*—in New York City and in Salt Lake City and other places in Utah, for example, that are wired for action.

Don't worry if you don't have access to a T1 line. It's not always necessary.

Home-based Web site designer Linda Shea says, "Because of what I do, I have to have a lot of equipment hooked up to the Internet. I have three phone lines. I have one dedicated fax line, one dedicated phone line, one dedicated computer line. I'm online all day. I resisted the temptation to get an ISDN line because I'm designing sites for people with very slow equipment. My computer is a heck of a lot faster than most others to begin with, so when I'm designing a site and it looks great on the screen, I need to know it's easy for someone else to work with, too. I have a 28.8 modem and a regular phone line so I can see how quickly something works. I could have a really nifty quick phone line, but it would be deceptive. I have to design for the lowest common denominator of computers, and I have to satisfy the most amount of people. There are 56K modems out there, but

I'm not designing for them; I'm designing sites for people with 14.4 and 28.8 modems. It's great to have a 56K modem, but the Internet is mostly used by people with the lowest speed modems. It may simply be that you have to upgrade the hard drive and memory. You may have a really fast modem and your computer is slow! You have to upgrade the one thing that will make the whole system go faster."

It's not always easy to know exactly what kinds of technology you will need or should have in your home office until you are working from home for a while.

"I eased into buying technology for my home office, but now I don't hesitate to experiment with all kinds of formats," says Cynthia Froggatt, principal of home-based Froggatt Consulting in New York City. "I waited a good year of working at home before I got my own computer because I worked so often at client sites. I made a concerted decision not to get a desktop computer so I could be mobile even inside of my apartment. For a while I resisted buying a printer because it was a serious piece of equipment to integrate into my home. The essential was the fax machine, and I've upgraded to a plain paper fax machine. I have a laser, color printer—a Cannon Multitask 2500, a good machine. I don't have a copy machine, and I see no need to have one. The copy centers around the neighborhood do a great job."

Although buying technology takes time, virtually all home-based workers say that they would rather spend their money on technology and marketing tools instead of making their work space aesthetically pleasing. But why? Technology allows the home-based worker to appear more professional to the outside world.

No doubt that new technologies continue to help home office workers put on a professional face while easing the financial and psychological burdens of working at home.

The latest personal computing and communications products mean home office workers often have the same resources available as those on the corporate campus. For example:

◆ The Internet and global e-mail capabilities mean that home-based workers have access to the same online resources and communications as their colleagues and competitors who work in traditional settings. (In fact, 1998 reports say Internet traffic doubles every 100 days!)

◆ The latest personal computers and networking have improved at a lower cost. While the average price of PCs purchased by home office households has remained between $1,500 and $2,200, capabilities of those machines have increased significantly over the past two years. Faster microprocessors, bigger hard drives, and removable storage are just some of the advanced capabilities vendors are including in computers targeted for home office use.

◆ Multifunctional products are becoming more popular. The latest generation of "all-in-one products" provides reliable printing, faxing, copying, and scanning at very affordable prices. The quality of output from a home-based business can now be equal to that of a Fortune 1000 firm.

◆ Advanced telephone services such as voice mail and messaging services available from local telephone companies mean a home office can have the same automated attendant capabilities as a major corporation.

Home office workers generally don't have an administrative support staff. Most home office workers don't believe that they need a support staff to thrive and look professional.

What many home office workers do believe is that knowing their way around technology increases their competitiveness by allowing them to more efficiently achieve key business objectives, such as accomplishing what large companies do—presenting a professional image and acquiring new customers.

A recent study by Xerox Desktop Document Systems found that technology-savvy SO/HO (small office, home office) professionals using state-of-the-art technology gain a competitive advantage in the marketplace. A full 86 percent of respondents using state-of-the-art office technology say that their investments have improved their efficiency and productivity levels, as compared to the 68 percent of those who have not invested in state-of-the-art equipment. Of the SO/HO professionals interviewed, 80 percent using state-of-the-art technology said that their investment has helped them to be more competitive, while only 64 percent using less than up-to-date equipment say that their investment has helped them be more competitive.

The computers of the self-employed are much more robustly equipped than the systems of their small office counterparts, according to a recent report by Computer Intelligence (CI), a source of information for the computer and communications industries. CI screened over 50,000 consumers to find 17,500 computer users who answered a detailed questionnaire on the subject. The study reveals significant usage differences between the self-employed and small office markets and demonstrates that a one-size-fits-all marketing approach will not work with both segments.

The study shows that a majority of self-employed computer users operate their businesses out of their homes, and they have much more demanding needs when it comes to computing systems, software, and communications. Nearly two-thirds of self-employed users' systems have CD-ROM drives, and more than 50 percent have external speakers or sound boards. By contrast, only 32 percent of small office systems have CD-ROM drives, and a mere 16 percent have external speakers.

Here's a comparison of the purchase of computer peripherals of the self-employed versus small office users:

Item	Self-Employed, Percent	Small Office (1-19 Employees), Percent
CD-ROM drive	62	32
Sound board	53	17
External speakers	51	16
Tape drive	17	20
Scanner/scanning device	16	7
Removable cartridge drive	11	9
LAN card	10	22

Source: Computer Intelligence, 1997.

The study showed that self-employed users are also running more applications than their small office counterparts. On average, computers of the self-employed have 6.5 applications per system, compared to only 4.5 on small office systems. The self-employed are also much heavier users of personal finance, integrated productivity, and desktop publishing software.

The amount of time spent on their computers further underscores the differences between small office and self-employed users. Small office users appear to be more task oriented, spending more time on their systems while using fewer applications. Thirty-seven percent of small office users spent 30 hours per week or more using their computers, while only 20 percent of self-employed users indicated they spent that much time. In fact, 30 percent of self-employed users reported logging fewer than 10 hours per week on their systems.

Other productivity and communications tools receive high usage by the self-employed. CI's research revealed that cellular phones, pagers, and the Internet are all widely used by the self-employed. Ironically, computing portability is not a major issue for either group, with only 9 percent of small office and 8 percent of self-employed users owning laptops or portables.

Here's a look at the percentage of home-based workers who use a variety of other products and services:

Product/Service	Percent Using
Cellular phones	56
Multiple phone lines	44
Internet access	43
Fax machines	42
Pagers	33
Data/fax lines	26
Copier	23

Source: Computer Intelligence, 1997.

Computers Still Popular, Fueling Home Officing

A national opinion survey of over 1,000 people across the country, conducted for Claris Corporation, reports that adults believe that by the year 2000, on average, 59 percent of Americans will use computers to work at home, compared to the 26 percent of Americans who are now using computers to work from home.

The survey also reports 68 percent of Americans credit technology with giving them the flexibility to choose where they work. Seventy-seven percent say technology has actually made their lives easier over the past 10 years.

Shop Smart: Plain Paper versus Thermal Paper Fax Machines

Most of us overlook the fact that every fax machine is also a copier, and no, you don't have to buy an expensive plain paper fax machine to get good-looking copies!

I grew so dependent on using a plain paper fax machine as a copier machine when

I worked for a company that I thought I needed one at home. So I thought that plain paper faxes were the only fax machines that made copies, and I knew I wasn't about to spend money on a personal copier for my office. I spent countless hours agonizing about which kind of fax machine to spend money on: a plain paper fax or thermal paper fax. I wanted the plain paper fax for its copying capabilities, but they were too expensive!

An OfficeMax salesperson who sensed my confusion over fax machines said the magic words: "All fax machines make copies."

Oh.

I didn't know that even after all these years of working in an office! And, I found out I'm not alone, many other friends didn't realize this fact, either!

So, I opted to buy the Brother IntelliFax 635 (see Figure 6-2), an older version with no bells and whistles except for a paper-cutter, on sale for $149, because I have the option to buy either cheap thermal paper or Therma-Plus, a higher-grade thermal paper made for Brother faxes that looks and feels just like plain paper! So when you make copies with this upgraded thermal paper (which isn't so inexpensive, actually, at $21 a box with two 164-inch-long rolls compared with regular generic OfficeMax thermal paper at $47 a box with six 164-inch-long rolls), copies come out looking as though you made them on a regular copier.

A friend of mine sends out copies to her clients that she makes on Therma-Plus paper, and she's heard no complaints. However, since the difference in great fax paper and industrial fax paper is about $2.70 a roll, I plan to start buying Therma-Plus after all.

Lesson from the Trenches: Have Supplies on Hand

Home-based workers don't have the luxury of storing supplies in a huge closet like the ones we may have taken for granted in the corporate office.

"The one thing I overlooked was having enough printer cartridges on hand. I had to run out to Staples in the middle of an important rush job. So now I have a backup supply," says telecommuter Brian McGuren.

Consultant Cynthia Froggatt learned this tip the hard way: "I learned a great lesson—have extra ink cartridges on hand for your fax or printer! One day I had to review a huge proposal that had to go out to the client for Monday delivery. The person I was working with on the proposal began faxing me the proposal for review on Friday at 5:00 p.m. when my ink jet ran out! For some reason, their machine wasn't interfacing with my laptop to fax by modem. So now, I have two ink cartridges on hand. I got caught that one time and was so embarrassed."

Do You Really Need a Copy Machine in Your Home Office

Marketing consultant Shannon Wilkinson says, "I don't have a copy machine, and that's a real problem. Aesthetically, I would not plunk a copy machine in the middle of my home office. If I do it, I would put it behind a screen or build a screen in front of it. I would not ruin the aesthetics of the space. But that's my own personal governing factor. I finally found a superb copy shop that delivers the large quantities I need copied. I spend over $5,000 a year in copying for my clients. Sometimes in the morning, I'll take a walk, drop something off to them, and they deliver it in the afternoon."

Having a copier (much like having a postage meter) in a home office is a luxury, and most of us don't have one because they are too expensive and too big. So we rely on friends and spouses to help us out with our copy needs, or, we shlep to Staples, Kinko's, or the local copy shop for their services, realizing that it's nice to get out of the house once in a while, anyway.

But, what about people who are lucky enough to have copiers in their home offices? What kind of copy machine do they have? And, do you need a copy machine?

"I just purchased a Cannon PC720—a little copier. I had one with a moving cartridge that I despised because it needed a big area in which to move," says Linda Shea, president of The Shea Company in Dallas, a home-based Web site design firm.

Shea is an exception. Almost 99 percent of the dozens of people I interviewed who have a home office don't own a copier, but they do own a what's called an "all-in-one" machine that combines fax, printer, scanner, and copier like the one shown in Figure 6-3.

Lucent Technologies telecommuter Brian McGuren says, "Because of my space requirements, I have a combination unit, a Hewlett Packard OfficeJet—fax/scanner/copier/printer. You can't churn out hundreds of copies at a clip, but you can churn out handfuls of copies at a clip. I use this machine quite a bit. In a corporate office, you copy stacks of forms, but here I wouldn't have any place to put them, and in my business I send out a lot of forms. To handle space requirements, I keep a master document, and if someone calls for one, then I copy and send it off. I rely on the machine; it's a good machine" (see Figure 6-3).

The only problem with owning an all-in-one machine is that if the machine goes on the blink, you are out of luck with faxing, printing, and copying at the same time! However, they are a good deal. A Hewlett Packard OfficeJet 500 with a color printer option can cost $499 regular price and $349 on sale at OfficeMax, for example, while personal copiers from Xerox can cost from $599 and up at the same superstore. A Brother all-in-one, without color, costs about $349.99.

The least-expensive small copier in the Winter 1997/98 OfficeMax catalog is the Xerox 5305T model with a list price of $695 and the store's price of $349.99. Of course, this model has absolutely no bells and whistles (no reduction or enlargement). It has barely any juice, which may be good for your electricity bill but frustrating since it takes 20 seconds to warm up and makes three copies in one minute (slow). Another model of the same price is the Canon PC320, but it makes 4 copies in one minute.

Figure 6-2. Not many home office workers have a dedicated copy machine in their work spaces like this at-home worker. We just don't have the space for it! On the bright side, local copy shops give most of us what we need: A chance to get out of the house and good-quality products at a fair price. (*MZS*)

Figure 6-3. Although most of us don't have copy machines in our home offices, many of you love all-in-one machines like the one featured here that combine fax, printer, scanner, and copier on your PCs. (*MZS*)

The Need for Surge Protectors:
Heed This Warning

No one knows how important surge protectors are more than Karen Gustafson, owner of a home-based public relations firm in New York City.

The day before Christmas Eve in 1995, Karen's prewar building lost its power due to a strange and unexplained power surge. Everyone in the building lost use of their appliances, but Gustafson's office equipment was left completely intact and safe. Why? She had surge protectors covering all her home office equipment. Not one database was lost, and she owes it all to smart planning on the technology front.

"Luckily the building was being rewired at the same time I was starting my business, so we rewired in the office and in the second room off the kitchen that we also use as an office," says Gustafson. "We thought we'd be the only apartment in the building with all this power. The only things in this apartment that weren't ruined during the power surge were the computers and fax machine. We have four business lines, a fax line, a modem line, and one personal house line. For all of this, we have special outlets in the walls of the home office and two surge protectors. Everyone should have surge protectors. My experience should be good enough reason."

Telecommuter Brian McGuren wasn't as lucky with his technology during a power surge. His technology in his basement home office was running fine until he went away for vacation: "I had a surge suppression unit for the electric lines, but I didn't get one to plug my phone lines into. Over the summer there must have been a surge in phone lines. It blew the internal modem in my computer. Luckily nothing else was affected. Internal modems are very sensitive, and it burned out and had to be replaced. To avoid that problem from repeating itself, I bought one suppresser that I can hook both electric and phone into," says McGuren.

A television spot for Staples, a major office supply retailer, delivers a strong message in support of electrical surge suppression. The commercial features a home-based entrepreneur connecting his word processor, printer/scanner/fax machine, and other equipment into the electrical power sockets. After plugging in, he's set to start business. But unfortunately at the same time he's ready to turn on his home office equipment, his teenage daughter switches on her electric hair dryer, causing an overload on the electric circuit.

The commercial ends with the screen fading to black as all his newly installed computer equipment loses its power, too. While the spot is intended to promote Staples' line of Canon home office products, it also underscores the importance of surge protection for electronic appliances and other equipment.

A transient voltage surge, or "transient," is a microsecond-length spike in the voltage that can destroy electrically operated equipment. There are products on the market to protect equipment by identifying and diverting excess transient energy. Such products are placed inline on the power circuit between the power source and the equipment to be protected.

The spot shows the "hero" plugging in the series of equipment into a power strip with numerous electric sockets. Too many real-life home office computer users also use similar power strips, many of which have some degree of surge suppression built in. However, many strip surge suppression products will leave computers, printers, modems, scanners, and other peripheral equipment at risk because of low peak surge current capabilities and high let-through voltages. All surge suppression units are not created equal because actual peak surge current capacities vary widely among products on the market.

Transient voltage surges can be generated in any power circuit by the simple action of switching on any other electric device connected to the circuit. The simple act of switching on a light or an air-conditioner can send substantial power surges through the line. Lightning strikes can also generate extremely strong surge levels. A series of smaller surges takes a cumulative toll on the circuits, which will ultimately cause the system to fail prematurely.

In order to be fully protected, a primary protection such as the installation of a surge suppression unit at the breaker panel should be supplemented by individual plug-in devices. The breaker panel unit serves to protect the system from the strongest surges, while the plug-in devices absorb any residual surges that may remain.

If you use a laser printer, know that those models use a lot of power during printing. In addition, each day a home experiences hundreds of microsecond voltage surges, some over 5,000 volts, that cause anything from a little blip on the computer screen or dip in lights to a full-fledged burnout. Many of today's desktop models store data on a spinning disk called a *hard drive,* which spins at a certain rate. Whenever there's a decrease in the electricity current, the spinning slows down or speeds up and data could be damaged, and the computer can't interpret the recorded data at warped speeds.

There are three forms of power interruption: a *voltage dip,* which occurs when motors of high-draw appliances come on (lights usually flicker); *electromagnetic interference,* which is everyday electrical activity that can scramble computer memory as mentioned above; and the *surge,* a rise in voltage that happens outside the house (electric company switches power from one zone to another) that can burn sensitive electronics.

To reduce the risk of corrupt data and shield computer drives from all the above power surges, telecommuters should invest in inexpensive (average $40) surge protector strips.

Inexpensive strips protect equipment from minor electrical disturbances, but for brief power interruptions, telecommuters would be wise to invest in an *uninterrupted power supply* (UPS) *device* that goes for about $150 and offers a few minutes of backup power and just enough time to save and shut down the computer. Look for a UL 1449 rating (which ensures the suppression of a 6,000-volt surge), an internal fuse for overwhelming surges, and a good warranty that will cover the cost of any damage a faulty suppresser caused (see Kearney, 1997).

Beyond the familiar plug-in outlet surge suppression strips for the home office, it's wise to invest in a *whole-house surge protector.* Doubling up on the surge suppression protects electronic equipment—including regular household appliances—from coming down unless it's hit directly by lightning. A whole-house surge protector uses only one-half watt of electricity, which costs only about 4 cents a month.

The design of whole-house surge protectors varies from a standard double circuit breaker that is easy to install to a unit mounted under the electric meter that uses a large metal oxide varistor component and that is sold through utility companies and requires professional installation (see Dulley, 1996) .

Other Ways to Disaster-Proof Your Home Office Technology

The Iomega Corporation, makers of software backup products declared that December 1 through December 5 of 1997 was National Disaster Proof Your Business Week.

They have the right idea. During the severe storm season, most computer damage occurs when ice or wind disrupts electric lines, causing power outages of a few minutes to several days. When power is restored, electrical transients can cause an uneven flow of electricity through the outlet, ultimately causing possible damage to microprocessors as well as to hard drives. Computer users may not be prepared for the resulting temporary or total hardware failure.

As part of Iomega's Disaster Proof Your Business Week, the company issued five important tips to help home office workers safeguard their computer investments:

◆ Save your entire system—operating systems, files, and applications—on a tape cartridge.

◆ Safeguard a second set of backup cartridges off-site in a protected area.

◆ Guard against infected software programs or possible virus downloads off the Internet by installing a virus protection program on your computer hard drive.

◆ Install a power surge suppression device to protect your computers and other electronic equipment from damaging lightning that can come directly through your outlets.

◆ Keep a fire extinguisher in the office.

How Can We Manage Our Wires While We're Trying to Manage Our Business?

If you have enough technology in your home office to require a surge suppression unit, you'll need wire management.

Wire management is a daunting term especially when we have so many other things we think we can't manage in our lives, much less in our home offices. Wire management is what you need when you have loads of wires dangling from the back of your desk. It looks bad, and that annoys you. It's a quick fix, however.

Most of us let our ugly wires dangle and languish under our desks because we don't know what else to do with them (Figures 6-4, 6-5, and 6-6). But there is something we can do about the problem. We can buy wire management tools. If the word *management* makes you feel uncomfortable and overwhelmed, just think of these products as "wire organizers."

Wire organizers come in many forms, from rubber piping to mesh bags (Figure 6-7) and plastic trays (Figure 6-8). If you really want to be economical, take some twist ties from your garbage bag drawer and simply tie wires together in numerous places to create some kind of tidy semblance down under. If you want another quick, inexpensive fix, go to your hardware store or The Home Depot, buy a short length of plastic gutter, attach it to the back or your desk and pile in your wires and surge suppression strip.

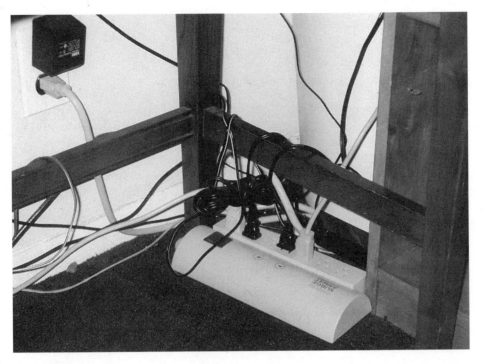

Figures 6-4 and 6-5. Although most of us have power surge protector strips, we still have a jumble of wires lurking underneath our desks. Note that pets love to chew on cords. To prevent this problem, rub the cords with a bar of strong laundry soap, and get a wire management system. (*MZS and Julie Taylor*)

Figures 6-6 and 6-7. Here's a great product, the Cable Keeper: A framed mesh-wire management bag. The bag is priced at $34.95 and is available through Watson Furniture Systems (see resources appendix). (*Watson Furniture*)

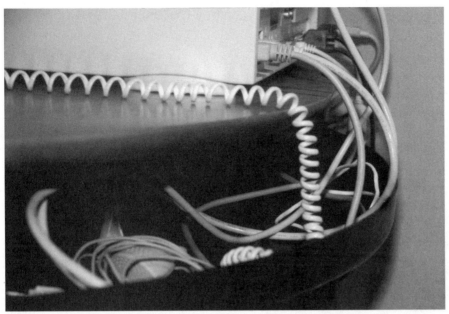

Figure 6-8. A plastic wire tray can be attached to the back of the desk for wire management. You can even use a simple piece of plastic gutter tray to get the same effect. (*Steve Syarto*)

Figure 6-9. Here's an elegant wire management solution: A desktop raceway system. The raceway snaps on and off. It comes in paintable white plastic or special-order wood laminate. It's U.L. listed and C.S.A. (Canada) approved. (*Wiremold*)

One new development from The Wiremold Company conceals wires and cables in a raceway, much like panel systems operate in a corporate office. The raceway conceals wiring in a decorative baseboard or chair-rail design with a cover that snaps off to add new wires or reposition outlets (Figure 6-9).

The raceway is easy enough: Just mount the base to any kind of surface and run the wires, then snap on the cover.

Maybe we can't have perfect home offices, but we can try to have perfect wire management like the home office in Figure 6-10.

Figure 6-10. This technology-intensive home office belongs to Web site designer Linda Shea, of Shea & Company. She manages to keep wires in order by placing everything against the wall. Wires are hidden by modesty panels on her Techline desking system. (*Linda Shea*)

How Many Phone Lines Do You Really Need?

The number of phone lines you need depends on whether you can tolerate answering your private line on a Sunday night at 11:00 p.m., only to find a business caller on the other end thinking she was about to leave you a voice-mail message on your corporate phone.

The second issue you will have to consider is whether there's a chance your little children will answer the phone if your business and your home phone number is one in the same.

"I have had a separate business phone ever since my four-year-old daughter followed me into the shower with the cordless phone," says Lisa Roberts, author of *How to Raise a Family and a Career Under One Roof.* "She yelled, 'Mommy, it's for you,' and I had to think for a minute, then I shut off the water, picked up the phone, and said hello, trying to sound professional. I knew it was time to separate home and business. Now nobody, I mean nobody, touches my business line and answering machine."

Whether it's a client, or a child who provokes you to get a second or third line, multi-line installations are on the rise. By 2001, close to one in three U.S. households could have two phone lines or more, and one of the primary drivers is the Internet, according to a recent report by International Data Corp. (IDC), a Framingham, Massachusetts, research outfit. IDC says that the demand for multiple-line installations is so great that people in some parts of the country are waiting up to six weeks to have a line installed after placing an order.

The telephone technician from SNET who installed my second line told me that in 1997, he saw a significant rise in the number of households that called for multiple lines. In fact, more than half of his orders are to install second or third, or even fourth and fifth lines, for home offices in the local area.

At the same time, phone companies are trying to offer versatile products to make life in the home office easier. For instance, Nortel (Northern Telecom) introduced its Cygic Home Office Suite, a unified communications package that enables home office entrepreneurs to handle multiple simultaneous calls, manage calls, build their contact list, and simplify messaging with integrated voice mail, e-mail, and fax.

Cygic Home Office Suite (CHOS) hopes to answer the following home office dilemmas:

◆ *Problem:* Only one caller at a time can get through.

   Solution: CHOS can handle up to five callers simultaneously, and the home office user chooses which call to take and in what order.

◆ *Problem:* Accessing voice mail requires dialing a separate number and listening to messages one by one.

   Solution: CHOS provides one on-screen message center for voice mail (with the caller identified) as well as fax and e-mail.

◆ *Problem:* Users can't connect to the Internet at the same time they are talking on the phone or sending/receiving a fax.

   Solution: Simultaneously surf the Internet and talk on the phone. All faxes arrive automatically, all using only one phone line.

Digital Subscriber Lines Mean Hope for the Future Home Office

In the near future, you might not even need to install multiple lines for your home office and home phones, faxes, and online activities.

A not-so-new, but newly available technology that works over regular phone lines, called digital subscriber line (DSL), allows you to download data up to 200 times faster than you could with conventional 28.8 modems.

DSL also opens the door for home office streamlining of video and desktop videoconferencing applications at affordable costs, much lower than traditional higher-bandwidth services.

In early 1998, Microsoft, Compaq, and Intel announced that these three giants in the computer industry joined with most of the nation's regional phone companies to offer DSL to consumers by the end of 1998. What this move hopes to do is negate the need for *integrated services digital network* (ISDN), a confounding, complicated technology of higher bandwidth that for years most phone companies have refused to install for a variety of political and practical reasons.

DSL, better known in the computer and telephony industry as *asymmetrical digital subscriber line* (ADSL), is an alternative to more expensive higher bandwidths. ADSL allows data speeds of up to 1.5 million bits per second, fast enough for pictures on the Web to pop up almost instantly. This compares to current speeds of 52,000 bits per second to stream through, which means an average photograph takes several seconds (or more) to appear.

Anything faster now requires ISDN or cable modems, which use coaxial cable and connect through cable TV companies. Fewer than 100,000 people have signed up for the cable modems.

ADSL technology has been under development for years, but competing standards have hindered its acceptance. US West has deployed it in limited areas such as Phoenix. That company's installation fee is $200, and the service costs about $40 a month. Today's fastest consumer modems cost about $150, and a net connection costs about $20 a month.

Home Office Technology Do's and Don'ts

Stuffing technology into a tight space—on- or off-site—can cause serious problems and may result in the loss of valuable stored information. Film and video professionals suggest the following tips to keep information on disks safe.

When disks are kept near the computer, retrieving information can be problematic. The disk says its damaged or there are errors, and most people have no idea why this happens. It's best to keep all audiotape and videotape a few feet away from electromagnetic sources such as a TV, radio, telephone, or computer screen.

Anything that is tape based or anything that records information such as computer disks should be kept as far away as possible from the computer screen, the unit itself, a phone, fax, radio, TV, or electric clock because electromagnetic waves emanating from any of these items, or even a speaker, will erase a tape or cause dropouts and noise. And if tapes are kept there long enough, eventually, the tape or computer disk will be erased. Over the course of a few days, you'll notice problems with the disk or tape. If you keep it right on top of the TV or speaker, you'll notice an increase in noise.

Even if the TV is off, eventually it will erase the tape. Keep all tapes 2 to 3 feet away. Don't put a disk right on a computer, don't put a tape right on top of a TV, and don't put a tape on top of a speaker or amplifier.

CDs are different; they are laser, light based. With anything that is tape based the electrons have been rearranged in the coded tape, so that anything electromagnetic will disturb the arrangement from the way in which it was done in the first place. Disks are similar.

Other Technology Snafus from Real-Life Home Office Workers

Do you keep your fax in your closet? Many people with little room for cumbersome technology are forced to do so (see Figure 6-11).

"The fax is in my closet with the ringer turned off so that in the middle of the night when my European clients fax me at 1 o'clock in the morning, I don't hear it, even when the paper cutter works," says home-based marketing director, Lisa Wendlinger.

Lack of storage is not a problem just for awkward equipment but also for the bulky boxes in which the technology came.

"I don't know where to put the boxes the computer came in," says Sandy Horowitz,* a home-based owner of a public relations firm in New York City. "The boxes don't fold, and there's no room under my bed. There's no room anywhere, and I don't know where to stash them. I was told to keep them as packing boxes in case I had to send the computer back to the manufacturer. I have to keep them for about a year."

That isn't Horowitz's only problem with technology. The telephone company and America Online seem to have her under a black cloud. Read about her confusing, confounding, and, unfortunately, common home office technology problems.

"I had six conversations with the phone company in a couple of days, and everyone contradicted one another," says Horowitz. " My screen froze while I was on AOL's help line. He was talking me through it, and the modem rang. I said, 'what's that?' And then my call waiting beeped. I told AOL to hold on a second, I answered my call waiting, and I came back to AOL, and he said your modem shouldn't ring unless you have call waiting on your computer line, and that could cause your screen to freeze because you're supposed to disable call waiting when you are online.

"I specifically told the phone company absolutely not to put call waiting on the computer line for that very reason. AOL said that the fact that it rang at the same time you had call waiting on the phone suggests that perhaps your lines are crossed. I called the phone company back an hour after the guy installed the line, and they said there was nothing wrong with the line but we will send someone anyway.

"Then they called back an hour later and said that I did have call waiting on my computer line when I specifically said not to do it. They said they didn't need to send someone out to fix it, and all I had to do was to call the business office, and they could do it from there. I called the business office, and I asked them to check it and they said that no, there was no call waiting on my computer line.

"So it's back and forth and back and forth. Then, they told me there was nothing wrong with the line itself, that something was wrong within the computer equipment!! Then, the technician came, told me I had crossed wires and a bad cable. And then he said he had another order here to check my phone line. I said, 'Hey, there's nothing wrong with my regular phone line,' but he said he had the order to test it. Then he tested it, called back and told me I had two bad cables.

"Do I believe this? I don't know what or whom to believe anymore."

And so this is the life of a home-based worker trying to troubleshoot his or her own technology snafus.

The problem is that when we work in a corporation, there are whole technology departments to help us get our computer to stop crashing, to fix our electrical hiccups, and facility managers to yell at the phone company for us.

Unfortunately vendors—from computer to telephone companies—frequently ignore the home office worker, forcing us to acquire expensive solutions designed for larger businesses.

Once again, we face the problem that we're on our own when we work at home, in more ways than one, and we must face alone the black hole of technology burnout.

Figure 6-11. For those of us who work in tiny home offices or who work in small city apartments, take heart. I've met many people who tuck their faxes into their closets so that they don't hear it ring and print out during the night. (*MZS*)

Every Home Office Worker's Favorite Piece of Technology: The Headset

"I got a Plantronics headset a couple of years ago, and it is *wonderful*!" writes a home-based worker on America Online.

"I spend the most time on the phone, and the greatest invention is the headset," says home-based journalist Barbara Mayer. "I would have a permanent crick in my neck if I didn't get them. I spent $175, a lot of money, to get a good headset, and I find they make all the difference in the world to me. I talk into a little microphone, and when I do my interviews, I'm able to type into my computer what they say. Those earphones are the most important thing in my home office."

Home-based public relations firm owner, Lesley Goddin, finally bought a headset so that she can comfortably handle lengthy telephone interviews.

"I've wanted a headset for a long time. I wrestled with which kind of headset would be best for me. The *Hello Direct* catalog has a great selection, but I couldn't get a lightweight headset and amp for less than about $150 to $160. Uniden has a headset that hooks into its cordless phone, so that you can carry the phone and the headset around the house with you. That's also about $179. And that's the one I was planning on buying."

Figure 6-12. Although shoulder rests are inexpensive, a phone headset, like the one journalist Barbara Mayer wears here, does a better job of reducing the stress on your neck, upper back, and shoulders. Phone headsets are increasing in popularity among home office and corporate office workers. They can run from $80 to $179. *(MZS)*

"But what I settled for was a budget version, the Plantronics PLX-500 for about $80. I was standing in Office Depot, and it was an immediate gratification issue. I was coming up on a week in which I knew I was going to do heavy-duty phone work, and I needed a headset *now*! It has a lightweight set (covers only one ear; ear piece is foam cushion; amp has mute button and volume control).

"So far it's okay. People have told me that I sound clearer to them than I do on the regular phone, or I sound very loud, and then I adjust the volume control. I figured I would work with this one for a while and see if it suits my needs, and then when I need to upgrade, I'll know better what my needs are."

Most ergonomic consultants celebrate the headset because it can save your neck and back muscles from becoming stressed.

"I use a headset, and that's been a big modification for me since my injury," says Ellen Kolber, ergonomic consultant and physical therapist.

"I have a cordless remote headset that is the best purchase that anyone can make. Why? Because you can stand and pace. In combination with a stand-up workstation, it's heaven. You're not tied to anything," says author and ergonomic consultant Deborah Quilter.

"The only potential drawback that I see is that the headset microphone may pick up environmental noise such as children and other family members passing by your office while you are on an important call. Of course, this is only a problem if your work space happens to be in the home and not well partitioned off from family quarters," writes another home-based worker chatting on America Online.

Troubleshooting Technology in the Home Office

When your computer crashes, the copier jams, the fax is out of toner, and your phone is on the fritz in the corporate office, you just dial up your technology services department or office manager and plea for immediate help.

At home, we are our own service department. Most home-based workers take pride in getting out of their own technical jams. Working at home with technology means you have to become strong and patient in matters of technology—you can no longer take the soft and easy route by calling the IS department. My own tip: Buy the *Macs* (or *PCs*) *for Dummies* book published by IDG (updated continously), a dog-eared, tear-stained book that lies next to my computer.

Another tip comes from Jessica Taper, a home-based public relations and marketing specialist: "When my technology breaks down, I usually panic. But now I have a backup plan with a friend. I have a key to a friend's house, and she has a key to mine. If something were to happen to either of our computers, we know we can go to the other person's house to save the day. We live within a mile of each other. She used my computer one time in a crisis like that. It helps to know you have someone there."

Always find a tech support service that is local so that you can run to them or call them into your home quickly to diagnose problems like monitor blowouts, disappearing hard drives, and the like. Independent support services can run anywhere from $40 to $100 an hour but it's worth it.

Support lines, such as the Microsoft, used to get 20,000 calls a day. Since Microsoft added an interactive Web site (www.microsoft.com/support/), it now gets 80,000 inquiries online (see Gallivan, 1997).

For those of us who have to rely on technical support via the phone, where it can take up to 45 minutes on hold before you talk to anyone, here are some key tips on getting good support:

◆ Always register your software so that it's on record with the manufacturer.

◆ Jot down all error codes and when it happened, what you were trying to do, any keys you think you may have accidentally hit.

◆ Call the support line using a phone next to the computer so that you don't have to run back and forth after the support person has given you an instruction.

◆ Try Microsoft's experimental Web site diagnostic tool that searches a system while the user is online and performs 10 different hardware and software checks: (www.microsoft.com/support/tshoot/multimedia.asp)

◆ Try Apple's support site: (http://support.info.apple.com/support/supportoptions/supportoptions.html)

One last word on technology: Unless you are a graphic or imaging specialist, you needn't feel pressured to keep up with every piece of technology that comes down the pike. (Graphic and imaging specialists have to keep up with new software and technology developments—oftentimes they buy programs together.)

Keep up with new technology developments by reading a magazine that won't overwhelm you with all the bells and whistles of new technology. My choices: *Home Office Computing Magazine* (they do a good job of basing their technology picks on the realistic needs of their readers) and *Fast Company* (this magazine taps into high-end gadgets, but it's fun to see what's going on in the world of high technology without feeling overwhelmed with information).

Don't worry about what other people buy, don't worry that you don't have the money for the tiniest cell phone available, don't worry that you can't keep up with expensive software that corporations are buying, and don't worry that you don't have a copier—that's why there is a Kinko's in your town. If something works for you but it's two years old and antiquated by anyone's standards, don't worry. Don't fix what's not broken!

Figure 7-1. As innocent as they look and in spite of the comfort they often provide, pets can be a diversion in your home office. (*Michael Laessle*)

How to Kid-, Spouse- and Pet-Proof Your Home Office

If you work at home, at some point during the day you inevitably share your office with kids, pets, and/or spouses, even when at times, you just want, and need, to be alone. It can be a tug of war when it comes to who uses your home office besides you. It's easier to demarcate your space from others when your home office is a dedicated room with a door you can shut. Sometimes, though, a door that's shut doesn't do the job.

You may have a triple-whammy of a problem trying to guard your work-at-home environment with children, pets, and a spouse under one roof, as did editor Jennifer Busch who works for *Contract Design* magazine in New York City and telecommutes from her home in New Jersey:

> I have a nanny come into my home five days a week even though I work only two days a week at home. I couldn't do it any other way.
>
> My home office is in the basement so I am able to shut the basement door, so I'm pretty far removed from activity upstairs. But the part of the basement I'm in is right under my dining room, and I can sometimes hear my daughter running around upstairs on the hardwood floors. That's when I'm distracted because when I hear her I end up going upstairs to cuddle her.
>
> I'm worried that when she gets older that she'll be able to find me in the basement office. She's too young now, so she doesn't really know where I am during the day. When she's 2 1/2 she will go to day care anyhow even though she will know where I am at that point and be able to open the basement door to call for me. I bring her into the basement only when I'm with her working on a baby computer program to play. She's not allowed down here because it's a pretty steep staircase. Luckily, she isn't interested in the tangled jumble of wires under my desk.
>
> My biggest problem is my pets. I have two cats. And their litter box is also down in the basement. I'm right down here in the thick of everything! They jump on my lap, jump on my keyboard, jump on my papers. I just pick them

up, put them down, and keep doing it till they get the hint or else I'll raise my voice a little bit and tell them to "get down" and then they sulk away. They love to hang out around me. As soon as they see me without my daughter, they come downstairs for attention because I give them less attention when my daughter is around. The worse thing they've done—so far—is jump on the keyboard when I'm typing and then I'll find goobly-gook on the computer screen.

I also have a problem with my husband coming into the home office space. He'll work on my computer at night and change something to accommodate what he's doing, but he'll forget to change it back. The next day, I'll go down there and I'll have a problem printing, or getting online, so I have to call him at work to help me fix it. I keep telling him that he has to stop messing around with my computer. He'll plug things in for peripherals but won't change it back to my settings. I'll go to print or fax something, and I'll find out I can't do it because it's reprogrammed. It's hard to reach the back of the computer to fix this. I'm furious when I lose a half hour because I can't fax or print. He's getting better after I shrieked about it last time this happened.

Busch is not alone in her juggling of kids, pets, and spouse in the home office. But the reality of the matter is that at times, many of you want to—and need to—embrace family into your home office space rather than forever trying to keep them at bay.

According to Lisa Roberts, author of the book *How to Raise a Family and a Career Under One Roof* (Bookhaven Press, 1997), your home office should be located in a place in the house that says "status."

Roberts writes in her book, "With the office in a prominent spot in the house, it reflects the prominent role it takes in the household, as well. Mom or Dad works at home. Simply put. This premise alone takes half the struggle out of keeping a home business up and running."

Roberts herself works in a commanding space—a large dedicated home office next to the kitchen and right off the living room. Although the office can be closed off, she often throws open the doors to connect with family as she works opening mail or answering e-mail.

Others, however, will do anything to keep family at arm's length and out of their home office. This chapter addresses both sides of the issue and presents subtle, and not-so-subtle, solutions to problems with children, pets, and spouses that may crop up along the way.

Keeping the Peace with Children While in Your Home Office

Though it may sound dramatic, there's a very real issue brewing in that many working parents fear another nanny crisis like the Eappen-Woodward manslaughter case in 1997. In light of inadequate child care, working parents are scrambling to find alternative work options that provide both a financially sound and emotionally secure home environment for their children.

"Despite all the hoopla of 'family-friendly' policies being instituted by corporate human resources, only a tiny fraction of employees are ever encouraged to take advantage of them," says Lisa Roberts. "Parents are discovering that it's a lot easier to turn their home into a family-friendly workplace and net the same income or more as a home-based professional."

As a solution, more and more parents are bringing their workplace into their homes. But with that solution come a host of problems, dilemmas, and issues for which parents are asking for help in handling.

Child-Proofing Your Home Office

One home office worker told me about her child's fascination with the fax machine. Her two-year-old son walked into her office when she wasn't in there, went over the fax machine where a document was coming through, and he promptly pulled hard on the fax paper as it was printing. She walked in on him to find this happening, and all she had left was a document with a blur of smeared ink. She called her client to refax and vowed to lock her door every time she left her office unattended.

Graphic designer Steven DeMartino found out firsthand how much toddlers love computers and wires:

> **My office used to be in the living room. The problem was that the office was set up in an L-shaped configuration where part of the workstation was exposed and part was against the wall.**
>
> **The key problem with that configuration was our son Robert, who is now three years old. Robby used to tug on the exposed wires, which made it too easy for him to get into trouble. To fix that, I moved my equipment and two desks side by side into the den-entertainment room.**
>
> **Now that Rob is three, he's not interested in wires anymore. Now the main thing that I have to keep safe is the software programs on my computer. Rob would click on the hard drive and change the name of the files on me. It got to the point where I didn't know what my files were called! They were named some random letters, like "a;alkdjf;alsdjk" and it made me nuts.**
>
> **I did find a solution—an After Dark screen saver with a password. Without the password, the mouse won't move anything on screen. However, a screen saver can't stop kids from sticking stuff in the keyboard or into the drives. But now Rob probably knows enough that he isn't supposed to touch my equipment. When he tries to move my mouse, a password icon pops up, and he knows he can't get any further into the computer.**

Lisa Roberts gives these time-tested tips on making your home office safe *for* your kids and keeping your home office safe *from* your kids:

> **The home office is akin to the kitchen when it comes to children. The kitchen and the home office are the two rooms in the home that children can get into the most trouble. In any other room, there aren't very many sharp objects. In the kitchen, there are a lot of appliances and electric voltage—the outlets are**

above adult waist height and pushed back out of the way onto the backsplash or even higher. Drawers have sharp things in it—put little locks on home office drawers just as you do when you baby-proof the rest of the house and the kitchen.

Anything located low to the floor is most dangerous for kids when they are babies and toddlers. By time they are three years old, they know the rules. When they are too young to understand, just don't put pencils and scissors in lower drawers, and don't put them in reachable desk drawers or on top of the desk. Put toys in the lower drawers so that when kids open them up, that's what they find instead of supplies. Just as in a kitchen when you have a lot of little things you don't want a kid to get into, you have in the home office—staples, pins, sharp pens. Just put this stuff into a box, and then put the box onto a high shelf. It's basic safety.

You have to child-proof the business, too! For instance, every time I had a neat stack of material for a client and I'd put it on the desk, over and over again, my kids would pull out a paper from the pile, and the papers would fall all over the desk and onto the floor, then they'd use crayons to draw all over the loose papers. From those experiences, I learned to have as many *high places* for stacking things as you can in a home office.

In my first home office, I had my kids draw a sign that said "mommy at work," and they decorated it with flowers and hung it on my door. They would tuck me into the office just as I tucked them into bed. The sign would have two sides. One side would tell them they weren't allowed to come in, and the other side would tell them it was okay to come in (see Figure 7-2).

Figure 7-2. One of Lisa Roberts's tricks: Have the kids make a sign that they can put on your home office door when you're working. (*Steve Syarto*)

> There was a very good reason for making that sign. My mother always said you can't walk away from your children, your children have to walk away from you. This applies to kids no matter how old they are. Even though you are working at home, they still need to know and feel that you are always there and they can safely walk away and not feel rejected if you're busy in your home office.
>
> There's no doubt in my mind that having kids walk away from your office is a lot easier than having you walk away from the kids to go work in your home office.

Home-based architect Mary Davis found an unexpected solution to keeping her five-year-old daughter at bay when it comes to her desire to work on the computer during the workday:

> Sally wants to use the computer all the time. I share the computer with her but not during working hours. She has to wait until I'm finished with it. What helped with this problem was the children's show *Arthur*. *Arthur* is a cartoon that approaches life's issues in ways little kids can understand.
>
> Just by luck, Arthur's mom is an accountant who works at home with a computer, and Arthur also has his games on the computer as Sally does. One of the episodes that Sally watched was about how Arthur wanted to use the computer during the day while his mother was using it. So his mother said, "Arthur, I'm using my computer for work." Sally saw this whole segment, and now she thinks that Arthur's mom's rule is also the rule for us! Arthur's father is a caterer who also works at home, so this helps explain things to kids.

Another last little tip to keep tiny hands and miscellaneous foreign objects out of computers (and VCRs): Attach a piece of plastic or acrylic over slots with self-adhesive Velcro. It's unsightly, but who cares!

Simple Solutions: Keep a Pretend Desk in Your Home Office for Kids

"I love to keep the office decorated with their artwork," continues Roberts who has four children. "When my daughter was three, for example, she would sit next to me in my old home office and do artwork. I would pull up a little desk for her, and she'd work while I worked, and I'd put stuff on her desk that I had on mine like Rolodexes. Kids love the Rolodex. It pays to get them their own!

"They also love Post-it notes, markers, and pens. I'd keep her desk stocked with things. My daughter become part of the whole home office experience, and I think that's the main goal when you work at home and have kids because your business is not just something that's happening to you, it's happening to your kids and to your spouse. The whole family is part of it, you're all one team. The whole idea is for you to be together. An inclusive attitude is most important when working at home."

Lessons from the Trenches: Kids and the Home Office Phone

"Kids always need something, and they always need it when you are on the phone," says architect Mary Davis who works at home. "They can be totally occupied, but when that phone rings, they need something. They have phone radar, especially when it's a business call. It's uncanny."

How does Peter Baylies, founder and editor of the North Andover, Massachusetts–based *At-Home Dad Newsletter* (see resources appendix), keep his cool when letting his kids work alongside him during the day:

> I do all the work while my two boys (age two and five) destroy the house. The biggest challenge for me is the phone. I am playing with my son, and suddenly the phone rings. When I'm trying to talk business, my well-behaved kid goes nuts and screams for my attention!
>
> How many times has this happened to you? Not only is your kid screaming, but the caller may think twice before visiting your home! Of course you can let the call go onto your answering machine and call back during nap time, but there are those times when you have to make or receive calls to get information when they are awake!
>
> Here are three things I've learned so that you can avoid the panic when the phone rings and you know it's a business call:
>
> ◆ Always have a favorite juice or snack ready to hand to your child.
>
> ◆ Always have a favorite video ready to pop into the VCR when necessary.
>
> ◆ If all else fails, and you must stay on the phone even though your kid is screaming, have ready to pull out two or three toys that your child has never seen before. This will almost always stop your child in his or her tracks.
>
> I've also learned that meeting clients at a local park or playground while you are watching your kids is an ideal, relaxed, stress-free atmosphere in which to talk business while your kids are happy playing.
>
> Another way to keep your child happy, if you have a two-year old or older child, is to set up his or her own desk so that your child can work alongside of you. Supply him or her with age-appropriate office "tools" to use so that they can be "just like daddy or mommy" (see Figures 7-3 and 7-4).
>
> If none of this helps, try conducting business over electronic-mail as much as possible.

You may never know how important having a separate business phone line is until your child picks up a call when you least expect it.

Lisa Roberts, author, association director, and mother of four young children, remembers this story:

> I have a separate business phone, and I have had one ever since my four-year-old daughter followed me into the shower with the cordless phone. She yelled, "mommy, it's for you." I had to stop and think for a minute and shut off the water; then I picked up the phone and tried to sound as professional as I could while dripping wet. I knew it was time to separate home and business phone lines. No one in my family touches my business line and answering machine.

Figure 7-3. Work-at-home dad, Peter Baylies, learned early on to set up a desk for his small son in the home office. That way children can celebrate their parents' work-at-home activities with them without getting in the way while the parents work. (*Peter Baylies*)

Figure 7-4. Always have on hand in your home office a choice of quiet toys for your children. Here's a silent plastic slinky (don't get noisy metal) and a noiseless magnetic sculpture (not for toddlers but for older kids) to keep them occupied while you try to work. (*Steve Syarto*)

Home-based media consultant Jennifer Taper had a similar experience:

> **Toward the end of my last pregnancy, I started to take little naps every now and then because my doctor told me I had to take it easy. One time I fell asleep on the couch with my cordless phone nearby. My cordless phone has the residential and the business lines on it and they both ring. As I dozed off, the office line rang, and my three-year-old daughter picked it up. But I thought she had picked up the home line. I heard her say "no, mommy's taking a nap," and I asked her who was on the phone. She handed me the phone, and I thought I was answering the home line. Of course, it was a client on the business line. I made light of it and told my client that my secretary is very honest, and she tells it like it is.**
>
> **Luckily, the client thought it was funny. We thought about disconnecting the office line on the remote phone, but I really need it. Since then, I keep better track of the cordless phone, and it hasn't been a huge problem.**

Both Roberts and Taper agree that the business world is becoming more tolerant and more fully accepting of the situation of a young child's answering the phone. After all, how many times do business people bring their own children into work with them?

Working at Home Isn't a Substitute for Child Care

Most home-based parents will be quick to say that you must have child-care provisions even if you work at home. This is one point that corporate telecommuting policies make crystal clear to anyone who applies to be a telecommuter. For most telecommuters, it's mandatory that upon signing a telecommuting agreement, they are making a promise to the company that they will continue their child-care arrangements even though they work at home one or more days a week. Generally, a company will screen a potential telecommuter by asking this question: "Are there any family distractions or obligations that will make working at home difficult?"

When an employee answers yes to that question, it immediately raises a red flag with managers. One telecommuting policy says the following about child care:

> **Although you have the opportunity to see and interact with your children or elders, you may tend to take care of them for longer hours since you don't have to spend time commuting to and from work. Please understand that telecommuting is never a substitute for child care. Please continue your current child- and elder-care arrangements should you be allowed to telecommute.**

"I tell people with kids that as a telecommuter, the needs of the business come first, and you can't be a substitute babysitter," says telecommuter Nancy Glenn, alternate work strategist at Lucent Technologies, and an advisor to the company's telecommuters. "People at Lucent tried to work as both telecommuters and babysitters, and it doesn't work. So now we have a screening process that lets us know if there will be a problem with child care."

It's tough to decide whether or not you want in-home child care or whether an off-site day-care center is the best choice for your work habits. An in-home nanny means you will no doubt hear your child or children, and you have to decide whether or not you can handle this without losing productivity.

Many choose on-site, in-home day-care, which only works if there's enough space for work and child-care activities. One New York City–based marketing director, Lisa Wendlinger, is lucky enough to have an apartment with a configuration conducive to working at home while her 14-month-old baby is in the next room. A door separates the main living area from the bedroom and bath, which is where Wendlinger's home office is situated. But she can still hear her baby, Gavin, through the walls:

> **My nanny comes at 8:30 in the morning, leaves 6:30 at night. I keep the door shut and stay in here, which is fine because there's a bathroom right here. If I go out there, he'll want to play with me, so he'll get upset if I disappear back into the office. Sometimes I find myself in here starving, and once I was so hungry that I called the nanny on the home line from my business line to ask her to bring the baby into his bedroom so I could leave my bedroom to get a bite to eat.**
>
> **We have a system where she knows that after his lunch, she's to take him into his room so I can come out and eat. If I've ordered food in and the doorman buzzes up for delivery, she knows I'll be emerging so she'll whisk him into his room or keep him occupied so he doesn't see me answer the door. It's very hard for me. In the beginning when they are really young, it's not that difficult because they are too busy playing on the floor. I had enough friends who warned me that when he turned a year old, I was going to have a problem. Now that he's older, I have to work away from him.**
>
> **Once in a while when I come out and he sees me, it's a little tough to get back in here for both of us. But he's still at the age where the nanny can distract him enough while I slip in. When I hear him crying, that's tough. But I trust my nanny and know that he's crying not because he's hurt but he's just crying. I guess after working in a newsroom atmosphere, which I did for years as a reporter, you can block anything out. I try to think of it as, "Okay, now I'm commuting and now I'm in the office away from home, and he's home with the nanny just like many other children, and I'm not here."**
>
> **I made the transition into the bedroom at just the right time. I'll be in here for a stretch of four to five hours at a time and the baby has no idea I'm home. When he gets closer to the age of two, he's going to probably start realizing I'm in here and start knocking on my door.**

Some home-based workers find that some nannies don't like the fact that the parents are home during the day, as Lisa Wendlinger found:

> **Some nannies don't like the mother home all the time because she'll be too involved with the baby during the day. But when I interviewed them, I was totally up front, and I told them that I'm home, but when I'm working I'm locked away and working in my bedroom and that they'd probably see me only once or twice a day.**
>
> **Luckily, I found a nanny that likes having me at home. It's great for her because when she's doing laundry, I can come out and watch him while she runs downstairs to the laundry room.**

I go out on appointments much of the time, so it's a nice balance. We've become friends, too. When I'm not busy, we find time to chitchat.

There's no doubt that working at home can bring you more confidence when it comes to child-care arrangements. Jessica Taper, home-based media consultant, talks about her experience:

When my second baby was born, we hired someone to be here during the day Monday through Thursday. But when I went to hire help, a lot of people didn't want to work here because I would be home working all day. That kind of scared me a bit, but I do understand that it's hard for them to forge a relationship with the baby if I'm in the house. When my babysitter started, I luckily had a lot of appointments out of the house so I wasn't around. Now I know they are good together so when the baby cries and I'm working at home, I don't panic. The great thing is that I can go out of my office, play with her a little bit, and then go right back into the office to work.

I have a lot of friends who are talking about starting an at-home business without a babysitter, and I think of how they will be absolutely shocked to experience that working from home is really not a substitute for child care."

If you have older kids, as in the case of former home-based medical transcriber Lauren McInally, you might be able to manage work while keeping an eye on your kids at the same time (see Figure 7-5).

McInally managed to transcribe and watch her three daughters by erecting a cubicle in her home as her home office. She found the cubicle secondhand, purchased from a bank that was emptying out its offices. She placed a toy chest for her three daughters right outside the cubicle where she could hear them if anything went wrong, but she could also hear her transcribing notes as well by using headphones.

The best part about having a home office cubicle? The kids knew they had to be quiet, but since it's so open, they also knew they could poke their heads around the corner to ask mom a question.

Figure 7-5. McInally bought a cubicle from a bank going out of business. A panel system can offer a parent the best of both worlds: You are accessible to your children, you can hear them since you aren't behind closed doors, you have visual privacy, and you have a good place to hang your children's artwork. (*MZS*)

Lessons from the Trenches: Sick Kids and Clients

Do work-at-home parents, sick kids, and clients mix well? Jessica Taper, home-based media consultant, once had a frustrating experience, but she realized that being honest about her work-at-home situation is the best policy when dealing with clients:

> I had an appointment with a business associate one day when my three-year-old woke up sick. That kind of thing normally happens when you have a crucial meeting. It was tough to reschedule, so my business associate said she wouldn't mind meeting me at my house. I warned her that my daughter was sick.
>
> Meanwhile, I'm home and the phone rings, and it's one of my clients in an absolute panic. There was an investigative reporter following around the president of the company, and she had cornered him in a parking lot. The president gave the reporter my phone number so I was waiting for the reporter to call and my associate to get to the house.
>
> Then, I used the bathroom, and it flooded! Now I'm home with a sick child, an associate on the way, and a determined investigative reporter—so what else could have gone wrong!
>
> The reporter called me in a frantic state because she didn't know why the client wouldn't talk to her. So she threatened to camp out on *my* doorstep! I told her, "That's fine, just bring a plunger." She was confused, so I told her that I worked out of my home, that my daughter was sick, that my toilet had flooded, and though I'd loved to have helped her at this point, I wasn't in the mood to help out. She never did show up at my house.

Safety Checklist for Children in the Home Office

◆ Kids love electrical cords so invest in wire management tools (see Chapter 6, "Technology")—if you don't, a child can easily tug on a cord and pull down the equipment.

◆ Cut all looped cords on your blinds or curtains into two separate cords to prevent strangulation.

◆ Install sufficient outlets in your home office so that you won't have to dangle or drag wires across the floor.

◆ Install inexpensive plastic outlet plugs or outlet covers with a spring-loaded sliding mechanism that covers outlets when they aren't in use.

◆ Make sure your toddler doesn't climb on your office chair—although a five-castor base chair is usually stable, it could topple over on its side if given enough force.

◆ Watch that your child doesn't get his or her head stuck in V-shaped arms on your chair.

◆ Keep finished projects and presentations for clients in high places.

◆ If you have a baby who crawls, put a heavy box of toys or something else in front of an exposed outlet—your baby can't reach the outlet or move the box.

◆ Bolt a bookcase in your home office to the wall so a toddler can't tip it over.

◆ Make sure your child can't get into an open top file drawer so that it doesn't tip over.

◆ Your child can trip on an open bottom file drawer.

◆ Keep vulnerable disk drives covered by putting a piece of hard plastic over the opening with self-adhesive Velcro.

Figure 7-6. Laptops are lightweight and can be easily toppled over by children. If your kids play or work on your laptop, try to put it on the floor (for short periods of time) or on a lower surface so that it doesn't go crashing to the floor. (*MZS*)

Spouse-Proofing Your Home Office

Oftentimes, spouses who don't work at home like to come into your office to "play." This can be frustrating.

> **My husband has a corporate office but he really just wants a home office Architect Mary Davis says: So I let him use my office for his special projects.**
> **My husband will come in here, and he'll throw stuff around in the little product sample cubicles I've designed, and then I'll have to dig through his stuff to get to my projects.**
> **My five-year-old daughter Sally doesn't even touch any of my projects the way my husband does. My husband, who is also an architect whose firm has a huge product sample library, will come into my home office and pick up a sample of some product and go "oh, what's this? It's nice!" Then he'll take it over to the other room, and before I know it, it's gone, and I'll be looking all over for my sample piece of granite. Sally wouldn't do that!**

Telecommuter Holly Gruske has the same problem with a husband who works outside of the home but nevertheless still likes to share in her home office space: "The problem is that I don't like sharing. My husband thinks he can walk into my home office and take possession of my things. It's a typical male trait. But they also tend to knock things over! I don't want my husband to share this office with me because he's such a clutterbug. So we arrived at an agreement for this sort of home office problem. My new workstation has two flipper doors. So I'm giving him one and I'll take the other."

My husband would constantly come into my home office while I was thick into concentrated writing. He'd come in there to borrow the calculator, get a stamp, pick up the scissors, use wrapping paper, find a pen, or whatever else he needed at the time.

Other times, I'd walk into my office and find him sitting in *my* chair with *his* feet on the desk, talking on the phone. I thought I solved the problem of space invasion by quitting my corporate job where we viewed everyone's cubicle as our own, share and share alike. Now, I had to contend with my husband!

The solution? My husband works in New York City, so he doesn't need a home office, but nonetheless, we refinished a rolltop desk that was languishing in the basement. We then moved my home office into a bigger room, and now he is the proud owner of a home office with his own calculator, stamps, scissors, paper, pens, and more! Now he sits in his own chair while he talks on the phone!

Finding Harmony with Pets While in Your Home Office

Most home office workers find extreme joy in having their pets by their side each day while they work—a luxury that can't be found in the corporate office. Cat lovers, especially, tend to warn clients who visit who may have allergies, but they let their cats wander freely even during meetings.

"When people come up to my home office to visit from the mill, I ask them if they are allergic to cats because I have two, and they are always in the way," says textile designer Michael Laessle. "They climb under and over the huge fabric blankets—they just get into everything. They run the office and the house. Sometimes they make me laugh so hard I just have to stop working and laugh with them."

Home-based publicist Lesley Goddin shares her own experiences about the joys of working with cats:

> **If I ever miss chewing the fat with other people in an office, I play with the cats, watch what they are doing, and I instantly feel better (see Figure 7-7).**
>
> **The cats come into the office and meow a lot. One likes to sit under the fax machine, settles down and goes to sleep. Or he likes to go onto my husband's office chair, so we put a pad on the chair for the cat hair. And they like to sit on my chair, but I take them off when I need to work.**
>
> **Bienito would try and chew the phone wires, but we discouraged him by yelling at him a lot. Sometimes both of them try to walk across my keyboard, which is not a good idea. But luckily they don't do anything distracting or disrupting.**

Figure 7-7. Cats love ergonomic chairs. Goddin puts down towels on the chairs so cat hairs don't cling to the fabric. (*Lesley Goddin*)

There are cat lovers, dog lovers, and...iguana lovers, too.

Architect Joe Eisner, based in New York City, is an iguana lover (see Figures 7-8 and 7-9). He has two that work side by side with him each day. Iguanas are extremely slow moving creatures that often stay still during the day. They will stay out of your way if you stay out of their way.

The only problems Joe has had with iguanas? They have the potential to scare clients (so he warns them first), and once in a while they get into vicious fights with each other—one time resulting in one biting the other's tail off.

Figures 7-8 and 7-9. Architect Joe Eisner keeps two most unusual pets in his apartment: iguanas. They move slowly and blend into the environment so much so that visiting clients sometimes don't even notice the iguanas are in the same room. (*MZS*)

Pet-Proofing Your Home Office

There are times when pets can be trying on you as you work.

"I work with my dog," says independent home-based film editor, Maxi Cohen. "When I have meetings, he can't stand it that he doesn't get attention, and he always gets attention because he's such a lovable dog. He likes to go into my garbage cans sometimes."

"I used to have a cat, Angel, that was fascinated with the fax machine," says Goddin. "She'd be sleeping in another room, and when she'd hear the noise of the fax machine, she'd run in and be right there as soon as the fax came through. Sometimes she'd sit on top of the fax machine. I was afraid she'd make the fax machine too hot or she'd get hair in it. So I'd have to take her off of it because she blocked incoming faxes, but for some reason she loved it—the fax machine was her favorite place.

"The only problem I have now is my laptop. The little trackball on the wrist rest gets dirty fast, which makes the cursor difficult to position properly. I think that may be due to having cats—all that hair gets trapped in the keyboard."

Another home office worker told me in passing that while she was on the phone doing an interview, her cat started making mysterious noises, but she knew what was coming. As she turned around to see the cat vomit into her fax machine, she quickly hung up the phone in the middle of an interview to take care of the mess. Needless to say, she had to buy a new fax machine.

My cat loves to play in my home office. I was especially startled one day when my cat jumped from the top of the file cabinet, then fell, into the open drawer of my lateral file cabinet resulting in numerous crumpled files and bent pendaflex folders.

On other days, my cat has been known to:

◆ Chew on paper

◆ Chew on Federal Express boxes lying around

◆ Walk all over my desk at the most inopportune times (hung up a call once by stepping on the wrong part of the phone)

◆ Meow her loudest when I'm on the phone on a business call

◆ Get her hair all over the task chairs (see Figure 7-14)

◆ Jump onto my lap when I'm on the phone on a business call

◆ Knead the rug in my home office

◆ Lick photos and slides that may be lying around

◆ Get up on her hind legs and paw me when she's hungry, of course when I'm on a business call

◆ Scream loudly when I send a fax through my computer (she hates the sound) or when I'm transcribing a tape with someone else's voice on it

…but she's awfully cute and wonderful and I can't stand it when she's not in my office when I'm working since she's my closest colleague! But this is just one cat and this is all she does during the course of a day when I'm in the office.

The one and only tip anyone can give you about handling pets in your home office is this: For a cat, always have catnip on hand if your pet doesn't like it when you are on the phone and won't take no for an answer when the door is shut; for a dog, always have a chew toy or bone on hand for the same reason! Dog owners say that even if your dog decides he absolutely must go outside at once when you are on a business call, he will be happy for a couple of minutes with a chew toy to make him forget all about his problem.

Figure 7-10. Here I caught my cat looking quite mischievous. One of the best tips for a restless cat in the home office? Have a catnip toy handy in your home office so your cat can play with it; soon it will put your pet into a deep slumber so you can work. (*MZS*)

Figure 7-11. Lots of pets are captivated with technology. Some cats are curious about fax machines; my cat, Gracie, is fascinated with my computer screen. She'll jump up when I'm typing and sit in front of the screen. Sometimes she accidentally steps on the mouse. (*MZS*)

Figure 7-12. My cat, Gracie, has a bad habit of lying down on a pile of paper, then chewing on the paper. Work-at-home parents have similar problems when their kids accidentally draw on important papers. A scanner can keep critical papers safe from being destroyed by kids or pets. (*MZS*)

Figure 7-13. Dogs can be easier to deal with in a home office because they obey orders whereas cats have an independent nature. However, unless a visiting colleague or client has an allergy or fear of pets, most home office workers say they let their pet come and go as they please. (*Sligh*)

Shop Smart: Fur Remover

It's tough to get pet hairs off of a desk chair that's covered in textured fabric. I have two commercial-quality chairs from Herman Miller and Knoll both covered in solid-color dark blue nubby fabric, which seems to attract my cat's fur even if she's standing a foot away (see Figure 7-14)!

If a lint brush and vacuuming won't remove pet hairs from your chair, buy this dry sponge from Gonzo. It costs about $5 (I bought mine at Caldor, a discount store) and quickly does the trick (see Figure 7-15).

Another solution to keeping pet hairs off of your nubby fabrics? Put a pad or pillow on the seat. Your pet will like it better, anyhow. It may seem like an obvious solution, but it didn't occur to me until my friend told me that's how she keeps cat hairs off of her home office chairs.

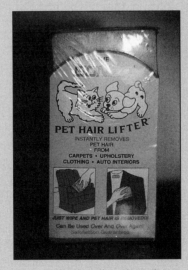

Figures 7-14 and 7-15. You and your pet can often compete for the office chair. If your pet wins out most of the time, eliminating pet hairs from nubby chair fabric can be difficult. The vacuum, tape, and a lint brush won't work as well as a Gonzo sponge. (*Steve Syarto*)

Privacy Providers When All Else Fails

You're working in your home office on the weekend or in the evening when the entire family is in the house. The dog is barking at the cat who is shrieking, your spouse is trying to calm down the kids as they run around the house, and you have to think!

When all else fails, and the radio or music you are playing in your home office to drown out sounds has become more of a nuisance than a help, buy a sound-masking device, the kind of white-noise maker that therapists use outside of their offices so you don't hear what's happening on the other side of the door. Corporations also use these types of devices in open-plan environments where sounds travel loudly from one open cubicle to the next.

This is the least expensive solution to reduce the penetration of noise both outside and inside your home office. Technically speaking, *sound masking* is a broad-band, low-level background sound that is precisely contoured to cover and mask unwanted noise. It's designed to mask out most frequencies of sound. Playing music can have the same effect, but it must be played loudly enough because it doesn't mask out most frequencies of sound at a low volume.

Either ask your therapist where he or she bought his or her white-noise machine, or visit The Sharper Image (1-800-344-4444) where they sell the Sound Soother in several versions priced from $100 to $140. You can also contact Dynasound (1-800-989-6275), a manufacturer of a large line of sound-masking systems that are used for commercial spaces (see Figure 7-16).

If you can't stand the neutral white noise that noise-masking machines make, you can get one that plays other sounds as well, such as sounds of the rain forest or ocean. Any sound-masking machine will let you work in peace.

Figure 7-16. Lots of devices can help you manage home office privacy in a busy house. Try a sound-masking machine like the one shown here from Dynasound, a wireless intercom so your kids can keep in contact with you, or caller ID so you don't accidentally answer a client's call when your kids are on a rampage. (*Dynasound*)

More Real-Life Home Office Dilemmas: How Others Cope

We've already read throughout this book about the many different dilemmas of real-life people who work at home. But there's more!

In this chapter you'll find profiles of how home office workers cope that may answer the same questions you may be asking yourself:

- ◆ Can I have a home office in a city?

- ◆ Can I work in a basement or a garage home office?

- ◆ Can I work in a small home office with my spouse?

- ◆ Can I work with an assistant in my home?

- ◆ Can I work at home in a rural setting?

- ◆ Can I allow customers or clients to come to my house?

- ◆ Can I afford a barrier-free office?

Can You Work at Home If You Live in a City?

Cynthia Froggatt, Principal
Froggatt Consulting, Strategic Facilities Management Planning Consultant
New York, New York

Too many people say they have no room in their city apartments in which to start a business. Maybe you're right—you don't have enough room and you can't move to larger quarters. So, how would you cope?

Cynthia Froggatt has learned how to cope. She has worked on staff at two of the country's largest architectural design firms. When Froggatt left the first firm, she had no intention of ever working at home. She wanted to take off four months and decide where she might like to work. At the end of four months, Froggatt couldn't think of one place where she would have liked to have worked full-time on staff. But she did start to think that it would be more fun to collaborate on projects with a variety of people. At that point, her clients found her, and Froggatt Consulting was born.

The only issue: Froggatt lives in a small one-bedroom apartment off of Central Park West, and where could she put a home office? Luckily, she lived in an apartment building that has a deck flanked by a shade tree growing up from the street. It's a welcoming and semiprivate spot where she can work during summer hours so she doesn't feel so hemmed into the apartment. That's a luxury for a New York City apartment dweller, however, and it's partly the reason Froggatt can easily work out of her small space.

Froggatt's home office is located in her dining area, on a table she used to clear every night so she could eat on it, but she has given up on that idea for some time. She's just too busy to clear off project work every night. But like most New York City apartment dwellers, she is strapped for space, and her fax is located in her closet, along with other office supplies.

Here's how she manages a successful business in a small city apartment:

> I had a big, big apartment when I lived in Michigan. I moved into my New York City apartment thinking I'd be here for three years, but I've lived here since 1989. I've never really bought anything for this apartment. You never think you're going to be somewhere permanently when you live in New York City. It never made sense to me to think about buying furniture for a small apartment because you would make such different decisions if you live in a bigger space.
>
> I'm not a designer at heart. I make do with what I have. I never thought of it as a permanent home, and sitting down and designing it would be a real commitment.
>
> Given the choice between furniture and technology, I'd spend my money on technology. I have such a long list of tools I would like to buy. But I'm concerned about ergonomics so a chair was important to me.
>
> I used to work on a straw chair with a pillow on it. The chair was all wrong for me. The height was wrong. A lot of people probably face this, but I didn't want my living space to look like an office—a lot of the serious chairs I looked at were too "offic-y". The upholstery I chose makes it integrate more into my apartment.
>
> During the warm months, I frequently work on my deck. I think furniture manufacturers would flip because I work on this director's chair and flimsy table on my deck. But you know what? This stuff works, although it doesn't work for long term. I'm trying to find nice deck furniture that will be good for outdoor work, too. But I can't find anything suitable.
>
> Frankly, I still haven't seen the right solution out there for me for my indoor office, either. There aren't any tables at the right height for full-time laptop users. I want to buy a mobile table/work surface for a laptop, one that tilts and has the provisions for peripherals. There are little tiny tables out there for laptops, but I need room for paper and a CD ROM drive. I haven't seen the right furniture out there small enough and interesting enough to be residential and also to accommodate what I want in terms of space.
>
> I don't think the New York City home office is a big market for the furniture manufacturers to think about. They are more interested in the people who live in houses with home offices off of their living room or in the bedroom.

Even if I did find furniture I like, it's a huge money issue to redesign the apartment. Plus, I can't stand the thought of how disruptive it would be to repaint my apartment and move in new furniture. My work was disrupted for four days when a plasterer did work in the building. I did a lot of work on the deck that week. On the other days I worked at friends' apartments. I was only 50 percent productive at that time.

It took me a good six months to get used to working at home. When I first started doing more of my work from home rather than more of my work at clients' offices, I used to have a lunch date every day. But that was really unproductive. I was taking two hours out of my day going on the subway to and from lunch plus time for lunch. I did that because I was afraid I'd get lonely every day. So I eased into it—I found other ways to be with people. I also have a lot of stay-at-home mom friends around during the day, so if I feel I need contact, it's there. And, going to the copy shop and joking with the guys that work there for a few minutes takes the place of having to have a full lunch out with someone every day.

The one thing this neighborhood is missing is a real hang-out place where I could take my work, like a café where I'd feel comfortable sitting and working alone, but also a place where I could walk in and there would be some sort of group of regulars I could bounce ideas off of. Barnes & Noble would be good, but I want a place where there are people who don't think the way I do and who don't do the same work I do.

Figure 8-1. If you live in a small city apartment and work at home, you know how confining your space can become if you work there day after day. Owning a laptop makes sense because it's space saving and you can take it with you when you need a change of scenery. (*MZS*)

Figure 8-2. Froggatt was lucky enough to find an apartment in New York City with room for an outdoor office. She can garden, cut herbs, and strategize on the phone at the same time. (*MZS*)

Figure 8-3. Rolling carts are the apartment dweller's best friend. They are offices-on-wheels that can be hidden into tiny spaces or closets when you are entertaining. When Froggatt decides to work outdoors on her terrace, she takes along her rolling cart of supplies and files. (*Maxi Cohen*)

Michael Laessle
Textile designer
Minneapolis, Minnesota

Michael Laessle is a textile designer who worked as an executive for the textile division of Knoll in New York City before personal reasons took him to his new home in Minneapolis where he started his own design business. While living in New York City, Laessle never had any desire to strike out on his own because he thrived on the energy and chaos at Knoll. But now, he not only runs out of one home office his own textile firm, he is the founder of the Michael D. Laessle Foundation for AIDS Care, which works to improve the quality of life through care-giving facilities. All of the royalties from the sales of his textile designs will be donated to his association.

The business of textile designers means being surrounded by fabrics—lots of it. But fabrics can either be bulky, or they can be little scraps and samples that can get lost and unorganized. In a corporate work space, there seems to be no end to the places in which to store fabrics, catalogs, color samples, and all the other paraphernalia it takes to run a textile design department. Laessle has some ideas that will solve his space crunch, but for now, he's fortunately too busy to put his plan into action:

This home office was already built in when I moved into the condominium. The space is wonderful; there's a circular open feeling to the room, but it can also be closed off.

What I love most about working from this condo is the light. I don't like lightboxes for color checking fabric samples. I prefer to use different artificial and natural lights, so I march around the apartment with fabrics to check color. I have gorgeous views from the 15th floor. Having a lot of light is important

to me. Light is good for me because I'm working alone without anyone else here to interact with, and having light and a window out into the city creates a feeling of having more contact with the world. Although there are lots of windows, it's never distracting because I can't focus on anything specific because I'm up high enough. I look over freeways and gardens and parks so it's pretty, but there's no street traffic noise. The other side of the building has the downtown skyline view, and that's probably distracting because of noisy horns.

Figure 8-4. Textile designer Michael Laessle says there's a distinct advantage to working at home in an apartment in the city: his friends' corporate offices are located nearby, so he can easily see them for lunch. (*Michael Laessle*)

My home office is square with large windows. The desk, storage, and filing are all built in right under the windows. What's great is that I have a wide and long work space that measures 14 inches wide by 15 feet long.

There's a very large closet that takes up three-quarters of the wall space with two heavy large paneled doors. It's one of the areas I want to attack and redesign for storage space. I want to store fabric samples, catalogs, and color samples in there. Now I store everything in boxes that are hard to get to and I can't get to them very fast. I have wire shelves in the closet now, but it's generally wasted space. I want to make every inch of that space useful because I don't have a basement or extra room to stash things.

When I finished my first textile collection for Pallas Textiles in June, I got rid of everything because I didn't have the space to store anything, and I wanted to keep whatever space I have open for new projects and developments. So I sent the big bulky fabric blankets back to the Pallas main office. Blankets are enormous—they include all the color combinations possible from all the fill and warp colors you wanted to try together. Sometimes there are over 400 colors on one blanket, and each color is 8 by 8 inches or even larger at 14 by 10 inches. The thing about blankets is that I have to live with the blanket, come back to it, then leave it alone quite a number of times until I'll whittle it down to 8 to 10 colors. And I have to take the blanket into different areas of the condo to see how different lighting conditions affect the colors. So running a textile design business definitely does take up room in a city condo.

Figure 8-5. Working at home in a high-rise isn't confining to Laessle. Views of the city from his home office help him feel connected to the world outside. (*Michael Laessle*)

Can You Turn Your Garage into a Home Office?

Maxi Cohen
Maxi Cohen Film and Video Productions
Venice, California

Maxi Cohen is an independent filmmaker who produces, writes, and directs feature films, documentaries, and videos. Some of her work includes *South Central Los Angeles: Inside Voices, Anger* (*Seven Women—Seven Sins*), and she has produced and directed several films for *Saturday Night Live* and the MTV Network.

Cohen has always worked at home because first and foremost, she likes to have dominion over her own world:

> I visit many offices for meetings, and I always think of those environments as being unhealthy, sterile, unimaginative, and uncozy places to work. The only great part of working in an office is that if you get lonely, there's always somebody to talk to.
>
> At a very early age I was independent. The very first project I did out of college was my own television show in a small town—Cape May, New Jersey. I produced, directed, shot, appeared in, and edited the show. It was the only local program in the community. I ran that out of my house, and I also ran a variety of related workshops out of my house. My house phone number was even the number for viewers to reach for feedback. For most of my life, I have worked out of the home, and it's by choice.
>
> I love to be able to get up in the morning and not worry about what I look like when I call Europe from LA. I can still wake up late and be in the office by 9:00 a.m. I can actually work in my pajamas all day long, and nobody would know. I can also get out of bed at 11:00 at night and call Europe, sit and write and work in my office until 3 o'clock in the morning totally undisturbed.
>
> I live in a house in Venice five blocks from the ocean. Before this house, I was living in a loft in NYC where I had a wonderful home office. When I moved out here into this house I wasn't really thrilled because it felt too dark to me. I figured I'm in LA, so why isn't it airy and light in this house?
>
> One day after I came back from a two-week trip to New York City, I came home to find a surprise waiting for me from my husband. He had converted the garage into an office! And he did it rather inexpensively. He laid out a beautiful inexpensive floor out of MDF with geometric shapes in it. He also built a deck over what used to be weeds to create a garden view for me (see Figures 8-6 and 8-7).
>
> I now have an office that is rather large, it's the size of a two-car garage except it doesn't look anything like a garage now. It has a high ceiling, windows on one side and big sliding glass doors on the other side that look into a garden. One of the criteria I always had about my office is that it has to have a view. I have to feel like I'm somehow connected to the outside world.

Figure 8-6. You would never know this home office was once a garage. (*Maxi Cohen*)

Figure 8-7. If you're thinking of converting your garage to a home office, you'll have to contend with cement and often oil-stained garage floors. The floor of this garage is covered in MDF, which has been cut in geometric patterns, then heavily varnished. (*Maxi Cohen*)

Right now I'm looking out at huge palm trees, the neighborhood, and my garden. The windows and doors are wide open, and I feel that connection to the outside (see Figure 8-8).

When you come into the office, you would never know it's in there, but there's a closet that kind of melts into the wall, and in there is my washer-dryer. I'm the only one that can make a deal and do my laundry at the same time.

Figure 8-8. The former view outside the garage was weeds. Part of renovating this formerly dark garage into a light-filled home office entailed tearing out weeds, and installing a deck, sliding doors, and outdoor furniture so that Cohen could have a view and an outdoor conferencing area. (*Maxi Cohen*)

Can You Literally Live in Your Home Office?

Shannon Wilkinson
President, Cultural Communications, A Marketing Firm Specializing in Art and Film
New York, New York

Shannon Wilkinson moved to New York City in the late 1980s and immediately immersed herself in the art world. Her dream was to find a job in the city that could blend her love of art and talent for writing. She became a publicist at the Guggenheim Museum on the Upper East Side of Manhattan.

She stayed at the Guggenheim for three years, soaking up knowledge of the high-powered art world. From the day she started to work at the Guggenheim, Wilkinson kept a file on starting her own business. At the same time, she began to write on a freelance basis.

Wilkinson has a unique way of looking at working at home in New York City, and her home office reflects her philosophies:

> I always dreamed of being a freelancer in New York City, but I didn't know what I'd be doing or when I'd do it. When I first moved here, I remember being struck by the fact that you can go out on the street at any given time during the workday, and there are hundreds of people who look intelligent, who are not working at 9-to-5 jobs. Instead, they're in Central Park exercising and having fun, and I began to wonder what they did for a living.
>
> When I was at the Guggenheim, I met artists in studios in SoHo who didn't have 9-to-5 jobs. These interesting people had wonderful lifestyles, and really started to think that this was the way to go if I wanted to live in the city. But, I didn't have my plan quite formulated so I just kept a file filled with things that I might call a "business."
>
> After three years at the Guggenheim, I got a job with a very well known public relations firm in their arts division. I was there for two years, and I continued to do a lot of freelance writing work. I started to feel I was missing out on great freelance opportunities because I had a staff job.
>
> I finally decided it might be time to freelance full-time, but I never really had the guts or money to do it until things in my personal life triggered a change. First, I knew I couldn't afford the kind of apartment I wanted to live in unless I had my own business and worked at home and could deduct part of it from taxes. That was a major motivation to freelance in itself. I realized that you can make $50,000 a year in New York City but still can barely afford a one-bedroom apartment—that's not right.
>
> Then, in 1989 three things happened that made me suddenly quit my job even though I only had $400 in the bank. My boyfriend broke up with me, one of my roommates left me in a lurch with a three-bedroom apartment with a lease in my name, and my request for a raise was turned down. I thought, why am I working so hard to climb four flights of stairs to live with three roommates?
>
> So I quit. I already knew how to support myself on a shoestring in New York because I had done it before. This city is worth being here if you are pursuing something you know will be satisfying and that will let you develop

your own way of life. Otherwise, it's too difficult and it's too expensive.

The home office to me is about shaping your life—shaping what kind of life you want and doing it your way. When you step out of the safety net of your routine and you open yourself up to opportunity, things happen that you would never dream of—*never.*

During one of the early days, I was sitting in my sad little desk in my ramshackle bedroom, and it was sad because my new roommates were off at work, and I sat there by myself wondering how in the world I was going to get jobs. There were mice running round the apartment, fire engines making a racket up Third Avenue, and then the phone rang. It was an art critic who needed to know the name of a consultant. That phone call came at the right time for me. I learned a lot about myself through working in corporations. My last corporate office was a small, institutional, but pleasant enough looking space in a hallway with six other identical offices. The ventilation was poor. The lights were fluorescent, and there was no natural light, which means on beautiful spring or summer days the air feels gritty, and I found it to be very glum. Through my jobs and freelance work, I met many people in New York who ran successful businesses from homes or apartments. After seeing all of this, I felt that life was too short to be cooped up in a glum office.

Before that, my office at the Guggenheim was a beautiful curved office designed by Frank Lloyd Wright. It was a joy to work there. Because I worked in publicity, we had racks of the latest publications like *Town & Country.* There were flowers on the desks. The art world is very civilized. And a friend of mine picked me up for lunch, and she looked at this gentile office, and she said, "Shannon, one day you are going to get out in the real world." I thought—*no I'm not!* I knew I wouldn't work in the kind of setting she was talking about, I knew it wasn't the life I wanted.

I started out in a tiny bedroom home office for one year before moving. I keep a picture of my past home office on my desk to remind me of where I came from. I hardly ever look at that picture because I'm so far away from that now. But there are times when there's the possibility you may not have income for a few months, or the economy hits a low. You never think it will happen, so this picture reminds me that it can happen, and you can't take money for granted.

When I started my business, I used to feel so overwhelmed to be alone, unknown, and no one around—go into meetings, and competing with people with staffs and offices and to leave and want the business. I thought it through very carefully of what image I wanted to project while building a business. The results and services I see are very impressive, and so I always want to do everything possible to dispel any image of a solo freelancer. Freelancers to me charge by the hour—they don't charge fees and retainers. From the time I started my business, I've only charged fees and retainers.

When I moved into my current apartment, I decided that I'd get rid of my bed. There was something about other home offices I lived in that always made me feel unprofessional. I realized it was because I could see my bed, and to me that was unbusinesslike.

So I made a lifestyle choice. I thought I could either have more of a home, or I can use the space to have more of a business. I do have meetings here, and

I wanted to feel more professional about it by having a more polished environment. Where do I sleep? I have a sofa bed. I just didn't want to look around my office and see a bed after I had just come back from a meeting where I talked about thousands of dollars worth of business.

My step-mother is an interior designer so she gave me some tips. She said to divide the space into three areas visually. She said I could do that by having a little chandelier and a round table at the entry. And I could also do it by having several sisal rugs. She said to keep all the furniture light in color, even the curtains. Everything should have a feeling of lightness so when you come in, you don't feel depressed.

The main work-space problems I have come up when there's a lot of business and the phones are ringing off the hook, and I have an assistant here four days in a row. I'm very aware that I could not have someone here five days a week. It's very difficult in this space for two people. It's too small for two people and constant noise. I'm always thinking of how to make my business grow, and it will probably lead me to a larger space and inevitably an office.

The other problem I have is that I'm working with wealthy clients who want to see my work space. But I feel it doesn't look as professional or opulent as it could.

I have superb clients who have hired me on my talents so they aren't judging me on where I work, and they probably don't care. It's funny because I work with a film director whose office looks broken down, so he wouldn't care. I've learned that my environment image is the least important because I wouldn't have these clients if they wanted someone with an office on Park Avenue. But it's important to me. I usually tell clients that I have a very modest office because I don't think this environment conveys to them the quality of my clients and of my work.

My dream, long-term goal, would be to have a larger space, preferably a townhouse. Until then, this is what I want to do to upgrade this work space. I want to upgrade its elegance by putting vintage photography in handsome, expensive dark wood frames. I'd replace the sisal rugs.

You should always listen to what others say about your work space. One art critic friend of mine said he was surprised I didn't have more art up with all the clients I have. He opened my eyes! I should have art! I was so busy getting my business going, I never thought of that.

I learned other lessons about productivity. When I first moved here, I used a long dining table as my main desk. But it was extremely wide, and I couldn't reach across it. Over a period of months, I kept notes on what I'd design if I could design something I needed. I always think long term and mobile. I'm going to eventually outgrow this, and I'll have to go somewhere, and I want to take things with me. Everything is built in units so that I can take it down and bring it with me. I could repaint it for a new interior, too.

I don't have a copy machine, and that's a real problem. Aesthetically, I would not plunk a copy machine into the space. If I do it, I would put it behind a screen so that it wouldn't ruin the aesthetics of the space. I cannot bear the thought of living in a place that looks like an office.

You have to have a lot of income in New York to maintain an office and a mortgage or rent and an office. But, as long as I'm single, I'll work at home.

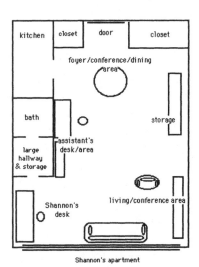

Figure 8-9. Wilkinson's entire apartment is arranged to look like an elegant office that just happens to be in a residential apartment building. Upon entering the apartment, this foyer with the round table and chairs looks like a welcoming reception area. Wilkinson also uses this area for dining and conferencing. (*MZS*)

Figure 8-10. Wilkinson divides her large studio into three parts. The first is the foyer. The second is the assistant's desk, which includes a library. The third part is Wilkinson's desk and conferencing area, which happens to double as her sleeper sofa. (*MZS*)

Figure 8-11. Wilkinson had her desk and shelving custom built because she needed lots of slots in which to pile papers and projects. She painted the components the same buttercup yellow color she painted her walls so that there would be minimal contrast in the apartment. (*MZS*)

Mimi Akins
Psychotherapist
New York, New York

Mimi Akins moved into her New York City apartment in 1975. What a great apartment it is! Two bedrooms, a living room, another "living room" area. Akins didn't set out to practice therapy in her own home, but it turned out to be the best set-up she could ask for.

Before Akins moved into this apartment with her four young children, the apartment was a doctor's office, so there are two front doors to the apartment. One door is an entrance into the apartment from the lobby, and another front door in the second "living room" space is a separate exit onto the street so that her patients don't have to bang into one another:

Never in a million years did I think I'd have a practice of my own when I moved into this apartment—I had four children under the age of 12. We picked the ground floor apartment in this building so that the kids wouldn't make noise up above anyone else. It was also a great apartment because they could get in and out of the house so easily.

I decided that in 1987, I would just use this room with the door to the sidewalk for a therapy room. I didn't have any ideas about how or what I wanted in here except that I needed two chairs and probably a couch. I get into conversations with people, and the set-up of my therapy room is conducive to that.

There are possibilities in the future that I will make my living room more of a therapy room. My living room is now used more as a waiting room. I totally redecorated the room—simplified it—recently because I think I'll be doing more group therapy, so I made it into a room where groups can feel comfortable. I had a lot of Victorian knickknacks around before, but now it's a more streamlined look. I'll probably put a door on the kitchen and onto the hallway entrance so it's an enclosed space for a group.

It's true, my business has taken over my whole apartment, but as my children have moved out, I have the whole apartment to myself. It's a good-sized apartment. But it all works even when the family is here during holidays. I'm never in the living room anyway. I live in the bedroom and the office, which are right across from each other in the hall.

My patients can even use my bathroom, although some people aren't comfortable having clients use their facilities. One man I spoke to who also practiced out of his home had a funny story. He has a great big rambling apartment, but the bathroom is on the other side of the house from the therapy room. He also has a lot of kids in the house. So if anyone asked to use the bathroom, he would fly down the hall to close the doors to his kids' rooms. He said that once clients went to the bathroom in his apartment, they never asked to do it again.

I feel comfortable with this set-up because both my parents were psychoanalysts, so I'm used to having people wander in and out of the house all the time. That's how it was in the Midwest; it was a small community, and you knew your patients and you socialized with your practitioners. It was no big deal. So I've always treated my clients as if they were guests in my home. I serve coffee, and it's comfortable when they are in my home. That's how Jung and Freud worked with their clients in their homes, too.

My philosophy of therapy also makes me comfortable with having my business spread out into my home. I don't work in a patriarchal system in which I'm the authority and you are some sick person coming here. I've set up the office so we are on even ground. The chairs are facing one another— but I have no formal seating arrangement. People sit wherever they choose to sit.

I gain a secondary benefit from working at home. If I did not work at home, I wouldn't be as orderly and as neat as I am. This place stays together, which I know it would not be if I were working away from the home.

I have no discipline whatsoever. Now, people literally come to the door for a session and that in itself disciplines me. I could not do another type job in this home. I can only do a job here that involves appointments.

Figure 8-12. Akins, a psychotherapist and hypnotherapist, lives in an apartment that was formerly a doctor's office. Here's the comfortable therapy room and office that has a door (next to a chair) that exits to the street. Akins uses her living room as a group therapy room. (*MZS*)

Can You Work from Home in a Really Rural Town?

Nancy Glenn
Alternate Work Strategist for Lucent Corporation
Hesperus, Colorado

Nancy Glenn, alternative work strategist for Lucent, moved to Hesperus, a small Colorado mountain town located 28 miles away from Durango, the nearest city. Glenn has telecommuted since 1992 for Lucent, but she had a much easier time of it when she lived in Denver.

When Glenn moved to rural Colorado in 1994, she bought a farmhouse on 7 acres of land. Her home office is located in an extra bedroom with two windows that provide an expansive view of farm country. She looks out over an old schoolhouse that's now a chicken coop, she says.

Though it sounds idyllic, it took Glenn three years to iron out the unanticipated kinks she encountered in putting together a home office in a rural area. Here's her story, and her advice for any would-be rural telecommuters or at-home entrepreneur:

> I live in farm country, and the nearest neighbor is a mile up the road. The kind of work that my husband does led us to move to this area, which we absolutely love, but there are some downsides to it if you're trying to work from home.
>
> Before moving here, I should have done some homework. Had I asked a few questions, I would have had an easier time setting up a home office. I live in an old farmhouse, and when we moved in, I asked the people who sold us the house whether or not I could get two business lines put into the house. They said, "oh, sure." But I didn't follow through with the local phone company. Although US West is the main phone company, there are also lots of little ma and pa phone companies I deal with. They just eliminated party lines about two years ago.
>
> It was quite a struggle with the local phone companies to get my lines up and running at all. It took six months to run lines because the county had a rule that you couldn't have cable laid out across the road. We have dirt roads and tractors out here. We had to hire a contractor to come out here and do some major drilling through rock on either side of the street in order to run cable through it. They also didn't have the proper cabling out here through the rural area that are found in the suburbs. They have what they call "six-pairs," which means we can get only two phone lines run in at once versus three or four lines. They also don't offer voice mail through the local phone companies. So I have to use hardware, and that is difficult when there are lightning storms that mess up the answering machine. The phone is my main connection to the rest of the world, so it has to be running properly.
>
> When I realized there were severe phone problems, I used my calling card to dial out on my home phone. I knew that solution wouldn't work for very long, but I had to sit tight till they figured out the phone line situation. One

of the problems I had was they could only give me two lines, and one had to be dedicated to my fax line. That was really frustrating because I also had to dial in through my modem. After six months of struggling with this, I suggest that people call the phone companies directly; don't rely on a neighbor to tell you about phone service!

I used to get phone bills with advertising inserts that said voice mail was available in my area, but when I called to find out, they said it wasn't available in *my* area of Durango. It was frustrating to get all these flyers in my phone bill, but none of the services applied to me!

Getting my Federal Express boxes is another huge problem in this rural area. I live in what they call a "black-out area." Their delivery time out here is not what it is in a suburb. My packages could come as late as 6 p.m. or the next day if the weather is bad. So if I'm waiting on a conference call and need a package to read through to better understand my client's needs, I work around it as best I can. Sometimes I run to town to pick up my own overnight deliveries. Airborne may not deliver a package to me for up to five days!

I live in the southwest part of Colorado and our house is at 7,000 feet above sea level. And we have mountains with 14,000-foot-high peaks. So we do get a heavy winter. The most annoying this is that if we have bad weather around here, I'll wake up to find the phones are dead. I may have a really important conference call, and I've had to jump in the truck and drive to the nearest pay phone—I've even gone to the middle school and used their pay phone to be on a call or to notify my boss that my lines are down. My husband and I finally invested in cell phones to back us up in case of severe weather conditions. The cell phones do work in our remote area, but, surprisingly, pagers don't!

People in the area don't think I'm strange for working at home. There are a lot of people moving into Durango because they want a better quality of life. They may have been middle management or are executives looking for a change. I'm also two hours from Telluride, which is very telecommuting and Internet savvy. I can't get ISDN now, but I'm trying to stay very active with local phone companies who are asking for input as to what customers will need in the future.

Our telecommuting program at Lucent is a volunteer one. So if you can't see the benefit in the program for you, don't do it. I say that because when I moved out here, the company said, "yes, you can have a home office in a rural area, but remember that you may have something that you may have to deal with that people in the city wouldn't."

For example, I tell people who are thinking of telecommuting from rural areas that their equipment may break. So, they have to be able to find a way to run their business while the equipment is being fixed or replaced. In my own case, I can't have a contracted tech support person drive here from Denver, which is 6 1/2 hours away, to fix my computer or fax machine. I will have to ship my computer to them.

Having done this for five years, I've learned some lessons because I've had equipment break down. Most towns, and we have one right here in

Durango, have office supply shops that rent out a fax machine on a month-to-month basis. I can rent a temporary replacement piece of equipment with my corporate credit card.

My work space is in a separate second bedroom. I have good lighting because I have two windows. I have a desktop PC, a laptop, shelves my husband built, and an ergonomic chair which is the most important thing you can have. It's a very dedicated work area, and I shut the door at the end of the day. I've learned things like how to turn my home phone ringers off in the morning and turn my business ringers on, and at night, to turn off my business and turn on my home ringers. It's my end-of-my-day ritual.

I wanted oak furniture for my home office, and I'm glad I have that instead of contract furniture. I am spread out in other parts of the house. For instance, I have a canning area in the basement with shelving, and it's become a control center to store supplies. I use my basement to store files.

Isolation can be an issue for me, but it's not that bad because I travel an average of two weeks out of the month during my busiest times. I also go to town twice a week to go to the post office.

Had I realized all the problems with phone and delivery service in this area, my husband and I would have revisited our choices. We would have probably rented an office space closer to town, and I would have stayed in constant touch with the phone company until they straightened out my lines.

Figure 8-13. Many of us want to ditch the rat race, move to a farmhouse in the open country, and make a living from home. It's not as idyllic as it sounds, says telecommuter Nancy Glenn, who had to learn the hard way that even the most basic telecommunications services aren't available in rural America. (*Steve Syarto*)

Can You Fit a Retail Business in Your Home?

Tom Gentry
Choo-Choos Trains & More
Plano, Texas

Home-based retail businesses thrive where zoning ordinances allow them to. But where do you put a retail business in your home? How do you deal with customers who want to use your facilities? Here's how one arts and crafts retailer handles those and other questions.

Tom Gentry worked for the government for years before finding his passion in trains. About eight years ago, he bought a train set for the Christmas tree because he had one as a child. He realized tinkering with one train set only on Christmas wouldn't satisfy his new-found love for toy trains. So he decided to open a business devoted to the art of toy trains:

> **The reason I decided to go into business in my home is because it's allowed in this town, and it would keep my overhead down because I didn't really know who in the world would buy toy trains from me in the first place.**
>
> **I started the business in my wife, Gayle's, home office for about the first four months. At the time, my garage was just a typical garage—dark and dirty. My customers were people I already knew because I hadn't yet advertised. Then, I started to convert the garage into a shop little by little by putting up shelves. The garage started out with the first train layout set up on a garbage can. I added a rug on the floor, added legs to the makeshift display, and had tiles on the side as a work surface and metal commercial shelving. It was all real basic.**
>
> **But we knew there was an interest in this business, so we started to remodel the garage within our own limits with shelving and train layouts, little work set up, and it was working. But, it was just okay for me. Then in 1997 Gayle redesigned the garage so that it's more functional, and it's a little too functional for me.**

Gayle, a registered nurse who is employed by a local hospital, is the "idea" person behind the business, says Gentry. She describes how she redesigned the garage to fit in a craft work area, retail space, and office space from which Gentry runs the business:

> **Because I'm around the business enough, I knew what the needs were for the office set-up and how it should be to function well. It was a long process, but the remodeling started in March of 1997. But two-week remodeling plans took more like six weeks to complete. Because the shop was originally a garage, everything looked great on paper, but it was much harder for contractors to actually get it done.**
>
> **It's an adobe house (an adobe is a large building brick made of clay and baked in the sun—irregular walls support large log roof beams), and that means that walls aren't square as they would be in a frame-built house.**
>
> **Some of the other challenges in renovating a garage into a work space have to do with the fact that garages have cement floors. Garage floors also slant**

toward the door, making the room even more uneven. To solve this problem, we used Wilsonart laminate flooring because it's a floating floor that's more forgiving of uneven surfaces. It worked out well, but it was tricky at first.

Adobe houses can cause all kinds of other problems. For instance, the shelves had to be put up and taken down from the walls so many times to get them level because the wall surface was uneven. We have wood beam ceilings, and they are round, and putting lighting up into the ceiling was quite a challenge.

The biggest challenge was fitting in all of Tom's needs into a relatively small space—it's a typical two-car garage measuring 20 by 22 feet. But, of course, we wanted this huge layout to somehow fit into the space. We wanted storage, work space, and retail areas all in this limited space. It's a lot of things to ask for in a two-car garage.

Some people can't possibly fathom giving up a garage to a home-based business. But Gentry doesn't mind using the garage for his shop because he never used his garage for cars, anyhow:

Setting up shop in the garage has improved the look of the house. Most people that come in want to know what room this was before it was the shop because it doesn't look anything like a garage.

It's a fun business. I'm not producing anything that anyone needs, it's more just another toy for mostly big boys. If they have a problem, they call me, but they aren't stranded somewhere or in serious trouble with anything—their lives don't depend on my business, and that's made my life relatively stress-free.

Figure 8-14. Before: A typical garage before the renovation into a retail home office. (*Joshua McHugh/Wilsonart*)

Figure 8-15. After: The new home of Choo-Choos Trains & More, a home-based retail business that sells, buys, and repairs toy trains. The former garage packs in shelving for train set displays, a display table for demonstrations, and an office and workshop area. (*Joshua McHugh/Wilsonart*)

Figure 8-16. After: Gentry's office and workshop area is located behind the counter, but not so out in the open that customers can see what he's working on. The key to organization is the laminate kitchen cabinets. Note the pull-out printer tray. (*Joshua McHugh/Wilsonart*)

Keeping Customers Safe in Your Home-Based Retail Space

About 10 people come through Choo-Choos Trains & More's space every week. Most customers are regulars. Gentry says it's almost like having a bar where people go to take care of their addiction. During the holiday seasons, his business picks up because he's listed in the yellow pages and people want trains for gifts.

"It's impossible to fully kid-proof a space like this, but we try the best we can. Most of the merchandise on the lower shelves is boxed, and Gayle designed a little corner of the space exclusively for kids where there are little play trains, books, gumball machines, stuff like that to attract them. The little tiny kids end up going to the kid's space because it's hands-on and okay. We also have portable steps for them to use so they don't get frustrated because they can't see anything," says Gentry.

The real problem was designing the space so that Gentry could sit at the workbench while customers browsed in the retail space:

> **I was most concerned about keeping tools out of the way and keeping customers safe. Before the redesign, the work space was situated right up front as soon as customers came into the shop. Tom had to get up out of the space to help a customer, and he really couldn't see if anyone went back into the space because it was partially hidden by shelving. He has all kinds of tools and chemicals, and he couldn't tell if a little kid was heading for that area. I knew that had to be addressed in the redesign.**
>
> **Now, Tom sits higher up at the countertop, he can see out, and his tools aren't out in the open anymore. He can help customers from where he sits. Kids tend to stay away from the area because the space is designed with a high partition so that it looks off limits. It's at the back of room, and it's not a desirable spot for kids to go to. His workstation is actually part of the shop, it's where he can see people but can continue to work. And people don't feel pressured by someone hovering over them asking if they need help.**

Owning a home-based retail business means that customers can potentially have public access to your home.

"Luckily, no one accidentally ventures into the house. I think because there are so many home-based businesses out here that people automatically know to call before coming over because they may not be there. It's different from a retail spot that's open with posted hours. Tom is open seven days a week, but people find him through word of mouth or the yellow pages, so people know to call first. We don't have our physical address in the yellow pages because it would be difficult if people showed up and we weren't here to meet them," says Gayle.

The Gentrys warn that a home-based retail business means the lines between home and work are constantly blurred by customers. Gentry is gracious enough to see customers seven days a week, even at night, and up till Christmas Eve for last-minute gifts.

But the biggest impact on personal space came as a surprise to Gayle. "I used to be very private about my own space. But we don't have restroom facilities like regular retail establishments. I understand that people drive a bit of a distance to get to us because we are a little far from the largest city. And people tend to spend a lot of time in the shop—they don't just breeze in and out. They spend on average an hour at a time here at least. It's been suggested we open up a snack area in the shop! But we've had to make our home available to customers who need a restroom. It's forced me to loosen up a bit about my own privacy. To get to the bathroom, people have to walk through the kitchen, the living room, and then down the hall. If we could change one thing, it would be to add a bathroom in the shop. It costs a lot of money to do that, though," adds Gayle.

Securing a retail home business set-up in a garage meant that the Gentrys had to eliminate the garage door. They replaced that door with double doors, but it wasn't secure enough. Eventually, the solution became a simple steel door with a dead bolt.

Quick Tips: The Right Surface for Working with Chemicals

"Before the redesign, I would do my model-making work on some floor tiles placed on top of a workbench. The only chemicals I use are spray paint and an alcohol-based cleaner, but I don't use acid-based chemicals. But just the same, you don't want a kid to get hold of a can of paint or cleaner," says Tom Gentry.

To solve the problem, Gentry now works on a Chemsurf chemical-resistant laminate surface from Wilsonart. There are a few benefits to using a surface like Chemsurf if you work with chemicals in your home office. The company that manufactures the surfacing material says that Chemsurf won't support bacterial growth and can't be contaminated by staph, *e-coli*, strep, or pneumonia. And that's good for food-related home businesses, as well.

Chemsurf is typically used in laboratories and hospitals, but can also be used in photography darkrooms and food-related home businesses, as well. The laminate comes in 20 colors in matte or pearlescent finishes.

Figure 8-17. Gentry used to build and repair trains on a make-shift table. Now he works on Wilsonart's Chemsurf Chemical Resistant Laminate so that chemicals won't eat through the material. The workshop is behind a high countertop so that little children can't get their hands on tools or chemicals. (*Joshua McHugh/Wilsonart*)

Can a Small Business (Four Employees) Thrive in an Apartment?

Karen Gustafson
President, The Gustafson Group
New York City, New York

For years, Karen Gustafson was an editor with a variety of design magazines, and she never thought about opening her own business even though she considers herself to have been an entrepreneurial child, always the one selling holiday cards door to door.

In 1987 she decided to open up her own public relations business out of her apartment in New York. When she started the business, it was just her alone in the office she set up in a room that had been meant to be the library at the entrance of her sprawling apartment.

During the first year she was in business, it began to get increasingly lonely in her home office. So Gustafson installed work surfaces along one of the walls so that she'd be ready to expand one day. Although Gustafson knew she wanted to expand, she never expected to have at times three to six employees (including interns) working in her apartment. With that many employees, she has had to utilize other areas of her apartment to accommodate her growing business:

I've expanded to have four people in the office, plus an intern from New York University. Originally, I didn't think I'd end up with this many people. I thought I'd end up with just one other person besides myself.

When other interns come in, we use other rooms in the apartment such as the dining room. Because of the expansion, right now I float and don't really sit in any one office. I used to have a desk, but now I just work on the dining room table. I might make the dining room into more of my own office. One of my ideas for the dining room would be to keep the dining table—we still need a big table for collating—but I would set up a desk by the window as my office. We haven't used the dining room as a dining room for a long time. We go out to dinner most of the time.

There is a second office that I had to set up in the room off the kitchen that is the original maid's room. My other interns work there, I store my clients' materials in there, as well.

Storage was a big issue for us, especially in dealing with materials for our clients. Each client has their own set of stationery, paper, press kits, photography, binders. I bought high, heavy-duty shelving.

The back area of the apartment consists of two bedrooms, which is our private living area. A door separates that space from the rest of the apartment. Sometimes people cook their lunches in the kitchen. It's nice to eat together during the day. I have one child grown and living on her own. I always thought it would be fun to have lots of children, so in a way, the business is like having a big family.

I don't think working for an employer who happens to be in a home office is for everyone. It depends on what stage an employee is at in his or her career and social life. They may want to work in that huge corporation where they can meet other people. I let prospective employees know right away that we are in a home office.

There have been times when I had bad colds, but I haven't been terribly sick since I started the business. Part of it is a mental attitude. I remember when I was an editor that I was sick and had to stay home. When you know it would be inconvenient to stay in bed ill while you know your business has to go on—and that it will go on in the same apartment—you just don't let yourself get too sick. If I get sick, it seems to always happen on a weekend.

You always have to be on your toes when you have employees in your home. My husband puts up with more than anyone. Sometimes there are reasons we need to be up and working at 8 o'clock in the morning or even earlier.

I've thought about moving the business out of my apartment and into an office. We've thought about which area to move to. Last year we thought about it because we were working on a cookbook to benefit the Momentum Aids Project—it's called *Delicious by Design—Architects and Designers in the Kitchen*. We gathered recipes from 80 architects and designers. It's taken up so much room. The dining room became the cookbook room.

Then there are other moments when we are working on trade show materials, and that means putting press kits together for each client, and then I think we need to have a huge loft space. But I go back and forth. There are some great advantages to staying here. It's comfortable. But there are times I that I think we could use another room. I haven't looked at spaces, but I thought about it. If we moved, it would be for my husband so that he could have the entire apartment back.

For now, I'm continuing to learn how to encourage everyone to have a say in how the office is laid out in its design. Charles has personalized his space to a degree, but I need to encourage that more with everyone. I'm encouraging everyone to give me ideas on how to reorganize and change things.

It's one thing to be the principal of the company, and it's another thing to have the office in your home. It's too easy for me to make all the decisions, and that's an intrusion on employees. You have to be aware of that issue.

In a way, it's like having our home in our office rather than having our office in our home.

Figure 8-18. The Gustafson Group teams at the conference table in the main home office. Gustafson feels as though her home is in her office rather than feeling as though her office is in her home. In reality, she has transformed most of her apartment into work quarters to accommodate her growing employee base. (*MZS*)

From Disaster to Efficiency: How One Small Business Got Organized

The home office of Ancient Sun, located in Corrales, New Mexico, was as about as inefficient as you can get. The home-based business that designed and created jewelry operated in a 400-square-foot work space that accommodated up to four people at one time while combining administrative, design, production, storage, shipping, and receiving bunched together without any rhyme or reason behind the layout.

A design team, Marie Henkel, ASID, and Janis LaFountain, ASID, of Design Works in Albuquerque, were called in for the overhaul. What needed to be done was to create a work space that effectively accommodated all the diverse activities in one small area.

Lots of built-in storage out of Wilsonart laminate and one big laminate worktable with drawers on the side to store inventory organized the Ancient Sun company.

Note the important change in seating. Old, worn-out kneeling chairs and hard-backed chairs were replaced with ergonomic seating from The Hon Company and task lighting from Tech Lighting.

Figures 8-19 and 8-20. Before Wilsonart came to the rescue, Ancient Sun, a jewelry manufacturing company, worked in make-shift quarters with materials thrown in rolling carts and hung on cork-boards. They also sat in poor seating and had inadequate lighting. *(Joshua McHugh/Wilsonart)*

Figures 8-21 and 8-22. After: Ancient Sun has a healthier work environment for the jewelry designers with ergonomic seating from HON plus overhead task lighting by Tech Lighting. A main work table with side drawers organizes materials used to make jewelry. (*Joshua McHugh/Wilsonart*)

Can You Afford a Barrier-Free Home Office?

David Grant Grimshaw
Cofounder of the Westport Gallery
Chairman of the ALS Association of Connecticut
Founder of the Artists Foundation
Black Rock, Connecticut

David Grant Grimshaw is a fine artist and writer, known for his esoteric oil paintings of landscapes and nudes. In 1996, Grimshaw was diagnosed with ALS (amyotrophic lateral sclerosis), a potentially fatal disease of the nervous system, also known as Lou Gehrig's disease, named after the baseball player who died of it in 1941.

Although Grimshaw has increasing problems with his mobility and ability to paint, he nevertheless leads a number of businesses from his home office. It's quite apparent when you visit Grimshaw that his quality of life is rich and full. He had a porch built overlooking the water of the Long Island Sound. The porch is accessible through a door from the home office, a room that is comfortable, cozy, and obviously productive.

In 1996, Grimshaw and his wife moved from their large house into a smaller house where it would be easier to move around as ALS progressed. Grimshaw knew he had to make sure the office could accommodate him once he began to use a wheelchair. Making an office barrier-free may not include as many expensive alterations as you may think:

> When I moved into this new house, I knew I had to make the office as barrier-free as possible due to my handicap. I may have to add structural changes around the house as the disease progresses, but I wanted to get the office done first since I am here so much of the day.
>
> I chose this room to be my home office because it is right next to the bedroom and the bathroom. I sought out a house that could give me this kind of configuration. I also knew I needed only one-level living. And I knew I wanted a house to look directly out over the water so that I could enjoy the views all the time.
>
> In the warmer weather I will go out on the porch all the time. Once I'm in the wheelchair, I'll have an easier time getting out onto the porch. Now I walk, but it's very precarious. We specifically added on the porch so that I could use it to draw, paint, and do work on.
>
> This office is unusual in that it combines a painting studio and an association office and an office where I write. Artists tend to work in a studio where they can slap paint on a canvas and it won't matter where else the paint lands. Because of my limited movement, I'm not as messy with my painting anymore. I used to spray paint and get it all over the place. I paint more gently now. Now I paint by putting a brace on my arm and the brush slides into it. I may go a week without painting now. Sometimes I paint every day. But I need help setting up and breaking down for painting so I'm somewhat limited by who is available to help me. Once you are committed to a pursuit, it's hard to leave it behind entirely.

Figure 8-23. Grimshaw gave great thought to how his home office should be arranged to accommodate his needs as his disease, ALS, weakens his motor skills. He will soon be using a motorized wheelchair, but he doesn't need to buy a new desk or widen the doorways. A motorized height-adjustable work surface is a good barrier-free solution, but it costs a lot of money. (*MZS*)

Figure 8-24. Grimshaw moved to a ranch house once he was diagnosed. He had a porch added and a door installed that lead to the outdoor area so that he can wheel outside directly from his home office during warmer months. Again, the door is a normal width and will accommodate a wheelchair. (*MZS*)

In the office, I made sure the hardwood floors would be bare with no carpeting so that I can get around when I start to use a wheelchair. I needed to make sure I had easy access to this porch so we added this doorway. I also have a ramp for handicap access—even though I don't use a wheelchair now, I will be soon.

I won't have to widen any of the doorways. It's perfectly wide enough for a wheelchair. Wheelchairs are only 21 to 28 inches wide, and most doors are 32 inches wide.

I might have needed more room if I were going to use my arms to wheel myself around. My arms are too weak to do that so I'll use a motorized wheelchair or someone will push me in.

When I start to use the wheelchair, I will have to move some miscellaneous furniture out of the way. The wheelchair is a little scary in that it is quite powerful so if you misjudge it a little, you can quite easily bang into things.

I'll be able to sit in the wheelchair using the same desk I have here now. I haven't practiced using the wheelchair yet, because I'll have time to practice soon enough. The desk is a little too narrow for a wheelchair to pull up close to the surface. But I don't use a keyboard for my computer anyhow, so it won't be too much of an issue. I have an onscreen keyboard. It tries to predict the word you are going to use after you use a mouse to click on a couple of letters and types it out.

In the world of ALS there are quite a few assistive technologies. There are support groups online that offer information on this (see resources appendix). I publish a monthly journal online for ALS and another one for assistive technology information.

With ALS, you tend to lose your voice. I don't have to stop using the phone, but I can have it broadcast directly onto the computer screen. If I lose the ability to use a mouse, I will be able to do all of this with eye movements. It's done not with a camera, but with a pair of eyeglasses.

There are always a lot of people coming in and out of the house. Between ALS business, and my community involvement, and gallery business, plus carpenters, and I have a home aide that comes regularly to help me exercise, I'm never lonely. People think I'm sitting around all by myself, but I'm hardly isolated or lonely. Isolation is never an issue.

Can You Work with an Assistant in Your Home Office?

Julie Taylor
Principal, Taylor & Company, Publicity and Marketing Firm
Beverly Hills, California

In the February/March 1998 issue of *Fast Company Magazine,* there's an all-too-true-to-life cartoon on page 30, titled "The Self-Employed." A man stands talking on the phone while in front of him sit his alert and attentive cat and dog. The man looks at the cat and dog and says over the phone, "I can't talk right now, I'm reorganizing my staff."

That's what self-employment is like—unless you have an assistant, which changes the dynamics of your work-at-home lifestyle.

Julie Taylor, a magazine editor in her former life, now runs a public relations and marketing consulting company and is the author of the book *Outdoor Rooms* (Rockport Press, 1998)

Her business has grown and diversified so much over the past year that she finally realized she'd have to share her home office with a much-needed assistant. Taylor has great insights, tips, and ideas about how to work with an assistant, and how to set up a work space so that two people can work together in harmony:

My home office is in the second bedroom of a two-bedroom apartment. My assistant comes in part-time, and she comes in two afternoons a week and all day Friday.

The second bedroom wasn't always the office. For two years, it was my art studio, and it slowly evolved into the office. What I really hated about the office was that there was no rhyme or reason as to how it was set up since I never planned it out. I never intended to have a home office, but my business grew, and it worked well.

About a month ago, I realized I had to upgrade this office. My assistant was in place for a couple of months before I reconfigured. But it gets to the point where you say to yourself that it can't go on like this one more day.

For starters, I didn't know where to put the computer I was getting for my assistant. And, it was to the point where my assistant and I were crawling all over each other because things were all over the place.

So I called up one of my clients, who is a space planner and architect, and pleaded for her to come over and tell me what to do. I told her I just don't know where to put furniture. She drew up a plan for an L-shaped work surface to support both me and my assistant in one space.

The new work surface that my client planned for me is simply white laminate crafted by a closet company, The Closet Warehouse in Los Angeles. They measured my walls, fabricated the work surfaces, made a 6-foot-long and 3-foot-high shelving unit to put over the work surface for more storage. They made and installed all of that for $500, and you *won't* believe how long it took.

I know a lot of furniture designers, but I realized I needed something quick, cheap, and fast. The closet company was able to do it quickly. I asked what the turnaround was, and she said "five."...and I was thinking five weeks? She meant five days! They measured twice. They had to come back the next day

after installation because when the guy was drilling the grommet for wires in the laminate, the drill went a little out of control and damaged a piece of laminate, but they came back the next day with a new piece.

I've learned quite a few things about working in a home office with an assistant. When I was looking for an assistant, the first thing I'd say to them on the initial phone call is first, this is a home office and second, I have a cat.

I know it's strange to say all that immediately, but I wanted to let them know up front that if they were looking for a corporate environment, this wouldn't be the right place for them and they wouldn't be happy. I wanted to find out if they were allergic to cats, too. That's the reality. I was completely clear about the working conditions.

The first interview with everyone I saw was held outside of the home office at Starbucks. When I narrowed the list down to who I wanted to see for a second interview, then they'd come to the apartment because I wanted them to see the office and get an idea of the clients involved. I also wanted to see if they got along with my cat because he owns the place.

One thing I had to know I could do before bringing in an assistant was afford a cleaning person every week. If you have people in your house and they are going to be there for a very long time, your home becomes their workplace, so you wanted to make sure it is neat and clean all the time.

I know what it's like to work with other people in their home. When I first moved to New York City, I worked in someone's home for two years—with the dogs, with the kids—and we worked on the kitchen table to put out a parents' magazine. I'd go to work 9-to-5 in their apartment, which was not remotely set up as an office. I worked on the table, in the living room, kids and dog running around—it was a magazine for parents, so if someone called and the kids were screaming, we'd say we had a day-care center there. If the dogs were barking, we'd say we had a kennel.

I knew from that experience that working in someone else's home could be strange at best. I try to be really respectful. There are those times when I'm in my scruffy clothes, and I have to change while my assistant is still working. It is what it is.

When my first assistant left after a month to move to San Francisco, I had my locks changed. She was terrific, but you just don't know someone well after a month. You really have to go on your intuition when hiring for a home office than in a corporate office.

More Suggestions for Making Your Home Office Employee-Friendly

"My boss would be waking up as I arrived in the morning. He started work in his bathrobe. I was constantly listening to family quarrels and being disturbed by barking dogs and the roar of the vacuum cleaner. I definitely didn't feel like I was in a career-building situation," says a writer who worked as an assistant to a writer in a Los Angeles home office (see Rushfield, 1997).

Figures 8-25 and 8-26. Before (above): Taylor and her assistant worked on slabs of porous wood. Taylor knew both she and her assistant needed a more efficient work space. After (below): Taylor now has an L-shaped work surface that houses computers on one part and free space for project work on the other side. Although at first Taylor didn't think the articulating keyboards would be beneficial, now she thinks they are indispensable. Trays get keyboards off the desk, giving Taylor and her assistant more work surface. (*Julie Taylor*)

Figures 8-27 and 8-28. The key to working in a home office with an assistant is the ability to share resources. Taylor never hoarded her Rolodexes and always kept them in a common area. But she took the next step by adding a flowchart (right) so that her assistant could keep track of where the projects were heading. An erasable flow chart like this has made working life much easier for Taylor and her assistant. (*Julie Taylor*)

What can you do to make your assistant feel comfortable?

◆ Keep family out of the home office.

◆ Outfit the home office as professionally as you can.

◆ Wake up at least an hour before your assistant is due to arrive.

◆ Don't work in your bathrobe around your assistant.

◆ Don't fight with family members when your assistant is around.

◆ Give your assistant a place of his or her own—even if it's a small space—and out of respect, give your assistant a good ergonomic chair.

◆ Try to locate your office where there is a separate entrance so that your assistant doesn't have to trudge through the house to get to work.

◆ Don't share romantic moments with your spouse in front of your assistant.

◆ Push your assistant to get out of the office and meet clients, do errands, or take personal time so that he or she won't feel as though the office is a prison.

◆ Let your assistant use your stove or refrigerator if he or she wants to.

◆ Keep your bathroom clear and free of dirty clothing or other personal items so that your assistant doesn't feel uncomfortable.

◆ Share supplies with your assistant.

◆ Make sure your assistant has a phone of his or her own and doesn't have to reach over you to make a call.

Can Marital Bliss Blossom in a Basement Home Office?

Elaine and Richard Turek
Owners, Big Daddy Digital, Imaging Specialists
Wallingford, Connecticut

As soon as their first child was born, Elaine and Richard Turek knew they wanted to own a home-based business together. Elaine had a high-profile job as a leather goods buyer for a retail store, Steinbach's, which included lots of travel overseas. Richard was a museum curator for a while until he learned the printing business. But Elaine knew she did not want to be "supermom" for long; she wanted to be at home with the kids.

The Tureks tried out a few home-based businesses over the years: They bought handyman special houses, fixed them up, and sold them, they tried the specialty foods business, and even had a day-care business for a year. Elaine Turek describes her experience this way:

> Everything I did was to be around the kids. Owning a business when kids are too young can put you in a compromising position. I couldn't develop enough time to get any business fully off the ground when I had young kids around. If the kids were home and I had an appointment, my priority was to stay with the kids. When the kids reached the ages of 10 and 13, I knew that they were okay when they got home from school because they were older and more independent. It was at that point we knew that owning our own home business would be feasible.
>
> We started this business the day the kids started school in September 1995. Rick and I are partners. He's the creative end, I'm the business end. This is the first time we've worked together, but it's what we've always wanted to do. We don't mind being together at all although he says sometimes that we need separate offices because he's concentrating on his work while I need to talk.
>
> We work so well together, but sometimes being together is a distraction. Sometimes we are challenged to stay focused so that we don't goof off and play for too long. One time we were both screaming at each other when he was trying to teach me his graphics programs. He's a good teacher, but with me he's impatient. We've had wars on this subject.
>
> But we don't get in each other's way. He listens to me while I'm on the phone. He'll coach me, and I can coach him. He'll tell me maybe I should have said something differently, or emphasize this, or you're too wishy-washy. Usually you know when someone's right. It's like having a coach there telling me how I'm doing.
>
> We have a three-bedroom house, so we worked in one of the bedrooms before we fixed up the basement for our office. Both of my children were in the same bedroom. We never even thought about putting an office in the cellar, but we were forced to because my kids wanted their own rooms now that they were older.

We work so much better down here in the basement. We were much too distracted upstairs. We are still distracted, but less so. We don't have a closed-door policy. The kids know when to be quiet—for instance, when we are on the phone with a client—since they are so used to our business now. We didn't have that many clients calling us when we were first got started so it was easy to train the kids on when to be quiet. You have to train them. We tell them they can't use line 2 until after 8:00 p.m., for instance. There are some things that they don't understand yet.

When we set up the office, Rick and I were going to sit with our backs to each other in case we didn't get along! But we both wanted windows. And the tables we bought dictated how we sit. Because of the equipment, we could spend no money on furniture. So we bought a $36 and a $48 folding table that sit side by side. Decor was a problem between Rick and I. I had curtains up at first. I love curtains; he hates curtains.

We realized the other side of the basement would make a great catch-all room where we could meet with clients. So we are remodeling that room, too. We haven't had any clients come here because we just didn't have the proper room for them to sit and talk. We've had to meet clients in parking lots! But we won't have to do that for much longer.

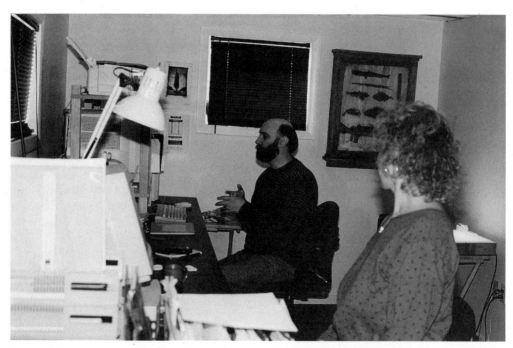

Figure 8-29. The Tureks work side by side in a basement home office. The key to working with your spouse in a small home office is that you must be best friends, says Elaine Turek. The downside of working with your best friend? There's too many opportunities for having fun and forgetting about work. *(MZS)*

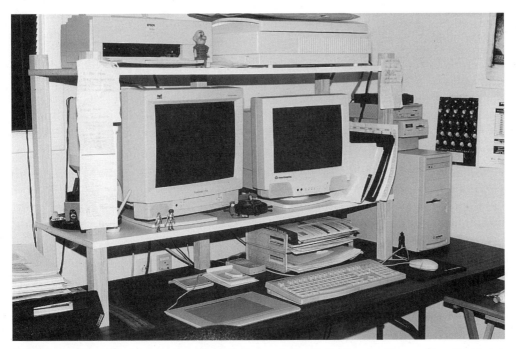

Figure 8-30. Richard Turek has thousands of dollars of equipment in the basement home office. The biggest mistake anyone can make when planning a basement home office? Putting your equipment right beneath pipes, as Richard admits to doing. He avoided problems by boxing in the pipes so that they wouldn't be so quick to leak onto equipment. (*MZS*)

Lessons to Remember about Basement Home Officing

The Tureks fixed up their basement into a home office in one month. In that time, they painted and hired an electrician to come in and rearrange some wiring and replace old plugs with grounded plugs for a cost of $400.

They are lucky because the office is in a part of the basement that isn't buried, so they don't feel confined. There are two windows that bring in lots of sunlight and a view. Although there are windows, the Tureks hated the way the basement looked before they removed the drop ceiling. "It looked like a catacomb down here," says Elaine Turek. "As soon as we took the ceiling down, we felt more comfortable down here."

When they took the ceiling down, they saw water stains on the wood. Richard Turek realized that the kitchen sink, directly above the basement room, probably leaked from time to time. So Richard decided to do a couple of things. He decided that everything, including wires on the ceiling, would be painted white to reduce the visual mess that drop ceilings tend to conceal.

"Because it was old basement wood, we had to paint it by hand, and give it two solid coats of Kilz brand stain blocker (around $10 a gallon), and as things bled through, we'd hit them again. I hit some of the knots six times and then used three coats of stain blocker so that brown water stains wouldn't leak through the paint two months later. This stain blocker helps to keep the ceiling looking crisp," says Richard.

For lighting the low ceiling of a basement, they chose to install two tracks of compact halogen lights because they are extra bright. Then they turn the bulbs so the light hits the wall and bounces light out into the rest of the space (see Figure 8-31).

Richard has some more lessons for anyone planning a home office in the basement:

- Take precautions, and don't put thousands of dollars worth of equipment directly under a pipe.

- If you are forced to put your equipment under a pipe, as in the case of the Tureks, do what Richard did to prevent leaks—box in the pipe with wood that can be easily removed—in case the pipe leaks, it won't pour onto the equipment.

- Be careful you don't put your equipment under a sink—if it accidentally overflows, it will leak down into the office.

- The Turek's washing machine overflowed, and they had to take up their office rug a few times to soak up the water—make sure you can easily take up your floor covering.

- If your basement is cool, don't use an electric heater—use an oil-filled one that doesn't have exposed coils.

Figure 8-31. The best way to brighten a basement home office is to paint the walls, ceiling, and pipes a bright white and then add halogen track lights. The Tureks added these mini-halogen-lights because the fixtures don't hang down low and they give off a bright light that washes the walls, then bounces out into the room so that it's not overlit. (*MZS*)

Can a Journalist Ever Find Enough Storage?

Barbara Mayer
Journalist and Author
Pound Ridge, New York

Barbara Mayer has worked as a journalist for years. She started as a full-time furniture reporter for the long-time published Fairchild publication, *Home Furnishings Daily*. When her family moved out of New York City, Mayer didn't want the commute into the city anymore, and she started to build her freelance career. She's the furniture reporter for the Associated Press, the author of two books, the editor of a gardening publication, and the writer of several other freelance projects.

Mayer has quite a busy journalism business, which means that she gathers a ferocious amount of papers, press kits, catalogs, books, magazines, and newspapers—you name it, she has it. Although she has always worked in an office that is located in a loft area of her custom-built, octagonal-shaped house designed by architect Buckminster Fuller, the lack of storage is becoming a problem for her because the house was built without a basement or a garage:

> **My home office was always upstairs. But more and more projects have made me take over the back of the loft space, and the entire upstairs has became my work space.**
>
> **Storage is a big problem. As a journalist with many projects, not only do I have a huge amount of materials such as books, notes, and articles on every subject, in addition, I have to file and come up with a story idea every day of the week, so I have to save a lot of stuff. I have four to five assignments I'm working on at a time. I make one pile per assignment.**
>
> **At this moment, my files are filled with stuff to be thrown away. Every once in a while I go through the files, and it's like a trip down memory lane, and I can hardly get rid of anything. I think to myself that maybe I'll throw those contracts away, but what if I need them, or what about notes from craft book material? I have a huge box up there with files from one book, but don't know what to do! One solution would be to rent storage space, take huge files and put them there. Two of the books I wrote created huge files that are in my file cabinet consuming the whole cabinet!**
>
> **To clean out my file cabinets to make room for stuff, it would take two weeks of my getting up every morning and doing nothing but cleaning out the drawers and organizing. It doesn't work for me to do an hour at a time. I have to do it at one time. I have a good time doing it, but it takes too long.**
>
> **I also get a huge amount of mail, and that's a terrible problem. I get so much mail that I have to stop the mail when I go away. As a freelancer, you give up having an office with services like having huge trash bins.**
>
> **I receive press materials, posters, and invitations in huge boxes. There was a phase where every company was sending invitations with confetti inside, so I'd open up the box or envelope and the confetti would go all over the place! I'd have to vacuum all the time. At the corporate office, you just leave confetti there and someone else cleans it up for you. Sometimes I get huge cartons of materials, and**

then I have to figure out how to throw that kind of thing in the garbage.

Books are another issue. I want a bookcase on castors, but I'm not sure if it will be too heavy to move. Right now, my bookshelves are leaning over.

My biggest problem is finding the time to clear the decks. Do I really need to keep an annual report I used for a story or book? Probably not. But I need to file so that I know where to retrieve materials for ideas. But that takes an inordinate amount of time and I don't have a secretary.

Figure 8-32. Mayer's home office is a loft area. Her desk and files divide the space. One side is the computer area. In back of the desk is the storage area for her books. (*MZS*)

Figure 8-33. Journalists like Mayer receive many books as press gifts, and they use many books for researching articles and other projects. Instead of putting these shelves against a wall, Mayer made the most out of a small space for her library of books by arranging the shelving at angles. (*MZS*)

Figure 8-34. Mayer is running out of shelving space for her books, so she takes the beautiful art books downstairs and gracefully stacks them in her living room. Note the box in the picture—journalists constantly receive boxes of press materials. Work-at-home journalists have to contend with the enormous amount of garbage this mail creates. (*MZS*)

Can an Architect Run a Business from a Tiny Home Office?

Mary Davis
Principal
Mary Davis Architect
New York, New York

Davis worked for one of the largest architectural design firms in the country, HLW, until she left a few years ago to have her first child. After some time went by, she felt ready to return to the working world, but she couldn't envision herself going back to being an associate in a large firm. Though she spoke to a few headhunters to find a position, she knew an associate's position would not allow her the flexibility she needed with a young daughter just starting school.

During the period she struggled with her decision to go back to work, she began to retain a couple of clients, so she decided to make a go of opening her own architectural practice in her apartment.

The home office is off of the living room, away from the "hub" of the house, which Davis considers to be her daughter Sally's room. Sally's room is on one end of the rambling apartment, and Davis's office is at the opposite side of the floor plan:

> **My business has evolved into a successful operation. I've had as many as three full-time clients at a time—one church and two residences. In addition, I let my husband use the office for special projects.**

Figure 8-35. Davis's home office is off of the living room, but far, far away from the kitchen and "hub" of the house, which she says is her young daughter Sally's room. The simple table here is a conferencing table at which Davis meets with visiting clients. (*MZS*)

The office is away from the hub of the home. The office phone rings only in the office, not throughout the rest of the house. Even in the kitchen, I can't hear the phone. I also have two voice-mail services to separate home and business. I know people who have home offices, and their phone rings everywhere, and they are always on the phone with clients, even with company over, and that infuriates me.

Sally's room is the hub of the house. But when she has a play date, I don't even hear them when I'm in my office. The guest bedroom next to her bedroom would have been an ideal home office, and it's bigger than the office I'm in now, and people ask why the office isn't in that room. But it's right next door to Sally's room.

Though my office is a small space and I'm busy, I'm actually very organized. I designed this shelving unit with cubicles designated to hold one project at a time. I have to be organized since having a five-year-old and working at home are two full-time jobs. The trick for me is to keep organized—I work best when everything is neat. When I finish a project, I just get rid of everything to clear the space.

The computer is the one single thing that has helped me. I have a virtually paperless office. I rely on e-mail, but I don't print out my e-mails.

When I worked for HLW, I worked in a pool. It was bright with lots of ambient lighting and four other architects in my area, plus a secretary for our pool. The things that make it difficult to work for myself are not having someone to go have coffee with and having to be self-sufficient without a support staff.

Figure 8-36. Davis has lots of work surface at the other end of the small home office. She purposely hid the computer and work space so that it couldn't be seen from the living room. There's enough space for an assistant to sit should she hire one in the future. (*MZS*)

For example, my lighting went out today. I don't have anyone to call to say, "Hey, come fix my lighting." I have no maintenance staff! If the computer is on the blink, I fix it! Or I'm on the phone with MCI, which takes up a huge chunk of time.

I can't just walk over to a copier and make a copy and come back to my desk. I find that when I'm making copies now, I'm buying milk, too. I am constantly organizing all the elements for efficiency. The number of things I have in my head at one time overwhelms me.

After saying all that, I still believe it's not easier for me to work in a corporation. I'm my own boss, and I have no one to answer to. The way I relate to my clients is very different now because I'm talking directly to them now. I don't have to seek approval from a boss in order to call and give a client information. When you work for a corporation, you are always operating under a corporate umbrella, representing a "we" and never just yourself. But now I can tell my clients what's on my mind—it made me a better salesperson.

Figure 8-37. Davis designed a series of cubbyholes, and she designates one cubbyhole per project. It's her way of keeping projects that involve bits and pieces of materials like stone or tile organized. You don't have to custom-build the cubicles as Mary did; you can use stacked baskets, bins, or cubes to the same benefit. (*MZS*)

Figure 9-1. The file tote: the symbol of telecommuting. It's a myth that telecommuters need only a computer to be productive. Oftentimes telecommuters have to tote files from office to home in order to work. (*Rubbermaid*)

9

Understanding the Telecommuter's World

Thanks to a memorable television commercial aired by MCI in 1996 and 1997 that depicts a telecommuter working from home in pajamas and slippers while teleconferencing with a room full of corporate workers dressed in crisp blue suits and wing tips, "telecommuting" has become a household word.

The word *telecommuting* is used quite loosely. Many people call themselves "telecommuters" when in fact they are really consultants and business owners who happen to work at home.

If you want to work at home but aren't ready to strike out on your own as a business owner, there is another option. You can telecommute for your current company. If your company has a formal telecommuting program, you are already familiar with the terminology and the concept.

If your company is in the dark ages and doesn't have a program, perhaps it's time for you to enlighten them and start your own informal telecommuting pilot within your department.

You wouldn't be reading this book if you didn't want to work at home. But before you march into your manager to ask him or her if you can telecommute, know the basics, read a book that specializes on telecommuting exclusively (see resources appendix), and talk to someone else who telecommutes. How you spend your days as a telecommuter would be quite different from how you would spend your days working as an at-home entrepreneur.

Telecommuters are one segment of the work-at-home market. Unfortunately, we tend to lump telecommuters together with work-at-home business owners. But they are two different "breeds" of the at-home worker.

First of all, let's define the word *telecommuter*. For most companies, a telecommuter or teleworker by definition is a corporate employee who works from home on a consistent basis—usually one or more days a week. Companies further define a part-time telecommuter as someone who works at home one to three days a week; a full-time telecommuter is someone who works from home five days a week.

Why Are Telecommuters Different from Home-Based Entrepreneurs?

"A telecommuting day is just like any other day at the corporate office, except that I'm working from a remote site," says Sara Smith,* a telecommuter from the New York Department of Transportation (DOT) at a seminar sponsored by the Telecommuting Advisory Council of New York. "The work hours are exactly the same as they would be if I were in the office, 8:00 a.m. to 4:00 p.m., but I have the opportunity to start a half hour earlier or later than my coworkers who are in the office."

Now how many home-based business owners do you know work only eight hours a day?

A telecommuter is still first and foremost a corporate employee. A telecommuter has one foot in the corporate office and one foot in the home office. But the bottom line is that telecommuters work for a company; they don't work for themselves. That should clear up the confusion about the difference between a telecommuter and business owner who both work from home.

There are other differences between the telecommuter and at-home business owner, too. A telecommuter is expected to be accessible by phone or computer 100 percent of the time. That means the phone is usually forwarded to the home line on the days the employee works at home so that a ringing phone doesn't add extra burden to nontelecommuting staff members.

"The problem with that is that once the calls are forwarded, you are expected to answer them, and no one is expected to answer the phone but you," says Smith*, the DOT telecommuter. "If you step away from your desk where the phone is, you have to run like mad whenever you hear the phone ringing.

"I moved into a new house and put the home office in the basement, but found I was running like crazy to get the phone every time it rang downstairs. I was losing weight from running up and down steps, but it wasn't working out."

This particular telecommuter found a solution to the phone problem. She switched her business line onto a cordless phone. "I take the cordless phone into the bathroom with me so I don't miss one call," she says. "I never go anywhere without my cordless phone."

Other companies discourage telecommuters from using portable phones because wandering around the house can distract a worker.

"I tried using the portable phone, and I feel I lost a lot of discipline with it," says telecommuter Nancy Glenn, an alternate work strategist for Lucent Technologies who helps the company's telecommuters in her region set up their home work spaces and work processes. "I need a stationary phone because it gives me that extra added discipline so that I have to answer my phone in my dedicated office area and I can't get up and walk around in the kitchen or anywhere else with the phone.

"I found that the people I set up with portable phones call me later to switch to a stationary phone," says Glenn. "They find using a portable phone is hard on them."

*Name has been changed.

They need the phone to stay put on the desk so that they are tied to the desk. You may think you are disciplined, but you need to have that extra system in place to help you stay even more disciplined. I don't even recommend cell phones to telecommuters because then you can start sitting outside, daydreaming, sloughing off, and you may not even know that you are doing it!"

Telecommuters are accountable for every moment of their day compared to an at-home business owner who is not bound by these rules. Telecommuters have to sign legal agreements that state when their day starts and when it ends and how many days they agree to work at home, along with other points that must be adhered to that have been drafted by managers and the heads of telecommuting program. Work-at-home business owners only have to commit to themselves.

Telecommuters are lucky in that most employers give them equipment, such as a computer, a fax machine, and an extra phone line with which to set up a home office. The business owner has to purchase his or her own equipment and furniture although it is tax deductible.

Telecommuters are also lucky in that they have a built-in help desk to troubleshoot equipment problems. Many of them are trained to troubleshoot their own problems, as well.

"We have our automation department show everyone how to troubleshoot computers," says Smith, the DOT telecommuter. "Before they leave to telecommute, they have to take apart equipment and put it back together in front of the automation department, no joke. All regional offices have the same kind of equipment as the telecommuters have so if there's a real problem when they are telecommuting, the automation department can tap into their system to guide them through the technical problems. It comes in very handy."

Home-based business owners don't have that kind of help: "We have a few computer consultants on hand who have come highly recommended, but we are always looking for more," says Karen Gustafson, president of the Gustafson Group in New York City. "Unfortunately, we go through them fast. We find an independent consultant that we like, and the next thing he or she tells us is that he or she has taken a permanent job some place and isn't available anymore."

Besides giving telecommuters equipment and troubleshooting help, employers may also give their work-at-home staff home office furniture.

The standards for furniture provisions for telecommuters are a little more blurry because every company has a different policy. Nevertheless, in setting up a home office, many telecommuters receive one of the following opportunities from their employer:

◆ The option to take home an unused desk, chair, or file cabinet from the corporate office

◆ A small stipend (anywhere from $500 to $2,500 depending on the company) to purchase home office furniture

◆ A choice of one of two home office furniture ensembles that is delivered to the home and assembled for the telecommuter (This is usually an option with the most progressive companies).

A Look at Telecommuting through Rose-Colored Glasses

You may think that a telecommuter has the best of both worlds. But it depends on your personality, whether you will prefer working as a telecommuter or as a home-based business owner.

I informally telecommuted from my staff job one or two days a week as needed. The company didn't have a telecommuting program, so I was on my own in setting up my home office. However, the company did pay for any business related phone calls and small supplies I needed to work at home. But I still had to pay out of my own pocket for printer ink, electricity, and even America Online though I used it for business. I will admit that trying to be reimbursed for the cost of one month of using my home-based AOL account for business purposes caused a problem with my manager.

When I telecommuted, I was held accountable for what I did on those days. I had to fill out a schedule sheet posted outside my boss's office that listed what I would be working on for the days I spent telecommuting. And I was accountable for handing in those projects completed when I came in the next day.

During the days I telecommuted, I checked my voice mail every hour or so and proceeded to return calls. The office would often call me at home asking me to "put my hands" on something they needed right away that was sitting on my desk at work, which was more than frustrating.

All in all, it was a positive experience to telecommute for three years for two different bosses who never telecommuted. But it is different from working at home as a business owner. Now I pay for everything out of my own pocket. The beauty of being an at-home business owner versus working as a telecommuter is that I don't have to be accountable to anyone else except myself. That's the beauty of owning your own business versus telecommuting where you are still working to produce for someone else's company instead of your own.

Although telecommuters have a company to back them up, some employers don't give their telecommuting programs enough resources to make the telecommuter completely confident in themselves when they work at home.

For instance, results from a Pacific Bell survey of 100 human resource managers randomly chosen from top California businesses indicate that, while almost all companies recognize the productivity and morale benefits associated with telecommuting, few have devoted enough resources needed to move it into the mainstream as a formal, company-wide business practice.

The survey shows that:

◆ Only one in five companies that practice telecommuting in California view telecommuting as part of long-term business strategy or as an official policy.

◆ Fewer than half (49 percent) of companies with a formal program reimburse employees for set up and ongoing costs related to telecommuting (computers, additional phone lines, supplies).

◆ The major roadblocks to effective telecommuting include providing telecommuters with a reliable computer and communications lifeline back to the office; training managers how to supervise telecommuting employees; and training telecommuters how to maximize personal productivity.

Telecommuters Find Relief in the Home Office

Even with a lack of resources and abundance of obstacles, telecommuters realize the benefits of telecommuting.

For example, Californians spent 300,000 hours daily sitting in traffic in 1996 to 1997, and 90,000 of those hours were wasted in a car by Bay Area commuters alone, according to The Northern California Telecommute America Team and Smart Valley, Inc., a Silicon Valley–based nonprofit organization.

One solution to this gridlock nightmare is telecommuting. But is telecommuting healthy for productivity? Is it a better way to live and work?

AT&T decided to ask those very same questions. Researchers of a study commissioned by AT&T randomly telephoned 12,000 U.S. households to screen for telecommuters who were willing to offer insight into the telecommuting lifestyle. From that group, they found 400 telecommuters who were willing to do in-depth interviews. Almost 100 percent of the group surveyed work at home an average of 11 days a month. Sixty percent of the interviewed teleworkers were aged between 30 and 49, 22 percent were over 50 years of age, and 14 percent were between the ages of 18 and 29.

◆ Demographics:

> 74 percent were married.
> 13 percent were single.
> 13 percent were divorced or widowed.
> 28 percent had a child in the house under 6 years old.
> 32 percent had a child in the house between the ages of 6 and 12.
> 25 percent had teenagers in the house aged 13 to 17.

◆ Impact on personal life:

> 73 percent said they have a more satisfying personal and family life than they had before telecommuting.
> 19 percent said there was no more or little satisfaction.
> 2 percent said they were less satisfied with their life than before telecommuting.
> 6 percent said they weren't sure if their life was more satisfying.

◆ Key factors of increased satisfaction (many cited more than one factor):

> 88 percent said their relationship with spouse or partner was better.
> 85 percent said they had more morale in their lives.
> 85 percent cited fewer sick days.
> 84 percent said their relationship with children was better.
> 83 percent said they had a better balance of work and family life.
> 80 percent said they had less stress.

◆ Effect on career:

> 63 percent said telecommuting has positively affected their careers.
> 33 percent said telecommuting has had no effect on their careers.
> 3 percent said telecommuting has had a negative effect on their careers.
> 1 percent said they weren't sure about the effects telecommuting has had on their careers.

◆ How have their careers been positively affected by telecommuting?

> 24 percent said they have gained more responsibility because they telecommute.
> 17 percent said they earn greater recognition for their work because they telecommute.
> 9 percent said telecommuting makes them more productive.
> 7 percent said they have received a promotion even though they telecommute.
> 7 percent said they have more flexibility on the job because they telecommute.

◆ Is the job more satisfying now that they telecommute?

> 71 percent said yes.
> 20 percent didn't see any change.
> 3 percent were less satisfied.
> 6 percent weren't sure.

◆ Have isolation issues increased since telecommuting?

> 62 percent said there has been no change in their feelings of isolation since telecommuting.
> 20 percent felt more isolated.
> 15 percent felt less isolated.
> 3 percent weren't sure.

◆ Reasons for feeling less isolated?

> 27 percent have more family contact.
> 27 percent have more contact with friends and neighbors.
> 18 percent said they have more communication with their supervisor.
> 8 percent said they communicate more with coworkers.

◆ Reasons for feeling more isolated?

> 68 percent say they communicate less with coworkers.
> 23 percent say they communicate less with supervisor.
> 14 percent miss office gossip.
> 9 percent miss office politics.

◆ Has productivity increased or decreased now that they telecommute?

> 30 percent say their productivity has increased an average of 22 percent.
> 50 percent say there has been no change in productivity.
> 11 percent say their productivity has decreased an average of 5 percent.
> 9 percent aren't sure.

◆ Reasons for increased productivity (multiple answers):

> 71 percent said they have more uninterrupted time and better concentration.
> 28 percent said they can work at peak times.
> 18 percent said they feel happier and more satisfied with life.
> 11 percent said they find fewer meetings means more productivity.

◆ Reasons for decreased productivity (multiple answers):

> 50 percent said too many interruptions.
> 14 percent said they don't have the right technology at home.
> 7 percent said they have difficulty with child and elder care.

◆ Would telecommuters go back to the corporate office if their telecommuting program were eliminated?

> 40 percent said they'd go back to the office.
> 29 percent said they'd look for another job where they could telecommute.
> 7 percent said they'd quit.
> 24 percent did not know what they'd do.

Source: AT&T Corporation, 1997 AT&T National Survey of Teleworker Attitudes and Workstyles.

Attitudes of Telecommuters

In spite of roadblocks telecommuters face in their daily jobs, they are generally a happy bunch.

In 1997, Find/SVP, AT&T, and Joanne H. Pratt Associates teamed up to conduct a national survey on teleworker attitudes and work styles.

Telecommuters in general are grateful for the opportunity to telecommute. They are corporate workers who relish the feeling that they aren't being forced to come into the office five days a week. So they generally self-report high productivity and satisfaction rates so that the telecommuting program can continue to flourish and they can continue working from home.

Most critics of telecommuting say that self-reporting high rates of productivity and satisfaction skew the realities of productivity. What is the difference whether a telecommuter self-reports a level of productivity and satisfaction or a company finds another way of measuring work? Doesn't it really matter that the employee perceives his or her job as satisfying, and out of that will come higher levels of productivity?

Many telecommuters will admit they work longer hours when they are at home. "Quite frankly, I'm working more hours now than I did when I was at the office. I'd try to get to the office by 8 a.m. or earlier, then leave for home about 5:15. I now get another 45 minutes of sleep and I'm in my office 7:30 a.m. and work till my wife comes home and gets supper ready till about 6:30. I could work here all night! I do pop in during the weekends to do work. I'm working so many more hours that I think the productivity gains to the company are very, very real," says Brian McGuren, a full-time telecommuter for Lucent Technologies.

AT&T commissioned the telework attitudes survey to find out more about the social, career, and productivity aspects of telecommuting. "The study confirms that telework arrangements can help employees gain control of, and increase satisfaction with, their business and personal lives," says Sue Sears, AT&T's telework project director.

Because telecommuters still have the support of a company behind them plus the opportunity to work from home, they are generally happy. Though it may seem they have less of a struggle than the at-home business owner when it comes to working at home, nevertheless telecommuters have their own issues they deal with on a daily basis.

For instance, they often feel the resentment from coworkers who don't telecommute. They also worry that their managers take their work less seriously because they telecommute. Telecommuters feel as though they are often left out of the loop when they work at home. Says Jennifer Busch, a telecommuting executive editor:

> **I often feel the prejudices as a telecommuter. It's an interesting psychological dynamic with people in the office. Plus, I'm a manager, so it's even more interesting. At times people may think I'm too far removed from a situation to know what's going on, and sometimes I feel that way too since you lose that consistency. Sometimes something happens on a day when you aren't in, and no one bothers to tell you about it.**
>
> **Communication is always a problem. I've never felt any resentment from them. People will call and say "sorry to bother you at home," and that's strange because I'm working.**
>
> **I'm trying to get people to understand that I'm just as accessible at home as I am in my office. Those kind of comments indicate to me that they don't think I'm really working when I'm at home. I refer most people to my voice mail, still, and I check in frequently.**
>
> **I don't expect my staff to make this work, I am the one who needs to make this work. It's not their personal choice, it's mine. I don't expect them to schedule everything around me. On days I work at home, I tend to come in for meetings or events because I don't feel that's fair if I don't. The arrangement shouldn't have an impact on them.**

Do Companies Cover a Telecommuter's Expenses?

Are you envious of telecommuters yet? It may sound like an ideal situation, but telecommuters aren't always handed the world on a silver platter, either.

On one hand, telecommuters have access to free office supplies. Supplies are expensive, but that's small potatoes when you realize that telecommuters can't deduct their home office from taxes because it's not their sole place of work. (This is untrue only in rare cases where the employer does not have a corporate office for the employee—perhaps because of diminished real estate—and it is a term of employment that the employee work at home full time in which case the IRS requires a letter from the company stating this.)

So are you willing to give up space in your home that you can't deduct for a tax break? However, many corporations require that telecommuters work from dedicated home offices.

"If clients call me and tell me they don't have room for a home office, I tell them not to do it," says Nancy Glenn, alternate work strategist for Lucent Technologies. "Lucent gives telecommuters all equipment and lines. People ask for payment of electricity because they see a definite rise in the costs of their power usage, but Lucent doesn't pay for that. Many people call and ask me if the company will pay for them to remodel their garage into a home office. The company is trying to reduce the bottom line so they have to be careful what expenses they incur."

But four issues remain constant and certain for most telecommuting programs:

◆ Companies will generally pay for any additional phone lines for business use and if necessary ISDN service or a modem.

◆ Any remodeling or electrical work for the home office is done at the employees' expense.

◆ Equipment such as faxes, copiers, and computers are tracked and retrievable assets.

◆ And no, the company is not responsible for picking up your heating or electricity consumption charges.

Telecommuters Work...Where?

There are a couple of widely divergent visions the public has of where the typical telecommuter works; from the beach to a fully outfitted, professionally designed home office. Just because a telecommuter has a corporate backup doesn't mean their home office will look any different from the office of a home-based entrepreneur who has just started out in business.

One furniture manufacturer, Herman Miller, found out how telecommuters really work by infiltrating the homes of real corporate telecommuters. Herman Miller had already come out with a major home office furniture collection in 1994, but they realized they needed to do additional research to come up with the perfect offering for a telecommuter's requirements.

The traditional route of questionnaires wouldn't do for this kind of research. Headed up by Marc Lohela, formerly the director of corporate telecommuting and the home office, Herman Miller decided it needed to find out firsthand what it felt like and looked like to work as a telecommuter (see Figure 9-2).

Figure 9-2. This is how the Herman Miller intervention team found one real-life telecommuter's home office. Although telecommuters are often supplied with equipment, it's a myth that every company gives telecommuters a stipend or actual furniture for their home offices. (*Herman Miller*)

So from 1995 through 1996, Herman Miller's "intervention research" project involved plucking 40 telecommuters from four companies—Amdahl, GTE, Atlantic Bell, and Nortel—from which they solicited 10 telecommuting volunteers from each company representing a wide range of geographical areas and diverse professions.

Lohela was able to see what it was like to telecommute from a 200-year-old farmhouse in upstate Connecticut to a three-year-old high-rise in central Los Angeles. You name it, telecommuters work on it. Kitchen tables, dining tables, or a door on two sawhorses. One man in the Herman Miller study worked in the corner of his living room on his well-worn rocking recliner—his work surfaces were folding TV tables and a larger box in which his computer had been packed.

To see how telecommuters work when their environments change, Herman Miller divided the group into three parts and asked the 40 telecommuters to work on other furniture the company provided at no cost. One-third of the group received Herman Miller contract office furniture from panel systems to desking systems. Another group worked on product purchased from local superstores. And the last third of the participants were asked to work on prototype furniture that Herman Miller commissioned to be designed by outside designers.

Lohela concluded that telecommuters expect equity in the way they are treated when they work at home, but they don't want parity in terms of furnishings. They don't want to work in a gray-paneled workstation at the end of their living room.

The result of this telecommuting study: the Beirise Collection of furniture that a majority of companies offer their telecommuters (see Figure 9-3).

Figure 9-3. Herman Miller is a popular choice with companies who offer telecommuters home office furniture. After intensive research of the way telecommuters work, Herman Miller designed the Beirise Collection with enough components to fit any configuration. Work surfaces are veneer or vinyl with radiused front edges and some melamine drawers and sides. (*Herman Miller*)

What Kinds of Furniture Do Employers Give to Telecommuters?

So you're still convinced that telecommuting is the route to a better quality of life and a chance to work at home to boot?

You may think that as a telecommuter, you will get a beautiful suite of home office furniture and top-of-the-line equipment delivered to your home gratis of the company for which you work. There are some instances in which this is true, but it's more the exception today than the rule.

Remember, there are many variations in a company's policy when it comes to the provision of furniture for the home office because the issue of standards is a new and evolving area for most companies.

For instance, there are companies that don't provide any type of furniture for their telecommuters. Since most telecommuting programs are voluntary, these companies feel it's better left to the employee to provide his or her own furniture for a home office.

Other companies, such as Tandem, deploy surplus furniture from downsized corporate offices to the telecommuter's home. Some of Tandem employees even take cubicles home. Tandem feels that it makes more sense to give this type of furniture to people who work at home than to sell it for next to nothing to a used furniture dealer. However, it's up to the Tandem employee to get the furniture home and assembled.

Up until now MCI, a company with over 800 telecommuters, never gave out stipends or had standards for home office furniture. But that may change in the future if one of two proposals becomes accepted. One proposal asks that telecommuters receive a $500 stipend to offset costs of setting up a home office. The second solution would be for the asset disposal group to make use of equipment and furniture that would be scrapped or turned over to a salvage dealer.

Another popular option for companies is to offer their telecommuters a cash stipend so that the employee can go out and purchase his or her own furniture. BellSouth Telecommunications gives each of its 500 telecommuters an allocation of $1,500 to furnish a home office. Since the company has standardized on Steelcase furniture for the corporate offices, telecommuters frequently go to the Steelcase dealerships in their cities to pick out their furniture and ergonomic accessories. By the year 2000, BellSouth Telecommunications forecasts that it will have 5,000 telecommuters, 2,000 of whom will be full time.

Northern Telecom (Nortel) doesn't believe in giving employees stipends for home office furniture. "The downsides of a stipend are many. First of all, there's no guarantee that they will use the money for furniture or equipment. The stipend then becomes a taxable benefit to the employee. And with a stipend we don't have control over the price points, which become a noncapitilizable item expensed at the time of purchase," says Tony Smith, manager of the company's telecommuting program that currently includes 2,500 telecommuters in North America and the United Kingdom, out of 60,000 total employees worldwide.

There is an increasing number of companies, like Nortel, that have more formalized standards for the telecommuter. These companies have decided to take control over what furniture packages their telecommuters will work in by offering them a choice of at maximum two different furniture collections. Two furniture manufacturers, Steelcase and Herman Miller, are aggressively helping companies arrange furniture standards for telecommuters.

Nortel decided to offer its telecommuters Steelcase Turnstone products and Herman Miller furniture because the diversity of aesthetics between the two lines gives employees a choice of style to fit their own home. To market choices to its employees, Nortel has set up a number of initiatives. For instance, Nortel built two miniature houses in two locations (in the corner of a cafeteria in its Research Triangle Park, North Carolina, and in it's "town square" in the new world headquarters in Ottawa, Canada). Within each structure, called "The Home," are two fully operational home offices with Steelcase and Herman Miller furniture, complete with phone lines, ISDN lines, and other technology a telecommuter typically uses (see Figures 9-4, 9-5, and 9-6).

Both Herman Miller and HON products are offered to telecommuters at St. Paul Companies in St. Paul, Minnesota. Each suite of home office furniture costs the company from $1,800 to $2,400 for each of its 800 telecommuters.

Employees can visit a mock-up of the Herman Miller and HON home office furniture lines to get a better idea of what they can choose. Employees are given sample fabric cards to take home so they can choose the right colors for their home. But they are discouraged from picking one piece of furniture from Herman Miller and another from HON because it results in double installation costs (see Figure 9-7).

Providing ergonomically correct seating is fast becoming a number 1 priority for home offices, however. But how do you ensure your telecommuters are sitting in the right chair if you provide a stipend?

Most companies that offer stipends for the purchase of correct seating emphasize, in the company's telecommuting guidelines, the correct use of height- and back-adjustable chairs with parallel armrests (see Figure 9-8).

Figures 9-4, 9-5, and 9-6. To give potential telecommuters a firsthand look at how their own home office can be set up, the facilities department at Nortel's North Carolina location built The Home, a miniature house that sits in the corner of the employee cafeteria in which there are two full-size mock-ups of home offices. One home office includes Herman Miller Beirise furniture, and the other shows employees what Steelcase's Turnstone furniture looks like. (*Northern Telecom*)

Figure 9-5.

Figure 9-6.

Figure 9-7. If you are a telecommuter at St. Paul Companies, you can choose furniture from HON's 38000 Series for your home office. The company offers this contract furniture line because it includes more filing options than other home office furniture collections, and, some employees like to carry the corporate office look into their homes. (*HON Industries*)

Figure 9-8. It's critical for companies to have some control over ergonomics in their telecommuters' home offices. Many companies give telecommuters chairs to take home. Select Seating in Somerset, New Jersey, sees an increase in the number of companies requesting ergonomic seating for home office workers. Its Stamina chair is popular for telecommuters because the scale is small enough for a home office. (*Select Seating*)

How Do Companies Deliver Home Office Furniture to Their Telecommuters?

After you choose your home office furniture, how will it get to your home? It hasn't been easy for the contract furniture market to come up with a perfect answer for the delivery of home office furniture. Herman Miller has persisted in trying to solve the delivery problem by setting up an arrangement with a residential goods delivery service that understands home deliveries. For Turnstone clients, the local commercial dealerships agree to deliver and set up the furniture in residences.

Telecommuters say that the main difficulty in delivery of home office furniture is in the scheduling of timely deliveries. The most frequent question a telecommuter will ask is why it takes two months or longer to get the furniture to their home. At Nortel, the toll-free Home Base Solution Line is set up for telecommuters to call in with their questions about the status of a delivery and installation.

The delivery of furniture became a nightmare for telecommuters at the St. Paul Companies. First, the company decided to take the least expensive route by letting the employee put the furniture together, but the company soon found out that wouldn't work because not everyone can muscle a 50-pound desk into place, nor is everyone a handyman. Most young people didn't own tools for assembling furniture.

Next, the company hired local install-and-assembly services for home office deliveries. That didn't work out because the services hire young people out on summer break, and they don't have the skills to put together contract furniture. Not only that, these services never accepted the responsibility if one of their employees damaged a telecommuter's walls or backed the delivery truck over the lawn.

As a result, the St. Paul Companies have all furniture deliveries made through the furniture manufacturer's dealer, an arrangement that works well because of the professional nature of dealers.

Will the Company Want to Inspect Your Home Office?

Once you have your home office set up, does the company come over to inspect it?

BellSouth believes that the company's responsibilities don't end when the home office furniture and the equipment are delivered to the telecommuter's home office. At BellSouth Telecommunications, a supervisor has the right to schedule a visit at any time to verify if a telecommuter's home office is set up properly. Audits are encouraged to discourage environments that may cause injury to the employee.

To ensure employees are working in ergonomically sound home office environments and to protect the company from issues of liability and worker's compensation, other companies feel that the best protection is to buy the furniture and/or accessories for the employee. That's why Nortel provides telecommuters with all the equipment and furniture so that all the precautions with ergonomics and safety are considered.

At Southern California Edison (SCE), employees participating in the telecommuting HomeWork program are well taken care of with ergonomic accessories and a chair from Herman Miller.

If a worker uses a computer for two hours or less per day on a consistent basis (three days a week), SCE doesn't consider him or her a risk. Over three hours a day and the employee is classified as a risk. That means that everything SCE gives its telecommuters has to meet every ergonomic standard that it would if that employee worked at the corporate facility. Workers at risk receive a fully adjustable keyboard, an ergonomic chair, a footrest, and a document holder. Even less risky employees receive keyboard trays because the cost is insignificant. If a telecommuter complains about mild pain in their wrists, SCE dispatches someone to the house immediately to have an evaluation done on the workstation.

What Happens If You Quit Your Job As a Telecommuter?

Since formal telecommuting programs are relatively new, most companies don't have much experience with reclaiming furniture and equipment from remote home offices. However, most companies do have a policy in place for future situations.

At Herman Miller, if an employee decides to cease telecommuting within two years, they are liable to pay back through a payroll program half of the $1,500 stipend given to them to purchase home office furniture.

But what happens to the furniture when a telecommuter leaves a company? The initial cost for a home office is $1,200 to $1,500 versus the significantly higher cost of $5,000 to $6,000 per employee for a corporate office work space. The cost it takes to track, retrieve, refurbish, repackage, inventory, and redeploy furniture has depreciated in value down to zero. As in many companies, it's an HR policy that upon termination of employment, the value of any outstanding resources—including equipment—that an employee may still be in possession of is deducted from a final paycheck.

For those companies that offer their work-at-home employees excess furniture from downsized offices, reclaiming the furniture doesn't make sense. A company won't chase down a file cabinet that would resell for $20.

It's a similar story at St. Paul Companies. The furniture is considered a perk and reverts to employee property. If the company tried to recover the furniture, it would have to pay someone to dismantle it, ship it, and refurbish it because it may have dings in it from two moves and warehousing. Then the company would have to store it until it was reassigned. It's a lot of expense to salvage used and battered products. In essence, a telecommuter is stuck with the furniture he or she receives from the company.

What's the Future of Telecommuting?

In spite of pressures from nontelecommuting coworkers and advocates of keeping workers chained to the corporate office, telecommuting is fast becoming a reality in Corporate America. Though there are many surveys that strive to prove that telecommuting is shrinking in its numbers, there are even more surveys that say the opposite is true.

In a recent nationwide survey commissioned by OfficeTeam, a staffing service specializing in temporary professionals asked 150 executives from the nation's 1,000 largest firms about their immediate future plans for telecommuting. A high 87 percent of executives predicted an increase during the next five years in the number of employees who will telecommute to work.

Respondents were asked to comment on whether the number of their employees who telecommute in their company will increase or decrease in the next five years. The break-out results are as follows:

	Percent
Will increase strongly	35
Increase somewhat	52
No change	9
Decrease somewhat	4
Decrease strongly	0

There's a rash of new research to support the claim that telecommuting is a fast-growing phenomenon (you can take these facts to your boss to help your case if you want to telecommute).

The research before 1997 is sort of jumbled, and many of the surveys disagree with each other's findings. Now that people have a better grasp on what and who a telecommuter really is, the research is beginning to become slightly more meaningful.

For example, according to a recent survey by the Industrial Development Research Council (IDRC), 20 percent of survey respondents have instituted a formal telecommuting program. Furthermore, consultants KPMG Peat Marwick surveyed 106 human resource executives at the largest U.S. companies. The results found that one in four (about 26 companies) have employees who regularly telecommute.

According to yet another study conducted by FIND/SVP market research company for Telecommute America (a group promoting telework), more than 11 million people reported working as telecommuters in 1997, that in comparison to 8 million in 1995.

There are so many studies on telecommuting that your head will begin to spin if you try to decipher what each one is really trying to say. The fact of the matter is that most medium to large companies in the U.S. are trying their hand at formal telecommuting programs. These programs may affect only 1 percent of the employee population (as is the case at American Express, for example), but nevertheless, it is happening around the country.

If you think telecommuting is for you, contact your human resource department to find out if there is a telecommuting program in place or ask if there's one on the agenda. If the answer is no, ask your manager if you can have a trial run at an informal telecommuting program in your own department.

Figure 9-9. Because the price and look are right, many companies use Turnstone to outfit their telecommuters' home offices. According to the Turnstone catalog, the suggested list price of this full setting is about $2,411 (without the chair). (*Steelcase*)

Figure 10-1. Corporate life often beckons even to tried-and-true home-based workers who miss the hustle and bustle of office work. (*Louis Syarto*)

10

Back at the Corporate Office ...
Could You Work There Again?

Could you work in a corporate setting again after tasting the freedoms, and the anxieties, of working in a home office? The bottom line: Never say never.

Though most people who work at home say they couldn't go back, others who have worked at home did go back to the corporate fold for a variety of reasons.

Even the quintessential home office pioneer Nick Sullivan, the celebrated columnist for *Home Office Computing Magazine* turned editor-in-chief of the magazine in 1997, made the transition into Corporate America, a move that drew him out of his rural home office in Massachusetts to the crowded streets of New York City.

"It's ironic that in order to find the best imaginable editor for this magazine we had to lure a maverick out of his home office and back into corporate work," said Hugh Roome, publisher of *HOC*, in his front-page welcome to Sullivan. Sullivan has since gone back to working from his home office, leaving New York City behind.

According to 1997 research by IDC/LINK, the strong U.S. economy has slowed down the growth of income-generating home offices. IDC/LINK research indicates successful home offices are expanding beyond the home to operate in commercial space as true small businesses. In fact, the company's latest survey indicates that 25 percent of all small companies began as home-based businesses.

The strong economy in 1997 has also provided opportunity to home office operators interested in returning to the corporate world. Those lacking the true entrepreneurial spirit but who started home-based businesses after leaving an employer, are being wooed back to traditional corporations. Fortune 1000 firms are adding staff in record numbers, making it easier for home workers to return to the self-described "leisurely" pace of traditional employment.

Take these and all other surveys on the home office with a grain of salt. Many home-based businesses remain hidden and anonymous, in part to evade constricting zoning issues, absurd taxing issues, and nosy neighbor issues.

However, there are those who leave the home office fold and step back into corporate life, or move their businesses to larger office quarters. This chapter explores the feelings of people who say that going back to work in a corporate office would be a step backward for them, and we'll hear from people who have moved out of their home office into a corporate office setting once again.

Just remember: it's *okay* to go through bouts of doubt about working from home. I went through a period where business was slow, and I thought I needed to go back to staff work. It wasn't until the opportunity to work on a staff arose that I realized I preferred working from home. Once I committed to staying freelance, doors began to open for me, and business is more than brisk.

How Do Home-Based Workers Feel about the Corporate World?

Most, if not everyone, interviewed in this book said they would have a difficult time working back in the confines of a corporate environment. They don't miss the commute, the office politics, and the stress of working on meaningless assignments, and they also don't miss having a windowless office or a tiny, crowded cubicle like the one in Figure 10-2.

Figure 10-2. For now, I couldn't trade in my 10- by 13-foot sunny yellow home office to go back to a cramped cubicle like the one I used to sit in when I worked for a magazine. My tiny work space was situated next to an empty cubicle that doubled as a storage area. (*MZS*)

"I spend time with clients in their boardrooms and offices, and I often wonder how they do it day in and day out," says a public relations firm owner who works at home. "A lot of people complain to me about their noisy work environments. They say they have to work on the weekends and at night to get the work done they couldn't do when they were at the office!"

The only important thing that home office workers seem to miss about working in an office is the camaraderie it offers, as we read about in Chapter 1.

After tasting the joys of working at home, it's difficult to transition back to a corporate work setting, unless it's designed to be quite special, and that doesn't just mean aesthetically pleasing. But the corporate workplace of the future must become an emotionally pleasing one if they want to recruit former home-based workers.

"I would only be able to work in a corporate environment again if it provided a range of different settings that was able to draw people to it rather than repel them like many corporate offices do," says Cynthia Froggatt, home-based strategic facilities planning consultant.

There are home-based workers who feel that working in a corporate environment makes one soft in their abilities in finding and clarifying their objectives and weak in their abilities to problem-solve. They feel that if they went back to a corporate setting, they would become too spoiled once again. Those are the thoughts of Lesley Goddin, a home-based writer who used to work in New York City for a large corporation:

> It's fun to work in a corporate office for a couple of years. It's fun to travel and eat out, but if that doesn't wear off after a couple of years, I have to wonder about the person who thrives on that.
>
> I was talking to someone about camping the other day. She asked me if I really liked to camp. I said, yes! Because for years all I did was go to really fancy places, sleep in fancy hotels, and eat fancy food, and I began to feel like a glutton. I couldn't enjoy it anymore, and to this day, it's still not a treat to eat out or stay at a fine hotel. You become jaded, take it for granted. You tend to think you *have* to eat this lobster when all you really want is a simple burger.
>
> Part of it was that I felt as though I was being drugged by all the luxury and perks of corporate life. You know, it's not good for people to eat all this rich food and drink all the time! I just don't want that anymore. So the camping thing is almost like an antidote, the total opposite. Go sleep on the ground in 39 degree weather and eat nuts and berries because there's no restaurant around and your food supply is a little too low. I think the corporate life can be too soft. And I used to think everyone lived like that! When I worked for a corporation, a group of us went to a very expensive restaurant and the bill was outrageous—we ordered so much fine wine—and the bill was being picked up by the company. It was incredible excess. And as we were leaving, we passed a homeless person, and everyone was clearly embarrassed. At that point I said, you know, I can't keep doing this. It's not real-world stuff. I feel sorry for the people who continue living this kind of high life because they have to keep living higher and higher to feel anything and to maintain that lifestyle.

Mandatory daily meetings, considered a waste of time by home-based workers—keep many away from seeking out staff jobs.

"I got tired of what I call 'blamestorming,' sitting around in a group discussing why a deadline was missed or a project failed, and who was responsible. It was a waste of time," says one former magazine editor, now a home-based writer, who doesn't want her name used.

Another home-based consultant doesn't want to get back into the pressure cooker. For years, Daniel Pink was chief speech writer to Al Gore, but he had "grown tired of politics in general and of office politics in particular, tired of doing assignments I didn't enjoy on a schedule I couldn't control, tired of wing tips that felt like vises and neckties that seemed like nooses," he says. Asked if he would return to the "traditional" corporate world, he says, "I can't imagine why" (see Pink, 1998).

Media consultant, Jessica Taper, of Taper Communications in Plano, Texas, wouldn't leave home, either. "I'm having fun doing things with my daughter's preschool. It's also amazing to me how much more efficient I am working out of the house than I ever was in a corporate office. Every now and then I go downtown to work out of the law office because they like having someone there, but it's amazing how much clearer my thoughts are when I work from home. I find that I'm also a lot more creative being away from that kind of environment and working in lots of different types of environments."

Home-based film and video editor Maxi Cohen feels that she already has a variety of places that she can write and work, including her home office, so she doesn't need to add one more to her list.

"I thought a number of times about getting a place to work outside the house," says Cohen. "Sometimes I do go away to write, anyhow. I went to an artist's colony for two months, people send me to various places like Hawaii for a week to write. Some of my best writing comes early in the morning, and I'd hate to give that up. I can't even move to the other end of the house [into her husband's old office] much less move into an office outside the house. My energy is best early in the morning or late at night so it's best not to waste any energy in order to get somewhere."

Marita Thomas, editor of *FFI* magazine (*Furniture Fashions International*), has worked from home for a couple of decades, sprinkled in with a couple of experiences working in a corporate setting. She's is blunt about her feelings of going back into the corporate world.

"I wouldn't be fit to work in a corporate office! I need to sit down with the phones off so I can work for a concentrated chunk of time. I absolutely enjoy people, but I don't enjoy commuting. I don't enjoy interruptions. I'm a very concentrated worker so the cohesion of my time is important. I don't think I'd enjoy it, quite honestly. When I want to socialize, I want to really sit down with someone and talk, but I'm not interested in asking if he or she wants me to pick up some coffee for him or her from the corner deli," says Thomas.

Finally, Tom Gentry, owner of home-based business Choo-Choos Trains & More, a retail operation based out of his remodeled garage, says this about the corporate world: "I'm too old now to take orders from anyone. I can't go back into any type of workforce, corporate or otherwise. I think if I went to work for McDonald's the whole experience would drive me crazy. A home-based business is it for me!"

How Would Telecommuters Feel If They Couldn't Work at Home Anymore?

Telecommuters keep one foot in the corporate environment and one foot in the home office. Does that mean they taste the fruits of both worlds, or do they have to deal with a double set of problems that each camp poses?

Clearly, telecommuters differ from full-time home-based workers who run their own businesses. Telecommuters work for a company that is not their own. So they must still take "orders" from a boss. So although telecommuters have the benefits of working at home, they also need to continue to carefully tread water in the corporate environment.

In any case, telecommuters say they feel privileged to work at home even though they may work at home one or more days a week. According to a Telecommute America poll released in 1997, telecommuters said that nothing, except perhaps doubling their salary, would convince them to give up their work style.

"If I had to work back in a corporate setting, I could. You have to do what you have to do. But if I had to commute out to New Jersey again, I couldn't do it. The commute took too much out of me," says Brian McGuren, a five-day-a-week telecommuter from Lucent Technologies.

Another Lucent telecommuter feels the same: "If I had to suddenly start driving to an office again every day, I'd become emotionally down about it because I know how much lost time it is. I know I'm healthier because I'm not dealing with the traffic. Could I work in a corporate office again? Well, my productivity is so high now that I know that driving to and from an office is a waste of time."

Why the Corporate Office Beckons to Others

Cathy Barto Meyer wouldn't mind going back to a corporate office because her prior experience was privileged, special, and holds fond memories for her.

"I wouldn't mind going back to a corporate environment. I liked it. The ad agency I worked for in New York City was a great place to work. We called it 'the high school.' We had a cafeteria where people sat in cliques, and there was a gym on the roof—it was a self-contained city with every conceivable service you'd want, and you can go into the building and never leave. We were given half-days on Fridays during summer, five weeks of vacation, personal days, and not only that, but if you gave blood in the annual blood drive, you'd get a day off! We even had snow days! You'd get all this and have it in the company of creative people. I miss that aspect of the corporate environment," says Meyer.

Then, there are those former home-based workers, like interior designer Michael Love, principal of Interior Options, who have leased out small offices to accommodate business growth or to ease isolation: "I was in my home office for seven years. I had to move to an office space because business was getting better, and there was no place to expand to in my one-bedroom apartment. I managed to cope with it for a while, but I needed more people for the business including a full-time assistant, bookkeeper, and student interns.

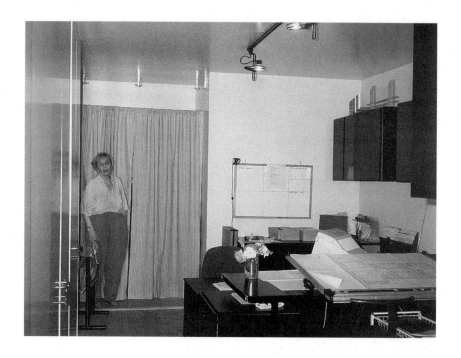

Figure 10-3. Interior designer Michael Love moved out of her home office into a small office because she was tired of having to transform her bedroom (the Murphy bed is behind the curtain) into a full-fledged working environment every day for staff and for herself. (*MZS*)

"My home office was in my bedroom, and that meant that whether I was healthy or sick, I'd have to get up at 7 in the morning, make my bed, push it up, pull the cart on wheels with the fax machine on it so that everyone could come into work.

"There was a feeling that I was on view every day in my own home. Now, here, if I'm really not feeling well, I can just go home. I had no place to go there. I also had vendors coming there to show me product, and I'd use my living room as the conference room. After seven years, it finally got to me."

Jerianne Fitzgerald Thomas, president of public relations firm Fitzgerald Thomas Communications, has this to say about why she moved out of her home office into a leased small office in a larger advertising agency:

> I found my work taking over the kitchen and the living room because I was putting press kits together and at the same time having other freelancers come in to help. I clearly needed more room.
>
> But the bottom line was that I just missed the interaction. I missed having a place to go, I missed sitting around having coffee with colleagues and asking them what movie they saw last night. I missed all that social stuff. I need that—that's where I get my energy from.
>
> At the time, I was working on four projects at once, and they were each growing by leaps and bounds. In December of 1996, I called a friend of mine who has a creative agency with a partner and who I've worked with in years past. I called and said, "Please tell me you have some office space, please tell me you have an empty desk somewhere." Fortunately, he did. I worked out a wonderful deal and was able to move in there right away.

> Today, I'm in an office that is within an advertising agency. So I have the luxury of being able to come and go as I please, it's my place and my set-up. And I have the benefit of going to the coffee pot and catching up with everybody else who works there, and these are people I've known before, so that makes it nice, too. It's the ideal situation.

Love and Thomas are not alone. These two women continue to own their own businesses, but they have chosen to run them in a corporate setting.

Transitioning from Home Office to Small Office:
Two Experiences

Lynn Bygott-Leahy started her pet-sitting business, Just Critters, eight years ago from a tiny sun porch in her house. At the time, she had a partner who also ran part of the business from her home office in another nearby town. When they started out, it was ideal to have zero overhead, but as the business grew, so did the confusion of running it from two home offices.

Bygott-Leahy and her partner dissolved the partnership, but she continued to work from a home she eventually rented that was zoned for commercial use, so that she could also put up a sign for her business outside the house. But the ideal situation soured slowly until finally the home office wasn't quite the sanctuary it once was:

> I will never, *ever* work at home again.
>
> It got to the point where clients were calling me at home in the middle of dinner, and my pasta would be half cold by time I got back to it.
>
> At the time, my office was in my living room so I'd find myself watching television and working on the computer at the same time at 8:00 at night. I always felt as though when I was in my house, I had to work. I'd eat dinner and go right back to work. I constantly felt guilty when I wasn't working because I had work staring at me when I was in the living room.
>
> The moment that I realized I needed to get out of the home office came at a time that one of my parents wasn't feeling well, and the phone rang at 2:00 a.m. My husband jumped out of bed and ran to get the phone. We were nervous that it was an emergency call from my parents. Well, it turned out that it was just a call from a drunk client calling me after she got back to her house in Westport from New York City to tell me that I needed to walk her dogs the next afternoon. My clients knew that I worked from a home office so what were they thinking calling me at 2:00 a.m. in the morning? That was it. I said enough. I just couldn't do it anymore.
>
> There were other problems, too. We had so many workers coming into the home! We'd have 13 people with keys to my house coming in at 11:00 at night, dropping off keys, knocking on the door saying hi. We had people doing

morning shifts coming in at 5:30 in the morning, and we'd hear the door bang and slam. We started to walk on eggshells. People were always around our house! I couldn't eat lunch because people would drop by to talk. Although my husband knew what he was getting into with my business, he got tired of it too, and he told me he couldn't walk around the house in a more casual way because too many people were always dropping by. I can't tell you how many times he'd come out of the shower with a towel wrapped around him, and he'd find someone in the hallways saying hi to him! It invades your privacy.

Not only was it an issue when we were home, but having employees come to the house was an issue even when we weren't home. When my husband and I did go away, it got to the point where I felt I had to hide some of my financial statements so that others wouldn't accidentally trip over them.

My employees like this arrangement better because they don't feel as if they are intruding in my life. Friday is pay day so everyone comes in that day and talks with everyone else. It's more of a workplace. It's more professional. Working out of your house is not professional, at least to me.

There are other things I hated about working at home. I always felt that my house had to be clean. I also didn't like being at home with my husband when he worked a few days a week at home. I didn't like looking at him 24 hours a day! I needed to get away into my own space.

But the bottom line is that I like having an office outside the home because I can shut the door, take my keys with me, and know I don't have to deal with any work until the next morning.

I worked in a corporate office once, and I can't do it. I don't like the lack of freedom. I am more disciplined with myself working for myself than I am when I work for someone else. My work ethic seems to be much higher, and I have higher standards when I work for myself versus working for someone else.

I'm more relaxed now that I don't have my office in my home. Now, no one has my home number. So we aren't interrupted with business anymore during dinner or at 2:00 in the morning.

Figure 10-4. At one point Lynn Bygott-Leahy, owner of Just Critters Pet Sitting Service, had 13 employees coming in and out of her house from early morning to late at night. She couldn't sacrifice her personal life anymore so she moved her business into a small 400-square-foot office in town where her assistant can bring her baby to work, as well. (*MZS*)

Although Bygott-Leahy didn't have isolation problems, Michele Foyer, president of Tropos, a marketing and imaging firm in San Francisco, moved out of her home office for more interaction. Foyer used to work for a medium-sized architectural firm in San Francisco until she realized she had had enough of corporate life. It wasn't until she started working at home that she realized she needed to put back into her life some of the daily rituals that come with working in a corporate office. Foyer explains:

> I loved working from home—at first. I enjoyed the fluidity of activity, but after two years the lack of interaction and isolation eventually got to me. It evolved into hate.
>
> Before starting my own company, I'd worked in a design firm that had a large open floor plan that brought many bright and interesting people into close proximity. Without realizing it, I'd become used to its communal nature, which suited my role in public relations and branding.
>
> I then became increasingly aware of my craving for solitary space—a good counterpoint to the open space—and necessary for intense writing and thinking. I thought that getting rid of the extraneous conversations would allow me to focus better. By working from home for myself, I wouldn't have to dress up, go out to lunch every day, or work by anyone else's schedule except my own biorhythms.
>
> But when "I got what I wanted," it was a great surprise to find that I missed the theater and drama of the office. I even missed dressing up! I longed for what I had rejected—camaraderie. I came to appreciate some of the rituals that office life offers, something that I had taken for granted.
>
> Ultimately, the benefits of seeing and talking with more people during the day were more important than the desire to realize additional profits by working from home, so I made the move into a small office. My business actually grew once I jumped back into "the thick of it."
>
> Now, during my 40-minute walk across San Francisco to work, I see colors and people and new things every day—something I did not see when I worked from home. As a creative person, I've learned that I thrive on change and stimuli. While this wasn't critical to the specific parameters of my work, I found it was essential to what fed me as a creative thinker and writer. I didn't like being in only one place when I worked at home.
>
> My office is in a building in the multimedia and design neighborhood of San Francisco. There's a part with a great café down the street where I meet with colleagues and clients. But there is also a conference room in my building that I use. My office is like a private one you might have in a company, except it has large 10-foot gridded industrial glass windows with an urban view of the city. There are also many entrepreneurs, graphics, advertising and high-tech people in the building for me to meet.
>
> I also missed the corporate infrastructure of a larger firm when I worked from home. I like having the reception desk, conference room, someone to handle Federal Express, delivery of mail and packages, and a copy machine. These are things I have now in my office. I also like being connected to a T-1 line via an ethernet 10 base T connection. Normally you'd find this in much larger companies, but I was able to tap into this because another tenant in the

building is an Internet service provider. For me, things go much more smoothly when these services are in place.

Because there are so many small businesses, we are starting up an organization in the springtime for more networking and to get people in, like accountants, to come speak to small business people in this building.

Though I like the privateness of my office in this building, I still feel we are all too separate from one another. So what's my ideal workplace? I've learned that it's one that balances privacy and people-to-people activity. The ideal office setting to me would be a space where there are five private offices for different businesses, but there would also be a common space nearby to encourage interaction and to share resources.

I'm able to pop into other people's offices. I see how other types of small businesses are expanding, I see those that don't make it. It exposes me to what's going on in the world, and how many different product and marketing applications there are out there. It's also fun to talk to these people about the latest books they're reading.

I could go back to working from home at some point in my life, but not right now.

The Fleeting Fantasy of Leaving the Home Office for a Small Office

Other home-based workers may look into leasing small office space but instead, realize the value of working at home. "What I found working at home is that a lot of times you fantasize about a larger space. So last spring someone in SoHo called me to let me know that half of an office was opening up and would I like to rent it? The rent was $700 a month. I really thought, hmmm, I can do that. I went down there, and the available space was almost as big as this office, and you know what? I came back here, and I thought, I have a beautiful, comfortable, pleasant place, and then I did number crunching. Such as, wouldn't I need someone there to answer the phones? And it made me look with renewed eyes at the value of a home office in New York City. My apartment is much more pleasant than any office you could pay $1,000 a month for anyway," says Shannon Wilkinson, president of art marketing firm, Cultural Communications.

"It would take some getting used to if I were to work in a corporate office again. Working for someone else at this point is a whole other issue. I would like to have an office and a full-time assistant, and I'd like to have a place to go to and a place to leave from.

"Sometimes I dream of my own office out of the home, and I see these cool buildings where I'd love to have an office—but at this point it's out of the question because it works so well right now at home. I don't want to put all that money into office space. And, office space has to be snazzy, and you can't get away with what you have in a home office," says Julie Taylor, principal of home-based marketing firm, Taylor & Company.

Figure 10-5. Some home-based workers have looked into small office space, but they couldn't justify the costs involved in working away from the home. Looking at the costs of real estate around town makes some people grateful that they can work at home. (*Global Industries*)

Web site designer, Linda Shea, of The Shea Company, did look at office space outside her home. "I looked at an executive suite, but the rental prices in Dallas are skyrocketing. Last time I did this, I had the fortune of good timing, Texas was in a real estate slump, and you could get office space for $9 a square foot. That same office space is going for about $27 a square foot today. My home office is roughly about 11- by 16-feet, and the executive suite space I'd move into would be smaller, yet I'd have to pay a lot more money to work there."

A Final Thought on Life in the Home Office versus the Corporate Office

So many of us are talking about working from home. There's one school of thought that says we will all be working from our home full-time; because the demise of the office is imminent. Still others say no one will be working at home in the future because we will crave the corporate setting once again.

None of this is true. None of it will be true. What will, no doubt, happen in the future is that we will want more variation in the way we work and where we work, and that most definitely includes working at home some or all of the time.

Though all of us won't be working at home all of the time while others will, the pull to work at home will be strong especially as the tools for working at home improve.

I think that business owners who work at home will continue to find outlets for socialization and to meet colleagues with whom to collaborate.

And although many critics of telecommuting are quick and happy to say that telecommuting is a trend that's come and gone, I disagree with that, as well. A survey from Wirthlin Worldwide said that Corporate America never bought into the concept of telecommuting and that the growth in numbers will slow from a 6 percent annual growth in 1997 to a 1 percent growth in 2003 and that today, 81 percent of companies don't allow telecommuting at all.

There are many other surveys that contradict the Wirthlin study, saying that telecommuting will rise in the future. However, I firmly believe that all the surveys that boast their counts of telecommuters across the country are dead wrong on their numbers.

The fact is that many surveys query human resource managers, facility managers, or executive management to find out how many people telecommute in their companies. Here's a reality check: There is no way a survey can account for all the closet telecommuters who work for companies without formalized programs.

And note that the small companies (under 50 employees) are never counted in surveys, and companies in this critical business category are firm believers in flexible work patterns and work environments, including the option to telecommute on a mostly informal basis.

I should know about being a closet telecommuter. I was one of them before working from home full-time. And I can assure you that I know dozens and dozens of others who are never counted in surveys about telecommuting or about home offices, but I do know that nevertheless, those numbers will continue to grow despite the latest survey numbers.

If you are, or are about to become, a work-at-home business owner or telecommuter, try to enjoy the process of settling into your lifestyle. All you have to know is that there are thousands upon thousands of others, some of whom you've met in the pages of this book, who share your joys and frustrations of the often-coveted, often-revered, and often-confounding work at home lifestyle.

Figure 10-6. Life is cyclical. Depending on where you are in your life path and in your career, you could find yourself attracted back into the world of big business. Don't dismantle your home office just yet because your company might allow you to telecommute! (*MechoShade Systems*)

Resources for the Home Office

Chapter 1, Miscellaneous Resources

Internal Revenue Service for information on
home-based businesses and Publication 587,
Business Use of Your Home
Ph: 703-321-8020
Web site: http.//www.irs.ustreas.gov
Fax back service: 703-487-4160

Pennywise Office Products
Ph: 800-942-3311; Washington, D.C.
area: 305-805-7733
Fax: 800-622-4411; Washington, D.C.
area: 301-805-0960
(Discount office product catalog. If you join Working
Today—see below—you'll get a "members only" catalog
with extra discounts. A few good hits in each catalog.)

General Associations for Home-Based Businesses

Working Today
Post Office Box 1261
Old Chelsea Box Station
New York, NY 10113
Ph: 212-366-6066
Fax: 212-366-6971
E-mail: working1@tiac.net
Web site: http://www.workingtoday.org
(For a $10 membership fee, you get a newsletter,
events list—New York City only—and listings for
discounts on products and services, such as
Pennywise Office Products listed above.)

The Cottage Industry Association
Jennifer Reed, Founder
1510 East Maryland Street
Bellingham, WA 98226
Ph: 360-671-4316
E-mail: crunchJ@aol.com
Web site: http://www.hotbooks.com/cottage/

Home Office Association of America
909 Third Avenue, Suite 990
New York, NY 10022
Ph: 800-809-4622
Fax: 800-315-4622
E-mail: HOAA@aol.com
Web site: http://www.hoaa.com/
(National organization for full-time home-based

professionals and telecommuters. Offers discounts
and newsletter. Membership is $49 a year.)

Magazines and Newsletters for Home-Based Businesses

Home Office Computing Magazine
156 West 56th Street
New York, NY 10019
Ph: 212-333-7600
Website: http://www.smalloffice.com

The Home Team Report Newsletter
Ph: 888-447-2632
Fax: 850-939-4953
E-mail: bookhome@gte.net
Web site: http://www.bookhome.com

Chapter 2, Planning Resources

Contacting Interior Designers for the Home Office

American Society of Interior Designers
608 Massachusetts Avenue, NE
Washington, D.C. 20002
Ph: 202-546-3480
Fax: 202-546-3240
Web site: http://www.asid.org
(Contact ASID for general information and
referrals to interior designers)

Susan Aiello, ASID
Interior Design Solutions
300 East 74th Street
New York, NY 10021
Ph: 212-628-2938

Maurice Blanks
Maurice Blanks Architecture, Inc.
2035 West Wabansia Avenue, No. 304
Chicago, IL 60647
Ph: 773-342-1717
Fax: 773-342-1692
(Project: closet home office in Chapter 2.)

Mary Overly Davis, AIA
Proprietor
Mary Davis Architecture and Interior Design
250 West 82nd Street
New York, NY 10024
Ph: 212-874-1718
Fax: 212-874-1720
E-mail: mary.davis@MCIONE.com
(Mary's home office is featured in Chapter 8.)

Gay Fly
6237 Cedar Creek
Houston, TX 77057
Ph: 713-461-6399
(Project: The Bear's Paw, Chapter 2.)

Marie Henkel, ASID
Janis LaFountain, ASID
Design Works
8244 Menaul NE
Albuquerque, NM 87110
Ph: 505-294-8866
(Project: Ancient Sun, Chapter 8.)

Michael Love, ASID
Interior Options
200 Lexington Avenue
New York, NY 10016
Ph: 212-545-0301
Fax: 212-689-4064
Web site: http://mlove@interioroptions.com

Janet Schirn, FASID
Janet Schirn Design Group
401 N. Franklin Street
Chicago, IL 60610
Ph: 312-222-0017
Fax: 312-222-1465
(Offices also in New York City and Washington, D.C.)

Miscellaneous

Patio Enclosures
70 East Highland Road
Post Office Box 186
Macedonia, OH 44056
Ph: 800-480-1966
Fax: 215-467-4297

The Container Store
Ph: Call for locations and/or catalog:
1-800-733-3532

Chapter 3, Ergonomic Resources

Ergonomic Consultants

Marlene Green
The Comfort Zone
331A Pavonia Avenue
Jersey City, NJ 07302
Ph: 201-659-4836
(A dealer of ergonomic furniture and products. Also
sells speech recognition equipment and software.)

Ellen Kolber. MS, MA, OTR, CHT,
ergonomic consultant
Diversified Ergonomics
127 West 24th Street
New York, NY 10011
Ph: 212-206-8925

Arlette Loeser, MA, OTR, ATP
The Ultimate Workspace
address: 360 Central Park West
New York, NY 10025
Ph/Fax: 212-865-7743
(Can do work-space assessments based on phone
interviews and photos.)

Books on Ergonomics and/or RSI

The Repetitive Strain Injury Recovery Book
By Deborah Quilter
Published by Walker & Company, New York

Repetitive Strain Injury: A Computer User's Guide
By Deborah Quilter and Emil Pacarelli, MD
Published by John Wiley & Company, New York

*Conquering Carpal Tunnel Syndrome & Other
Repetitive Strain Injuries: A Self-Care Program*
By Sharon Butler
Published by New Harbinger:

Ergonomic Furniture Showroom and/or Retailer

BP Associates
200 Lexington Avenue
New York, NY 10016
Ph: 212-679-0800
Fax: 212-679-9284
(Showroom; call for appointment.)

The Relax the Back Store
229 East Lancaster Avenue

Ardmore, PA 19003
Ph: 610-896-5515
(Opening stores around the country featuring
affordable price points for at-home professionals.)

Ergonomic Web sites

(The following three Web sites will link you with
practically everything there is to know about
ergonomics, carpal tunnel syndrome, and RSI.)

http://www.cb1.com/cb1/john/links/rsi.html
(All the links you need to learn about ergonomics.)

http://www.ergonomics.com.au/ergolinks.htm
(Links, societies, journals, and papers on ergonomics.)

Typing Injury, Frequently Asked Questions
http://www.tifaq.com/
(The RSI Community's Online Resource:
Information about furniture, alternative keyboards, and speech recognition.)

Ergonomic Furniture and Product Manufacturers

HAG, Inc.
108 Landmark Drive
Greensboro, NC 27409
Ph: 919-668-9544
Fax: 919-668-7331

ErgoSystems, Inc.
71 George Street
East Hartford, CT 06108
Ph: 860-282-9767
Fax: 860-289-2386
(Sells ergonomic keyboard trays and computer
workstations.)

Hello Direct Catalogue
5893 Rue Ferrari
San Jose, CA 95138-1858
Ph: 800-444-3556
Fax: 408-972-8155
E-mail: xpressit@hihello.com
Web site: http://www.hello-direct.com
(Catalog sells phone accessories, phone
conferencing products, and headsets.)

Task2
500 Bragato Road
Belmont, CA 94002
Ph: 800-592-ERGO
Fax: 415-592-7755
(Sells ergonomic articulating keyboards.)

Chapter 4, Feng Shui Resources

Feng Shui Practitioners

Deborah Meyer
Cinnabar
Ph: 610-527-4996
Fax: 610-527-5457

William Spear
24 Village Green Drive
Litchfield, CT 06759
Ph: 860-567-8801
Fax: 860-567-3304

Edgar Sung
Feng Shui Practitioner and Teacher
Ph: 415-681-1182
E-mail: MJEP2578@aol.com

R.D. Chin
Space Alignment
308 West 30th Street
New York, NY 10001
Ph: 212-695-2147
Fax: 212-465-8690
(Author of: *Feng Shui Revealed*)

The Yun Lin Temple
2959 Russell Street
Berkeley, CA 94705
Ph: 415-841-2347
(Intensive courses in feng shui, founded by master
Lin Yun in 1986; source for referrals.)

International Feng Shui Centre
1340 Marshall Street
Boulder, CO 80302
Ph: 303-939-0033
Fax: 303-939-0044
Web site: www.fengshui2000.com/
(Web site includes a list of feng shui practitioners
around the country.) Practitioner Referral List on this
Web site: fengshuiguild.com/ or ph: 303-444-1548

Feng Shui Workshops

New York Open Center
83 Spring Street
New York, NY 10012
Ph: 212-219-2527
Fax: 212-226-4056

Feng Shui Products

Feng Shui Warehouse
Ph: 800-399-1599
(Catalog of feng shui–related items.)
Feng Shui Emporium
Inner House/Outer House
Charlottesville, VA 22906-6701
Ph: 703-526-9588
Web site: http://www.luckycat.com/

Feng Shui Books

Feng Shui Made Easy: Designing Your Life with the Ancient Art of Placement
By William Spear
Published by Harper Collins, San Francisco
(Simple workbooklike format; good for use in applying basic cures.)

Feng Shui: The Chinese Art of Placement
By Sarah Rossbach
Published by Arkana/Penguin Books, New York
(Sarah studied feng shui with renowned practitioner Lin Yun. This book explains overall concepts of the ancient art of placement.)

Interior Design with Feng Shui
By Sarah Rossbach
Published by Arkana/Penguin Books, New York
(Building upon what Sarah wrote in her first book, she goes deeper into feng shui, explaining further cures used in interior design.)

Sacred Space: Clearing & Enhancing the Energy of Your Home
By Denise Linn
Published by Ballantine Books, New York
(Unique book about the energies in your home; chapter on feng shui included.)

Chapter 5, Furnishings Resources

Office Furniture Liquidators

Office Furniture Heaven
22 West 19th Street, Seventh Floor
New York, NY 10011
Ph: 212-989-8600
Fax: 212-727-8028

The Business Outlet, Inc.
200 Penn Avenue
West Reading, PA 19610
Fax for information: 1-800-752-2946
(Sells remanufactured Herman Miller furniture.)

Corporate Liquidators
110 West 40th Street, No. 1407
New York, NY 10036
Ph: 212-764-1160
(Offers Steelcase furniture.)

Home Office Solutions
1500 West Cypress Creek Road, No. 505
Fort Lauderdale, FL 33309
Ph: 800-933-3453
E-mail: officef@worldnet.att.net
Web site: http://www.furntogo.com/
(Sells contract office furniture at wholesale prices to the public retail customer. When looking at furniture, be sure to ask for brands to determine the value of product. Brands aren't listed on the Web site.)

Furniture Alliance
6312 Airport Freeway, Third floor
Bedford, TX 76022
Ph: 817-540-3700
Fax: 817-545-3701
E-mail: wesellfurniture@mindspring.com
Web site:
http://www.furniture-alliance.com/index.html
(Sells all types of commercial furniture at remanufactured prices.)

Davies Office Refurbishing
40 Loudonville Road
Albany, NY 12204
Ph: 518-449-2040
(Ask about the furniture in their warehouse on Six Simmons Lane in Albany. This refurbisher sells an original $800 Ergon office chair from Herman Miller for $265 reconditioned.)

Home Office Furnishings Retailers

The Container Store
Ph: Call for locations and/or catalog: 1-800-733-3532
(Twenty locations include Atlanta, Washington, D.C., area, Chicago area, San Diego, Dallas and other large cities in Texas, and Denver.)

Ikea
Ph: Call for locations across the country and/or catalog: 908-352-1550
(Twelve locations include Houston, Philadelphia,

Washington, D.C., Baltimore, Pittsburgh, Elizabeth, Long Island, Burbank, Carson, Tustin, City of Industry, and Seattle.)

Furniture at Work
Ph: Call for locations in Texas, California, and Florida. Call Office Depot for nearest location 1-800-685-8800.
California Closets/Room2Work division for home offices
Ph: Call for locations: 800-274-6754
Web site: http://www.calclosets.com/index.html
(There are 150 stores in the United States, Canada, and overseas. They've been in business since 1978, and recently they expanded their custom home organization services into the home office.)

Closets By Design
Ph: 800-293-3744
Web site:
http://www.closets-by-design.com/Home.htm
(A custom home office solutions company that offers home office furniture in a variety of finishes.)

InHouse Home*Home Office*Furniture & Design
343 Vermont Street
San Francisco, CA 94103
Ph: 415-554-1950
Fax: 415-554-1955

Home Works Furniture
Veterans Square Plaza
1265 Veterans Boulevard
Redwood City, CA 94063
Ph: 650-365-7800
E-mail: info@homeworksfurniture.com
Web site:
http://www.homeworksfurniture.com/main-menu.html

Home Office Furnishings Catalogs

Levenger
Ph: 800-544-0800
(This catalog carries some home office furniture and the Herman Miller Aeron chair for under $1,000.)

Reliable Home Office
Ph: 800-869-6000
(This catalog specializes in value-priced, good-looking furnishings, products, and electronics for the home office worker.)

Home Office and Office Furniture Manufacturers

Ready-to-Assemble

Blu Dot Design & Manufacturing, Inc.
1500 Jackson Street, NE
Minneapolis, MN 55413
Ph: 612-782-1844
Fax: 612-782-1845
Studio RTA
2067 East 55th Street
Vernon, CA 90058
Ph: 213-583-8882

Sauder Woodworking
Ph: Call to find out where to buy Sauder furniture in your area: 800-523-3987

Busch Industries, Inc.
One Mason Drive
Post Office Box 460
Jamestown, NY 14702-0460
Ph: 716-665-2510
Fax: 716-665-2074

Anthro Computer Furniture
10450 SW Manhasset Drive
Tualatin, OR 97062
Ph: 503-691-2556
Fax: 503-691-2409

Newell Office Products
2102 Business Center Drive
Irvine, CA 92612
Ph: 800-822-4287
(Product: Snapease desks and hutches, formerly Rubbermaid products.)

Armoires

The Office
The Summerland Group
3451 South East Court Drive
Stuart, FL 34997
Ph: 561-219-0455
Fax: 800-282-4805
E-mail: info@the-office.com
Web site: http://www.the-office.com/
(Good resource for cutting-edge home office products and children's computer furniture.)

Frogbench
Manfred Petri
3589 Spencer
Marietta, GA 30066
Ph: 800-899-FROG

ConSole
Linkworks
Ph: 416-921-4409
Fax: 416-961-2019
E-mail: linkworks@msn.com
Sligh Furniture Co.
1201 Industrial Avenue
Holland, MI 49423
Ph: 616-392-7101
Fax: 616-392-9495
Web site: http://www.sligh.com

Techline
Ph: Call for store locations: 800-666-0947
Web site: http://www.techline-furn.com

Commercial- or Contract-Quality Furniture

Herman Miller (for the Aeron chair and Beirise
home office furniture)
855 East Main Road
Zeeland, MI 49464
Ph: 800-851-1196
Web site: http://www.hermanmiller.com

Knoll (for the SoHo chair)
105 Wooster Street
New York, NY 10012
Ph: 212-343-4180
Web site: http://www.knoll.com/

The HON Company
Post Office Box 1109
Muscatine, Iowa 52761-0769
Ph: 319-264-7100

Steelcase (for Turnstone furniture)
901 44th Street, SE
Grand Rapids, MI 49508
Ph: 800-333-9939
Web site: http://www.steelcase.com/

Kinderlink children's computer furniture
Skools, Inc.
40 Fifth Avenue, Suite 15A
New York, NY 10011
Ph: 212-674-1150
Fax: 212-674-2426
E-mail: skoolsinc@aol.com
Web site: http://www.kinderlink.com

Chapter 6, Technology Resources

Cable Keeper
Watson Furniture Systems
Ph: 800-426-1202
Web site: http://www. cablekeeper.com
Microsoft
http://www.microsoft.com/support/
http://www.microsoft.com/support/tshoot/multi-media.asp

Apple
http://www.support.info.apple.com/support/supportoptions/supportoptions.html

US Robotics
http://www.usr.com/home/software/software.html

Chapter 7, Family-Proofing Resources

Products

Gonzo Pet Hair Lifter
The Gonzo Corporation
Canton, MA 02021
Ph: 800-221-0061

Books, Newsletters, or Forums on Raising Children While Working at Home

How to Raise Your Kids and Have a Career Under the Same Roof
By Lisa Roberts
Published by Bookhaven Press, Coraopolis,
Pennsylvania
(Lisa's Entrepreneurial Parent Web site: www.en-parent.com is a work-family resource for home-based entrepreneurs.)

At Home: The Newsletter for Parents Who Work From Home
Post Office Box 487
Mendon, MA 01756-0487
Ph: 508-634-3989

At-Home Dad Newsletter
Peter Baylies, Editor
61 Brightwood Avenue
North Andover, MA 01845-1702
E-mail: athomedad@aol.com
Web site: http://www.parentsplace.com/read-room/athomedad/index.html

(The quarterly newsletter costs $12 a year. The Web site is entertaining, understanding, and sympathetic at the same time.)

America Online
Keyword: Moms Online
(Sympathy for work-at-home moms.)

Chapter 8, How Others Cope

Barrier-Free Resources

ALS Association
21021 Ventura Boulevard, Suite 321
Woodland Hills, CA 91364
Patients' ph: 800-782-4747
Others' ph: 818-340-7500
E-mail: EAJC27B@Prodigy.com
Web site: http://www.alsa.org/HOME.html

Phoebe Tucker, MA, CCC
AAC Evaluation and Treatment
45 Honeybee Lane
Shelton, CT 06484
Ph: 203-929-6455
Fax: 203-926-6003
(Specializes in technology and computer assessments and consultations. Extensive experience with adults with disabilities.)

National Organization on Disability
910 16th Street, NW
Washington, DC 20006
Ph: 202-293-5960

The Barrier Free Design Centre
2075 Bay View Avenue
Toronto, Ontario M4N355
Ph: 416-480-6000
(Nonprofit consulting organization, provides education, information, and technical assistance.)

Chapter 9, Telecommuter Resources

Associations for Telecommuters

International Telework Association
204 East Street, NE
Washington, DC 20002
Ph: 202-547-6157

Fax: 202-546-3289
E-mail: tac4dc@aol.com
Web site: http://www.telecomute.org/
(Annual individual membership fee is $125, and with that you get a comprehensive quarterly newsletter and information on the association's annual conference.)

Newsletter for telecommuters

Telecommuting Review Newsletter
Gil Gordon, Editor and Publisher
10 Donner Court
Monmouth Junction, NJ 08852
Ph: 732-329-2266
Fax: 732-329-2703
E-mail: gil@gilgordon.com
Web site: http://www.gilgordon.com
(Gordon's award-winning Web site gives you all the answers and information you will ever want to know about telecommuting. The monthly newsletter is $177 for a year's subscription and worth the money to find more in-depth information on telecommuting. Gordon holds an annual conference on telecommuting, as well.)

Books on Telecommuting

For a complete listing of every book published on the subject of telecommuting, visit this Web site: http://www.gilgordon.com/gga/amazon.html.

The Telecommuter's Advisor
By June Langhoff
Published by Aegis Publishing, Newport, Rhode Island

Telecommuting: A Manager's Guide to Flexible Work Arrangements
By Joel Kugelmass
Published by Lexington Books, New York

Telecommute: Go to Work Without Leaving Home
By Lisa Shaw
Published by John Wiley & Sons, New York

The Telecommuter's Handbook: How to Work for a Salary Without Ever Leaving the House
By Brad and Debra Schepp
Published by McGraw-Hill, New York

Index

About the Author

Marilyn Zelinsky is an author and a real-life home-office worker. She was formerly with *Interiors* magazine and has written for *Home Office Computing* magazine. She holds degrees in journalism and communications from New York University and the Fashion Institute of Technology. She is the author of *New Workplaces for New Workstyles*, also from McGraw-Hill.

"Willingness to trust the unknown takes courage."

A Guide to the I Ching

by Carol Anthony